Microsoft® Silverlight® 4
Step by Step

Laurence Moroney

Published with the authorization of Microsoft Corporation by:

O'Reilly Media, Inc.
1005 Gravenstein Highway North
Sebastopol, CA 95472

1 2 3 4 5 6 7 8 9 WCT 5 4 3 2 1 0

Acquisitions and Developmental Editor: Russell Jones
Production Editor: Loranah Dimant
Copy Editor: Matt Graven
Editorial Production: OTSI, Inc.
Technical Reviewer: John Grieb
Compositor: Ron Bilodeau
Illustrator: Robert Romano
Indexer: Seth Maislin

978-0-735-63887-7

While it's only a few words, I hope they describe the enormity of what you mean to me. I dedicate this book to those that mean the most to me—my wife, Rebecca, and my children, Claudia and Christopher. You guys are just the most amazing people in my world. Thanks for being who you are.

I also want to thank the One who makes it all possible: The God of Abraham, Isaac, Jacob and Jesus, for giving us life, love, happiness, and hope.

Table of Contents

What do you think of this book? We want to hear from you!

Microsoft is interested in hearing your feedback so we can continually improve our books and learning resources for you. To participate in a brief online survey, please visit:

www.microsoft.com/learning/booksurvey/

Acknowledgments

Thanks to the entire staff at Microsoft Press and O'Reilly for putting this book together. Thanks in particular to Russell Jones and Loranah Dimant, who held my hand every step of the way, and to whom I owe a huge debt of gratitude for keeping me honest and on path. I'd also like to thank the technical reviewer, John Grieb, copy editor, Matt Graven, and indexer, Seth Maislin. You guys rock!

Introduction

To paraphrase a famous character from one of my favorite movies: Silverlight is what Silverlight does. And Silverlight does a *lot*. It's a platform that's designed to allow you to build rich applications that are delivered over the web. It isn't limited to browser-based applications, but instead allows you to build applications that are powered by the Internet. These can run in the browser like a typical Rich Internet Application (RIA), or can run on the desktop like a typical Rich Client Application. Being Internet-powered, Silverlight applications are cross-platform, cross-browser and cross-device.

Using Silverlight, you can build applications that run on your PC using Windows or Linux, your Mac, and even a range of mobile devices. If you want your applications to run only within the browser, you can reach all the major browsers, including Internet Explorer, Firefox, Safari, and Chrome.

In this book, you will proceed step by step through the procedures required to build, deploy, and maintain Silverlight applications. This book is broken down into a number of different areas that Silverlight addresses.

Each chapter is a step by step learning experience for a particular functional area of Silverlight. While later chapters build on the content from earlier chapters, if you have prior Silverlight experience, you should be able to dip into the areas that you're interested in without having to read all the preceding chapters first.

System Requirements

Supported Operating Systems:

- Windows 7
- Windows Vista Service Pack 2
- Windows XP Service Pack 3

Visual Studio Requirements, either:

- Microsoft Visual Studio 2010 with the Visual Web Developer feature, or
- Microsoft Visual Web Developer 2010 Express

Support for This Book

Every effort has been made to ensure the accuracy of this book and the contents of the companion CD. As corrections or changes are collected, they will be added to a Microsoft Knowledge Base article. Microsoft Press provides support for books and companion CDs at the following Web site:

http://www.microsoft.com/learning/support/books/

If you have comments, questions, or ideas regarding the book or the companion CD, or questions that are not answered by visiting the sites previously mentioned, please send them to Microsoft Press by sending an e-mail message to *mspinput@microsoft.com*.

Please note that Microsoft software product support is not offered through the preceding address.

We Want to Hear from You

We welcome your feedback about this book. Please share your comments and ideas via the following short survey:

http://www.microsoft.com/learning/booksurvey

Your participation will help Microsoft Press create books that better meet your needs and standards.

> **Note** We hope that you will give us detailed feedback via our survey. If you have questions about our publishing program, upcoming titles, or Microsoft Press in general, we encourage you to interact with us via Twitter at *http://twitter.com/MicrosoftPress*. For support issues, use only the e-mail address shown above.

Foreword

It's an exciting time to be a Silverlight developer, and it has recently become even more exciting with the announcements about and releases of new Silverlight development tools for the upcoming Windows Phone series. The excitement we're seeing among developers is palpable and we're looking forward to seeing the applications that you build using Visual Studio tools.

In my opinion, the Visual Studio developer tools are the best on the planet for building applications. Silverlight is a terrific runtime for building rich, fast applications that run on your desktop, in your browser, and now even on your phone. And not only is Silverlight free, the Visual Studio 2010 Express editions are also free! So you can start building today and it won't cost you a penny.

Based on the Microsoft .NET Framework, Silverlight is available for both Windows and the Mac and is supported on a variety of upcoming Windows Phone devices. Linux users can also capitalize on Silverlight, using the compatible Moonlight plug-in from Novell.

Silverlight is a robust development platform, offering extensive layout and styling options, powerful communications protocols, flexible data access, and high-definition media. It helps you produce fast, smooth, and visually rich experiences for your users.

Last year's Olympics produced some of the largest online media events in history—and if you watched the games online, you did so using Silverlight. Already, Silverlight has been used by major organizations for critical projects: by NASA for its Mars Rovers; by MGM to promote its great TV show 'Stargate Universe'; by Hard Rock International to make its extensive collections of rock and roll memorabilia available online in high detail; and by many, many more companies needing to offer rich user experiences.

These are just a few examples of the many thousands of applications that are available today. And you have the tools in your hands to build applications that are just as good as these, if not better!

This book, written by my colleague, Laurence Moroney, will get you started building Silverlight applications quickly. Whether you are an experienced .NET developer or are relatively new to Visual Studio tools, you'll rapidly find out how to create the applications that will power the future Web. Each chapter in this book employs the tried-and-true step-by-step method, walking you through examples. It's very approachable, and the standalone nature of the following chapters will make it easy for you to pick up the book and start learning from any point.

In Chapter 1, you'll learn about the Web Platform Installer, which offers a one-click way to install the entire Microsoft Web Stack and tools, including IIS Web server, SQL Server Express, ASP.NET extensions, Visual Web Developer Express, and Silverlight. After installing the software, you'll put the platform to use right away by building a basic application using some of the built-in Silverlight controls.

Chapter 2 drills down into many of the controls that are built into Silverlight. You'll see how the control model works and you'll learn about common properties, methods, and events across many controls. Additionally, you'll start to learn the methodology for building Silverlight applications, getting a first-hand look at how simple it is to use powerful controls, such as the *ListBox* control.

Chapter 3 delves into layout and styling, exploring how layout controls such as the *Canvas*, *Grid*, and *StackPanel* work. And you'll discover how to use styles and templates to render controls on the screen the way you want them.

Chapter 4 changes gears to explore a new methodology for building business applications, called *RIA Services*, which is being released with Silverlight 4. You'll see how to build a SQL Server database and create services that expose its data to Silverlight. You'll also see how to build a Silverlight application that provides basic view and update methodology.

Chapter 5 teaches you how to use the rich imaging functionality available in Silverlight using Photosynth. You'll learn how to use this to build applications like those used by NASA, MGM, and the Hard Rock Café.

Silverlight is a terrific media platform, so rendering media using the *MediaElement* control is both easy and powerful. In Chapter 6 you'll learn about the object model of the *MediaElement* and how to use it to provide media control and playback features in your applications. This includes consuming markers encoded into the media. You'll also see the new webcam support that Silverlight 4 provides and how you can use it to create Webcam-based applications.

You design Silverlight's graphics and user interfaces using a powerful XML-based language, called XAML. Though you can write and modify XAML by hand, visual tools, such as Expression Blend, simplify and automate the process. Chapter 7 introduces you to the transformation and animation engines in Silverlight and shows how you can add life to your applications using them.

Silverlight isn't just a browser technology. It also allows you to build out-of-browser applications that run on the desktop. Silverlight exposes some simple APIs for such scenarios that can detect network availability and take advantage of such features as isolated storage and elevated trust. You'll also learn how to debug out-of-browser applications. Chapter 8 takes you through all these capabilities and much more!

In addition to running out of the browser, Silverlight, of course, also runs *in* the browser. But it isn't just a black-box within the browser—Silverlight can integrate and interoperate with other assets running in the browser. For instance, you may have made substantial investments in JavaScript-based libraries. Well, Chapter 9 shows how to use the browser bridge to access everything in the browser. To delve into this, you'll work with JavaScript and the Bing Maps API.

Chapter 10 shows you how to build network-connected applications. You'll build some services that run on a server and then you'll learn how to use the network APIs in Silverlight to call them, retrieve results, and render the data on-screen. As an example, you'll build a Silverlight client that lets users retrieve real stock quotes.

Chapter 11 shows you how to get the tools for Windows Phone development and how to use the Windows Phone emulator to test your applications. You'll use this to build an application similar to that in Chapter 10, but this time you'll make a client that can get a stock quote on a phone.

Chapter 12 takes you on a tour of some of the features that are specific to the Windows Phone platform. You'll see how to detect the phone's orientation and write applications that respond to orientation changes. You'll look at the hardware Back button that's built into every Windows Phone device and learn how to use it in your applications. You'll learn how to build application bars that provide always-available buttons and menus in your applications. And you will learn about Input Scope and how to use it to create a better user experience when users have to use a virtual keyboard to enter text on the phone. Finally, this chapter also covers programming for multi-touch interfaces.

Chapter 13 introduces Expression Blend for phone development. It walks you through a basic example that uses Expression Blend to build an animation. And it explains how to run that animation on the phone emulator.

The final chapter, Chapter 14, introduces XNA and demonstrates how to use the XNA framework to write games. You'll write a basic game that uses many of the techniques and attributes used to create a real-world game. You will create an animated player character that the user can control with the keyboard and an automated non-player character (NPC), configure collision detection, use sprite sheets, and even incorporate audio effects!

That's a lot of material to cover. I hope this book and the lessons it offers can help you to become the next great Silverlight developer.

After you've worked your way through this book and have a great application to share, drop us a line at our blogs.

Scott: *http://weblogs.asp.net/scottgu*

Laurence: *http://blogs.msdn.com/webnext*

I look forward to hearing from you and seeing the great applications you build using Silverlight.

Scott Guthrie

April 10, 2010

Chapter 1
Introducing Silverlight

After completing this chapter, you will be able to:

- Use Microsoft Web Platform Installer to install and configure the Web Platform, database, and tools.
- Install Visual Web Developer 2010 Express for creating Silverlight applications.
- Build your first Silverlight application.

Get the Tools

The easiest way to get started with Microsoft Silverlight development is to use Microsoft Web Platform Installer (Web PI). This provides a single application that can be used to install and configure a variety of things, including tools, servers, databases, programming APIs, and applications.

Work with Web Platform Installer

1. Web PI is available as a free download at *http://www.microsoft.com/web*. After you install and launch Web PI, you'll see a screen something like the one shown on the next page. Select the Web Platform tab.

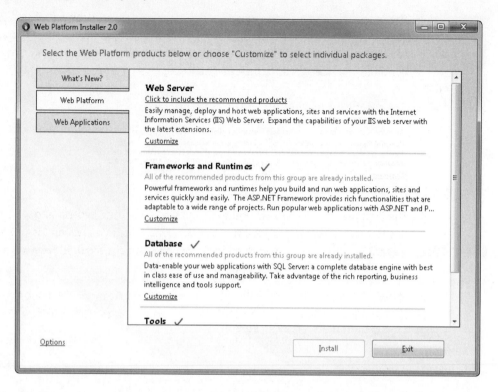

2. The first section, Web Server, allows you to install the Internet Information Services (IIS) Web server as well as a number of options, including those for application development, common HTTP features, compatibility with previous versions, deployment and publishing, health and diagnostics, management, and performance and security. Under Web Server, there is a link called Click To Include The Recommended Products. Click this link and you'll see a check mark.

3. The second section is Frameworks And Runtimes. Here you can install and configure the various development features of the Microsoft Web Platform, including ASP.NET, ASP.NET MVC, and PHP. If the green check isn't already shown beside Frameworks And Runtimes, click the Click To Include The Recommended Products link.

Frameworks and Runtimes ✓
All of the recommended products from this group are already installed.
Powerful frameworks and runtimes help you build and run web applications, sites and services quickly and easily. The ASP.NET Framework provides rich functionalities that are adaptable to a wide range of projects. Run popular web applications with ASP.NET and P...
Customize

4. The Database section allows you to install the SQL Server Express engine. You can use this to add a database to your Web applications, which you will use as you work your way through this book. You need to do two things here, though, because you will be using some tools that are not part of the default list.

a. First, if there is no green check box beside Database, click the Click To Include The Recommended Products link. If this link isn't available, you already have the recommended tools, so don't worry.

abase
 to include the recommended products
-enable your web applications with SQL Server: a complete database engine with best
ss ease of use and manageability. Take advantage of the rich reporting, business
igence and tools support.
omize

Database ✓
Click to remove the included products
Data-enable your web applications with SQL Server: a complete database engine with best
in class ease of use and manageability. Take advantage of the rich reporting, business
intelligence and tools support.
Customize

b. Now click the Customize link at the bottom of the text. This will take you to the screen that allows you to customize which parts of SQL Server you are going to install. You'll see that SQL Server Express 2008 With Service Pack 1 is already selected, but SQL Server 2008 Management Studio Express is not.

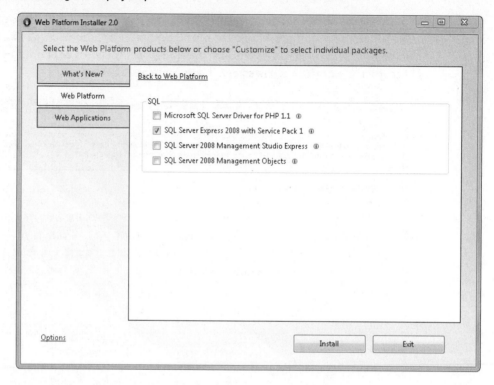

c. Select the SQL Server 2008 Management Studio Express check box, and then click Back To Web Platform.

d. Do *not* click Install yet!

5. The final section is Tools. This allows you to install and configure development tools for ASP.NET, Silverlight, JavaScript, and more. As discussed earlier in this section, if there is no green check mark beside Tools, you will see Click To Include The Recommended Products link. Click this link, the green checkmark will appear, and you'll have everything you need to get going.

Tools ✓
Click to remove the included products
Increase productivity with tooling support for ASP.NET, Silverlight, Javascript, Web standards and more. Visual Web Developer provides a complete environment for developing and testing standards-based web applications, sites and services.
Customize

6. At this point, you are ready to get started, so click Install at the bottom of the window. Web PI will display a list of each of the items you have chosen to install that require you to accept their license terms. You can accept the license terms all at once by clicking I Accept at the bottom of the screen if you want to continue.

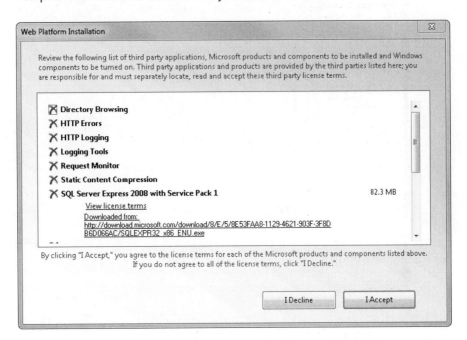

7. Since you have chosen to install SQL Server Express, another dialog box will appear. This will ask how you want its security to be set up. There are two options. The first is Windows Integrated Authentication, which will allow your Windows account to be used to log in to the database. The second is Mixed Mode Authentication, which will support Windows Integrated Authentication as well as allow SQL Server to have its own login system. Choose Mixed Mode Authentication and provide a password for the administrator account. For this book, use **sasa123!** as the password.

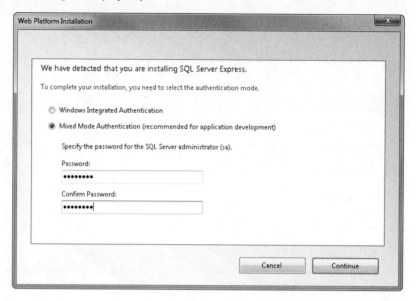

8. Click Continue, and Web PI will download and install the components. This may take a few minutes.

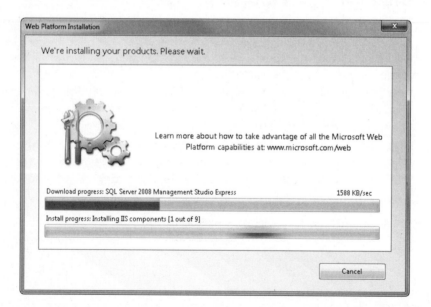

9. When you're done, you'll have installed the Microsoft Web Platform, the database, and all the dependencies you need to start developing. Note that on some versions of Windows 7 you may get a message informing you that SQL Server 2008 Management Studio Express has known issues with Windows 7. If you see this message, just click Run to get it to continue.

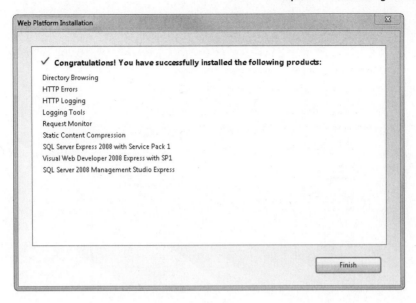

Install Visual Web Developer Express

Although the Microsoft Visual Studio suite is a set of premium tools designed for developers, free versions of the apps are available as Express editions.

A number of Express editions are available:

- Microsoft Visual Basic 2010 Express
- Microsoft Visual C# 2010 Express
- Microsoft Visual C++ 2010 Express
- Microsoft Visual Web Developer 2010 Express

Note For this book, you'll be using Visual Web Developer 2010 Express.

Install Visual Web Developer 2010 Express

1. Download Visual Web Developer from *http://www.microsoft.com/express/Web* and launch the vwd_web.exe program.

2. Click Next to continue to the next screen and you'll see the license terms. If you accept these terms, select that option and click Next.

3. The next screen lets you select where you'd like to install Visual Web Developer. Either keep the default setting or choose a new directory and then click Install.

4. The installer will then download and install everything you need.

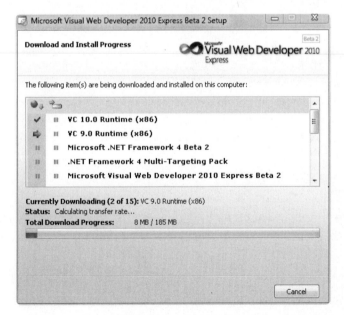

5. You may need to restart your system to ensure that the Microsoft .NET Framework is properly installed. When you're done, you'll see the Setup Complete screen.

The next step is to install the Silverlight Tools for Visual Studio. You'll see how to do that in the next section.

Install the Silverlight Tools

Silverlight is a rapidly evolving platform, so some of the details discussed here may change by the time you read this book! Regardless, the best source for the latest information on Silverlight is *http://www.silverlight.net*. The best place to download the latest version of the Silverlight Tools is *http://www.silverlight.net/getstarted*—just look for information about the Silverlight 4 download on this page.

Install the Silverlight Tools

1. Download the Silverlight 4 Tools for Visual Studio from *http://www.silverlight.net/getstarted* and run the installation. You'll see a screen that outlines what you will be installing:

- The Silverlight runtime

- The Silverlight Tools for Visual Studio (this provides the integration and templates that allow you to easily build Silverlight applications)

- The Silverlight SDK

- Some add-on controls

- The WCF RIA Services package (this allows you to build business applications)

2. Click Next and the installer will download and install everything. When you're done, you'll see a confirmation screen. You're now ready to build Silverlight applications!

Create Your First Silverlight Application

Now that you have everything installed, it's time to start creating your first application. In this section, you will create a simple Silverlight application and explore its anatomy.

Build a Simple Silverlight application

1. Open the Start menu and launch Visual Web Developer 2010 Express.

2. To create a new Silverlight application, select New Project from the File menu.

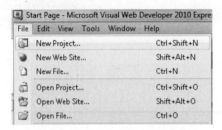

3. The New Project dialog box will list the installed templates. A template is a skeleton of an application. When you select a template for your application, Visual Web Developer creates all the files necessary for that application. The templates are organized according to language, with versions of each template available for Visual Basic and Visual C#. Open the Visual C# folder. You will see a number of different application types, including Windows, Web, Cloud Service, and Silverlight.

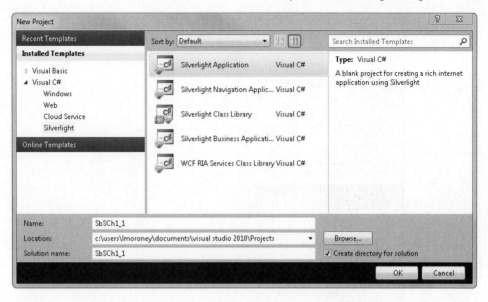

4. Select the Silverlight Application template. Enter the name **SbSCh1_1** and click OK. Visual Web Developer will start creating a Silverlight application for you. A Silverlight application runs on the Web, so it needs a Web site in which to run. Visual Web Developer can create that for you also.

5. The New Silverlight Application dialog box will appear, asking whether you want to host the application in a new Web site. Make sure you select that check box. Silverlight will then create a Web project with the same name as your Silverlight project but with a postfix of .Web. Leave the other options set to their defaults for now and click OK.

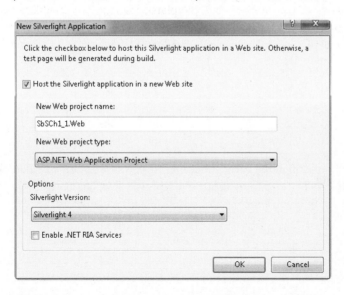

Visual Web Developer will create a new solution, which is how it organizes different projects. Your solution will contain two projects: the Silverlight application and a Web site for hosting the Silverlight application. You can see these in Solution Explorer.

6. The Silverlight application uses Extensible Application Markup Language (XAML) files for its user interface. The *MainPage.xaml* file contains the default UI. Double-click this file to open it in the designer. Along the left edge of the screen, you should see vertical tabs that read Toolbox, CSS Properties, and Manage Styles. Open the Toolbox tab.

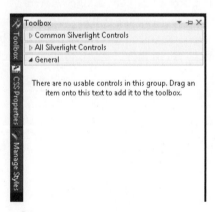

7. Click the pushpin icon in the top right corner to keep the Toolbox pinned open on the screen. The Tabs will move to the bottom of this window. Click the Common Silverlight Controls section and you'll see a list of simple Silverlight controls.

8. Your first application will use two Label controls, a TextBox control, and a Button control. Start by adding the first Label control by double-clicking Label in the Toolbox. You'll notice that two things happen.

   ■ First, Silverlight adds a visual representation of the Label to the design surface.

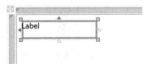

   ■ Second, it adds the markup code for the Label to the XAML.

```
Design    ↑↓    XAML
<UserControl x:Class="SbSCh1_1.MainPage"
    xmlns="http://schemas.microsoft.com/winfx/2006/xaml/presentation"
    xmlns:x="http://schemas.microsoft.com/winfx/2006/xaml"
    xmlns:d="http://schemas.microsoft.com/expression/blend/2008"
    xmlns:mc="http://schemas.openxmlformats.org/markup-compatibility/2006"
    mc:Ignorable="d"
    d:DesignHeight="300" d:DesignWidth="400" xmlns:dataInput="clr-namespace:System.Windows.Controls;assembly=System.Windows.Controls.Data.Input">

    <Grid x:Name="LayoutRoot" Background="White">
        <dataInput:Label Height="28" HorizontalAlignment="Left" Margin="10,10,0,0" Name="label1" VerticalAlignment="Top" Width="120" />
    </Grid>
</UserControl>
```

 Note When creating Silverlight applications, Visual Web Developer lets you design visually and design in code, with the tool keeping the two synchronized.

9. Now you need to edit the Label so that it says something other than "Label". There are two ways you can do this. You can use the Properties window to change the value of the Content property. (The Properties window should be at the bottom right of your screen.) Type **What is your Name?**.

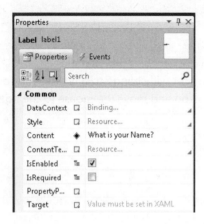

Alternatively, you can edit the XAML. To do this, add an *attribute* called *Content* and set its value to *What is your Name?*. Notice that when you use the Properties window approach, the *attribute* is automatically added to the XAML.

```
<Grid x:Name="LayoutRoot" Background="White">
    <dataInput:Label Height="28" HorizontalAlignment="Left" Margin="10,10,0,0" Name="label1"
                     VerticalAlignment="Top" Width="120"
                     Content="What is your Name?" />
</Grid>
```

You've just added and configured your first Silverlight control! Now you need to repeat the steps to add the other controls.

Configure more Silverlight controls

1. Double-click TextBox in the Toolbox to add a TextBox control to the designer. Notice that the TextBox is added immediately below the Label you already created. You can use your mouse to drag the TextBox so that it's to the right of the Label.

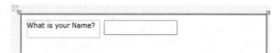

2. Repeat the process again to add a Button control. Drag it to the right of the TextBox, and change its Content property to read Go instead of the Button. Note that despite Button being a different control type, the process for adding and configuring its Content property is identical to editing the Label control.

3. The last UI element you need to add is another Label. Double-click Label in the Toolbox to add the new control. You'll see that it has been added beneath your original Label. Leave it in its position, but use the mouse to drag out the right side of the Label to make it wider. You'll see a little round dot on the right edge of the Label. If you move your mouse pointer over this, the pointer will change to a left-right arrow. Once you see this, hold down the left mouse button and move the mouse to the right.

4. Take a close look at your XAML code. Look for the *Name* property on each of the controls. By default, Visual Web Developer names controls as the control type followed by a number. The first Label control you place on your design will be called *label1*, the next *label2*, and so on. So you'll find that you have controls called *label1*, *label2*, *textBox1*, and *button1* in your application. In practice, it's a good idea to give your controls more meaningful names, but for now you can keep the defaults.

5. Now it's time to add a little code to make your application do something. Double-click the Go button and you'll see that the designer goes away and is replaced by a code window. This is because you are moving into the code-editing mode.

    Visual Web Developer creates a stub function called *button1_Click*. This is where you will write the code that executes whenever a user presses the button.

Add functionality to your button

1. Within the *button1_Click* function, start typing the word **label2**. After a couple keystrokes, the IntelliSense menu will pop up.

2. IntelliSense figures out what the possibilities are based on the installed classes in the .NET Framework and on the instances of controls in your application. Because the only things you could code against that begin with "Lab" are the *Label* class (in the .NET Framework) and the label1 and label2 controls within the current application, IntelliSense narrows the choices down to these three items. You can either finish typing **label2** at this point or just select that entry on the menu.

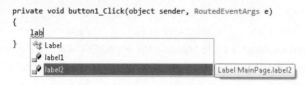

```
private void button1_Click(object sender, RoutedEventArgs e)
{
    lab|
}
```

3. You address properties on a control in the .NET Framework by using dot syntax. So in code, for example, the Content property of label2 that you edited earlier in the designer becomes *label2.Content*. As soon as you type a period for the dot, IntelliSense will kick in again, listing the properties you can address. Pick the *Content* property (or just type it) and you're ready to go to the next step.

4. Finish the line of code. It should look like this:

```
private void button1_Click(object sender, RoutedEventArgs e)
{
    label2.Content = "Hello World, " + textBox1.Text;
}
```

Whenever a user types text into a TextBox, the entered text gets stored in the *Text* property. The code you've just written says "Change the content of label2 to read 'Hello World,' plus whatever the user typed in the TextBox." This code will run when the user presses the button.

5. Press F5 to run the application. Your default browser will open and display your new Silverlight application. Type your name into the text box and click Go. You'll see that the label2 text will change so it reads "Hello World," plus your name.

Congratulations! You've just created, designed, coded, compiled, deployed, and run your first Silverlight application.

Key Points

- You learned how to download, install, and use the Microsoft Web Platform Installer to install and configure the software, database, and tools you need to create Silverlight applications.

- You got an introduction to the Visual Web Developer 2010 Express tools that you will be using to create the Silverlight applications in this book.

- You learned where to obtain and how to install the latest version of the Silverlight Tools for Visual Studio.

- You built a Silverlight application, learning the steps involved in the process.

Chapter 2
Silverlight Controls

After completing this chapter, you will be able to:

- Understand the Silverlight control model and how events are wired up to controls.
- Understand what content controls are and how they work.
- Use common Silverlight controls.
- Recognize similarities between the properties and events of various controls.

Learning Silverlight Controls

In Chapter 1, "Introducing Silverlight," you learned that Silverlight lets you create rich experiences and user interfaces that run within a Web browser. In this chapter, you'll explore the controls, properties, and events that allow you to create more sophisticated user interfaces.

Understanding the Control Model

In Chapter 1, you created a simple Silverlight application. When you typed your name into a text box and clicked a button, this application rendered "Hello World" followed by your name. What you did not see is how Silverlight knows to map the code to the button click.

In this chapter, you'll create another simple application so you can explore how Silverlight maps code to control events. First, you'll create a simple application that updates the button's text caption when you click the button.

Create the sample application

1. Launch Microsoft Visual Web Developer 2010 Express and select the New Project entry on the File menu.
2. Under Visual C#, select Silverlight Application and enter the name **SbSCh2_1**. Click OK.

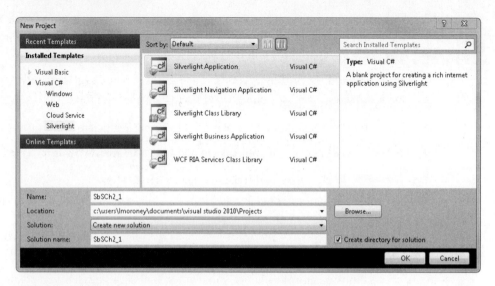

3. Visual Web Developer will present the New Silverlight Application dialog box and ask whether you want to create a Web application project. Keep the default settings and click OK to continue.

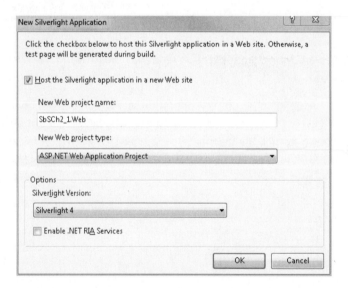

4. Visual Web Developer will create your application and open a XAML page named MainPage.xaml in the designer. This is the first page that Silverlight will render, so any changes you make here will show up immediately when you run the application.

5. From the Toolbox, double-click the *Button* control to add a button to your XAML page. If you don't see the Toolbox, review the tutorial at the end of Chapter 1 that demonstrates how to "pin" the Toolbox to your designer window.

When you add the button to your page, the XAML is updated to include the code that declares the button. The code should look something like this:

```
<Grid x:Name="LayoutRoot" Background="White">
    <Button Content="Button" Height="23" HorizontalAlignment="Left"
            Margin="10,10,0,0" Name="button1"
            VerticalAlignment="Top" Width="75" />
</Grid>
```

6. In the designer window, double-click the button. The designer will go away and the code window will open. Don't worry, your design hasn't disappeared! Visual Web Developer has opened a new file, called the code-behind file. Whenever you create a page, Visual Web Developer creates a code-behind file with the same name, but with a .cs extension if you're using C# and a .vb extension if you're using Visual Basic. In this project, for example, when you created MainPage.xaml, Visual Web Developer will have created the file MainPage.xaml.cs. So the associated code file is simply opened when you double-click in the designer and the tab for the MainPage.xaml designer file is still available at the top of the page.

```
MainPage.xaml.cs × MainPage.xaml*
    4   using System.Net;
    5   using System.Windows;
    6   using System.Windows.Controls;
    7   using System.Windows.Documents;
```

Solution Explorer will also indicate that MainPage.xaml.cs is open. You'll explore MainPage.xaml in more detail in a moment, but for now, you need to edit some code.

7. First, look at the *MainPage* function. If you are familiar with C# or other object-oriented languages, such as Java or C++, you probably know that a constructor function has the same name as the class that contains it. And the constructor function runs whenever an instance of the class is created. Thus, for all intents and purposes, this is the first code that will run when you launch the application.

Add a single line of code to the *MainPage* function that sets the *Content* property of the button to "0". When you run the application, the button will render and you'll see "0" as the button's caption.

```
public MainPage()
{
    InitializeComponent();
    button1.Content = "0";
}
```

8. Next, you need to add some code that will do something when the button is pressed. Note that when you double-clicked the button in the designer, Visual Web Developer created a *button1_Click* event handler stub. This is because when you double-click a control in the designer, Visual Web Developer assumes you want the most commonly used event for that control. And for a button, the *Click* event is the most commonly used event.

9. The following code retrieves the number currently used for the button's caption, and adds 1 to that number. It then sets the button's caption to the new value, effectively adding 1 to the value of the caption every time you press the button.

```
private void button1_Click(object sender, RoutedEventArgs e)
{
    int n = Convert.ToInt16(button1.Content.ToString());
    n++;
    button1.Content = n;
}
```

10. Now press F5 to execute the application. You'll see the button and you'll be able to click it to increase the value of the number in its caption.

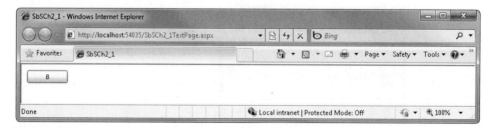

Exploring the Control and Event Model

The application you just built handles two events: one that initializes the button when the application loads and renders for the first time and another that fires in response to a user action—clicking the button. Now you'll explore the application to see how these events are "wired up." This will help you more clearly understand the control and event model.

Explore the control and event model

1. Using Visual Web Developer, select the MainPage.xaml tab to display the designer so you can edit the application visually.

2. Select the *Button* control. Take a look at the Properties window on the lower right-hand side. There are two tabs at the top, one for Properties and one for Events. Select the Events tab and you'll see that the code specified to handle the *Click* event is called *button1_Click*.

Note The de facto naming convention for events is the control name followed by an underscore followed by the event name. Visual Web Developer Express uses this naming convention.

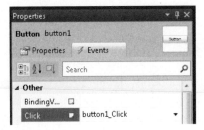

3. Change the text that reads button1_Click to **addIt**. As soon as you press Enter, the code window will open and you'll see the new *addIt* function.

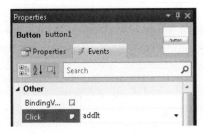

4. Close the code window and return to the designer. Take a look at the code and inspect the button's XAML. It should look something like this:

```
<Button Content="Button" Height="23" HorizontalAlignment="Left"
        Margin="10,10,0,0" Name="button1"
        VerticalAlignment="Top" Width="75" Click="addIt" />
```

Note that Visual Web Developer added the *Click="addIt"* code at the end of the *Button* element. Code like this is called an *attribute*. XAML uses attributes to specify the event handlers that Silverlight calls when a particular event occurs.

5. Place your cursor in the text of the *Click* attribute (immediately to the right of the first quotation mark) and type something. It doesn't matter what you type, just press any key.

6. You'll see a menu drop down that contains the function names of every event handler function within the code-behind, giving you the option to easily map to one of the existing handlers. Alternatively, you can elect to create a new event handler.

7. In this case, create a new event handler by double-clicking the New Event Handler menu option. Visual Web Developer will create a new event handler called *button1_Click_1* (because *button1_Click* was already used). Any code you write in that function will execute whenever the user clicks the button.

8. The name *button1_Click_1* is not a particularly intuitive name, so go back to the *Click* event attribute and type anywhere in the value. When the pop-up menu appears, select addIt to switch the button's *Click* event handler back to the *addIt* function.

9. You haven't written the *addIt* function yet. So you need to switch back to the code window by selecting the MainPage.xaml.cs tab at the top of the page (or by double-clicking the file in Solution Explorer).

10. The *addIt* function is empty, so you should add the following code to it. Note that this time you're adding *2* to *n*, instead of *1*.

```
private void addIt(object sender, RoutedEventArgs e)

{
    int n = Convert.ToInt16(button1.Content.ToString());
    n+=2;
    button1.Content = n;
}
```

11. Press F5 to run the application. When you press the button, you will see the application add *2* to the value shown on the button.

This application demonstrates an important concept in Silverlight programming—one that can lead to many hard-to-find bugs if you aren't careful. It's easy to fall into the habit of expecting all event handlers to use the standard naming convention (control name, underscore, event name), but that may not always be the case. You should always check, by using either the properties inspector or by looking at the XAML code, to see how the event handler is declared.

Using the Silverlight Controls

The previous section showed how the Silverlight control model works, how it associates events with event handlers, and how to use properties to determine a control's appearance. In this section you will explore several of the most common controls. Most of these controls have some properties and events in common; you'll explore those first with the already-familiar *Button* control. You should read the following section, "Using the *Button* Control," before reading the other sections, because it will cover the common properties.

Using the *Button* Control

You've already used the *Button* control to see how you can run code in response to user actions, such as clicking on a button. But the *Button* control is capable of far more customization than simply altering its caption. And it supports many more events than just the *Click* event. Here's a look at some more events the *Button* control can support and how you can use them.

Content in Controls

The two previous examples in this chapter placed text on a button. You learned how to change the text both manually and by using the *Content* property. However, the *Content* property is useful for far more than simple text. In fact the *Content* property stores XAML, which means you can define a button's content by using the same language that you use to define the overall user interface. For example, you'll often see user interfaces that incorporate buttons with pictures. Here's a look at how you can build a picture button by using XAML.

Build a picture button

1. Create a new Silverlight project called **SbSCh2_2**.

2. Double-click the *Button* control in the Toolbox to add a new *Button* control instance.

3. Click the sizing handle at the lower-right corner of the button and drag the mouse to make the button larger.

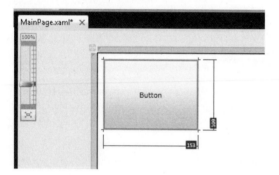

The XAML for the *Button* will now look something like this:

```
<Grid x:Name="LayoutRoot" Background="White">
    <Button Content="Button" Height="107"
            HorizontalAlignment="Left" Margin="10,10,0,0"
            Name="button1" VerticalAlignment="Top" Width="170" />
</Grid>
```

4. Delete the *Content="Button"* attribute and replace the slash and angle bracket (/>) shown on the fourth line with a single angle bracket (>). Then add the full </Button> closing tag. After you do that, your XAML should look like this:

```
<Grid x:Name="LayoutRoot" Background="White">
    <Button Height="107"
            HorizontalAlignment="Left" Margin="10,10,0,0"
            Name="button1" VerticalAlignment="Top" Width="170">
    </Button>
</Grid>
```

5. Now, add an *Image* control to the application. You won't use the *Image* control directly, but adding one to the designer gives you a nice shortcut for adding an *Image* to your project with the added advantage of making sure that it's in the correct place for any other *Image* control to load it.

6. Double-click the Image tool to add an *Image*.

7. After adding the *Image* control, click it, and look for its *Source* property in the Properties window. You'll see that it has a caret button (one with ellipsis "...") beside it.

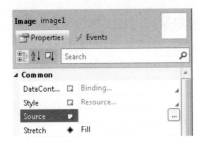

8. Click the caret button, and you'll see a dialog box that asks which picture to use. If there are any images within your solution, they'll be listed here. You haven't put any images in yet, so the list will be empty.

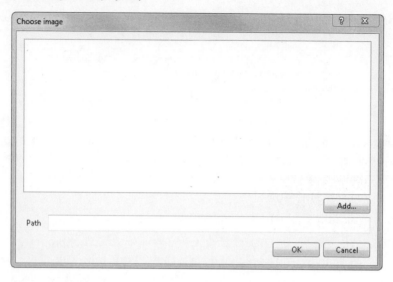

9. Click the Add... button to add a new image to your solution.

10. Visual Web Developer will display a common dialog box that lets you select an image in one of the two formats Silverlight supports: .jpg or .png. Select an image and click OK.

11. The Choose Image dialog will display an image. The Path field will show how you can reference the image in the XAML for your Silverlight application. Click OK and the Image control will load the selected image.

12. In the designer window, resize the image so that it is smaller than the button.

13. Looking at the XAML, you'll see that the *Button* declaration and the *Image* declaration are siblings. That means they are beside each other, and neither is nested within the other.

When editing the content of the button earlier, you modified an attribute whose value was a string, which you deleted. Another way to describe the content is to use a *child node*—in other words, one node within another. In XAML, you do this by using dot syntax, so the *Content* declaration uses a *Button.Content* child, like this:

```
<Button Height="107" HorizontalAlignment="Left" Margin="10,10,0,0"
        Name="button1" VerticalAlignment="Top" Width="170">
    <Button.Content>
        <!-- Content will go here-->
    </Button.Content>
</Button>
```

14. Now you can place XAML inside the *Button.Content* tags for the button. Remember the *Image* control you just created? Cut its XAML and paste that inside the tag. The image should now appear within the button.

Note If you moved the image around in the designer window, the Margin property may have been set. As a result, you may not see the image within the button at this point. If this happens, simply delete the *Margin* attribute and then you should see the image within the button.

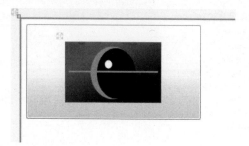

Notice the placement of the XAML within the *Button.Content* tags in the following code:

```
<Grid x:Name="LayoutRoot" Background="White">
    <Button Height="148" HorizontalAlignment="Left" Margin="10,10,0,0"
            Name="button1" VerticalAlignment="Top" Width="205">
        <Button.Content>
            <Image Height="95" HorizontalAlignment="Left"
                Name="image1" Stretch="Fill"
                VerticalAlignment="Top" Width="156"
                Source="/SbSCh2_2;component/Images/front-logo.jpg" />
        </Button.Content>
    </Button>
</Grid>
```

15. If you try to add more XAML elements to the *Button.Content* tag, you'll discover that Visual Web Developer flags an error by underlining the second element. This is because the property can only hold one XAML element. That may sound limiting, but it really isn't. The single XAML element can be a container control, which, in turn, can hold multiple XAML controls. One such container is the *StackPanel* control.

16. Add a *StackPanel* element as the first child of the *Button.Content* node. The XAML editor will automatically close your tag, so it looks like this:

```
<Button.Content>
    <StackPanel></StackPanel>
    <Image Height="95" HorizontalAlignment="Left"
        Name="image1" Stretch="Fill"
        VerticalAlignment="Top" Width="156"
        Source="/SbSCh2_2;component/Images/front-logo.jpg" />
</Button.Content>
```

17. The preceding code is invalid because the *Button.Content* element has two children (*StackPanel* and *Image*). So cut the *Image* tag and paste it between the *StackPanel* tags. Your XAML should now look like this:

```
<Button.Content>
    <StackPanel>
        <Image Height="95" HorizontalAlignment="Left"
               Name="image1" Stretch="Fill"
               VerticalAlignment="Top" Width="156"
               Source="/SbSCh2_2;component/Images/front-logo.jpg" />
    </StackPanel>
</Button.Content>
```

18. A *StackPanel* control can have multiple children, allowing you to add another control as a sibling to the *Image* control. Place the cursor before the closing *</StackPanel>* tag and type the following:

```
<TextBlock Text="Laurence's Books"></TextBlock>
```

The XAML for the button's content now contains two controls: an *Image* control and a *TextBlock* control.

19. By default, the *StackPanel* control stacks its children vertically. If you want them stacked horizontally (placing the text to the right of the image, rather than beneath it) you can use the *Orientation* property of the *StackPanel*. Set it to *Horizontal* to see the effect.

You've now seen how content controls work. This might be a bit of a departure from what you are used to, where a control holds a specific data type, such as a text caption on a button. You'll find that many Silverlight controls are content controls, making it easy to build complex scenarios, such as an image list, a video button, and so on.

Handling Mouse Events

Until now you've programmed only the *Click* event, which happens whenever a user clicks your control. User interfaces need to support many more mouse events, such as tracking when the mouse moves over an element, when the mouse enters an element, when the mouse leaves an element, and which mouse button is pressed. This section looks at these mouse events, and demonstrates how to program against them, using the *Button* control as an example.

The *Click* Event

The *Click* event applies only to *Button* controls and controls derived from *Button*, such as *HyperlinkButton* and *RepeatButton* controls. The *Click* event fires when a user clicks the button.

> **Note** A click is defined as both pressing and releasing the mouse button while the mouse cursor is over a control. The mouse cursor must remain over the same control when both the press and release events occur.

You can configure the occurrence of this event by using the *ClickMode* property. The default mode is *Release*, but you can set it to *Hover*, which generates the *Click* event when the mouse moves over the button. You can also set it to *Press*, which generates the event as soon as the user presses the mouse button while the mouse is over the button. Experiment with these a little.

The *MouseMove* Event

The *MouseMove* event fires whenever a user moves the mouse over a control. When this event fires, Silverlight provides some data about the mouse event, such as the mouse coordinates. Here's a look at how to build a simple application that uses the *MouseMove* event to track mouse coordinates.

Build an application using the *MouseMove* event

1. Create a new Silverlight application and name it **SbS2_3**.

2. In the designer, add a *Rectangle* control and two *TextBlock* controls to the new application's MainPage.xaml.

3. Select the *Rectangle* and find the *Fill* property.

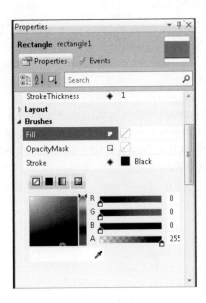

4. Select a color using the color palette. (For this sample, it doesn't matter what color you choose, as long as it stands out.)

5. Next, select the Events tab at the top of the Properties window. Find the *MouseMove* event and double-click it. Visual Web Developer will create the event handler.

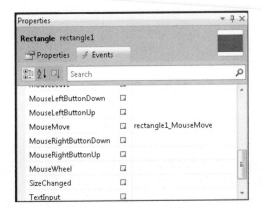

6. Take a look at the code-behind page (MainPage.xaml.cs). You'll see the *rectangle1_MouseMove* event handler declaration. Add the following line of code to the event handler:

```
textBlock1.Text = e.GetPosition(this).X.ToString();
```

This code sets the text of the first *TextBlock*. The value is derived from *e*, which is the *MouseEventArgs* argument passed into the function. This object, as its name suggests, contains the *arguments* (data) associated with the event. The *MouseEventArgs* class exposes a function named *GetPosition* that returns the *X* and *Y* value of the mouse's position when the event fired. Note that the *X* and *Y* values returned from the *GetPosition* function are of type *double*, which you'll need to convert to a *string* to use in a *TextBlock*. In other words, the code you just added will set the text of the first *TextBlock* to the *X* value of the mouse whenever you move the mouse over the *Rectangle*.

7. Can you guess how you would place the *Y* coordinate of the mouse into the second *TextBlock*? Give it a try. In case you need a little help, here's the answer:

```
textBlock2.Text = e.GetPosition(this).Y.ToString();
```

8. Press F5 to run the application and move the mouse around the rectangle. You'll see the mouse coordinates render in the *TextBlock* controls as you move the mouse.

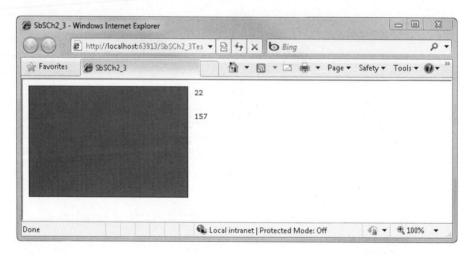

You might have some questions about this application. First, you might be wondering "why don't you see screen coordinates as opposed to the coordinates relative to the rectangle?" This is because you passed the *this* parameter to the *GetPosition* function.

You might also be asking "why don't you see the position *0,0* when you reach the top left corner of the rectangle?" The answer to this question lies in the *Margin* parameter for the *Rectangle*, which defaults to having a 10-pixel margin at the top and left. If you change the

Margin property to **0,0,0,0**, you'll see that the *MouseMove* event handler will then display 0,0 when you move the mouse to the top-left corner of the *Rectangle*.

> **Further Exploration** You should also explore the *MouseEnter* and *MouseLeave* events, which fire as the mouse enters and leaves the control, respectively. These events also expose a *MouseEventArgs* object that you can use to trap the mouse coordinates.

The Right Mouse Button

New in Silverlight 4 is support for the right mouse button. You can program event handlers that fire when a user holds the right button down and when the user lets the right button go over a control. The latter cannot happen without the former happening first. The two events are called *MouseRightButtonDown* and *MouseRightButtonUp*, respectively. (Note that there is no right mouse *Click* event.)

Use the *MouseRightButton* and *MouseRightButtonUp* events

1. Start by opening the SbSCh2_3 project you created in the previous section.

2. Select the Rectangle in the designer window and locate the *MouseRightButtonDown* property in the Events tab of the Properties window.

3. Double-click the property to add a *rectangle1_MouseRightButtonDown* event handler. The code window will open. Close it and return to the designer window. (You'll add code to handle the event in a minute.)

4. Find the *MouseRightButtonUp* property on the Events tab of the Properties window. Double-click it to add the *rectangle1_MouseRightButtonUp* event handler.

5. Now, in the code window, find the *rectangle1_MouseRightButtonDown* event handler and add the following two lines of code to it:

```
rectangle1.Fill = new SolidColorBrush(Colors.Yellow);
e.Handled = true;
```

The first line fills the *Rectangle* with a yellow color. Silverlight uses the concept of brushes for colors, so the code creates a new yellow brush and assigns that to the *Fill* property of the *Rectangle*.

The second line is quite interesting. The default experience in Silverlight is to render the Silverlight "About" menu whenever the user right-clicks on the application. By setting the *Handled* property of *e* to true, you tell the runtime that you've already handled the event so it doesn't need to bother!

6. Find the *rectangle1_MouseRightButtonUp* event handler and add the following line of code to it:

```
rectangle1.Fill = new SolidColorBrush(Colors.Green);
```

You now have an application that will turn the rectangle yellow when you hold down the right button over it and change it to green when you let go of the right button. Press F5 and try it out!

> **Further Exploration** Try wiring up the *MouseLeftButtonDown* and *MouseLeftButtonUp* events. They function the same way as the right mouse button events, but for the left mouse button.

The *MouseWheel* Event

Many mice have wheels that can be used to scroll through large sets of data quickly. Silverlight allows you to write code for the mouse wheel in your applications by trapping the *MouseWheel* event. This event takes a *MouseWheelEventArgs* instance as a parameter, which lets you track what the user does with the wheel through its *Delta* property. Here's a short exercise that will give you a better idea of how the *MouseWheel* event can be used.

Trap and program mouse and wheel events

1. Open the SbSCh2_3 project. Select the *Rectangle* and find the *MouseWheel* event on the Events tab of the Properties window. Double-click it to generate the event handler.

2. Add the following code to *the MouseWheel even*t handler:

```
if (e.Delta > 0)
{
    textBlock1.Text = "Up";
}
else
{
    textBlock1.Text = "Down";
}
```

3. Press F5 to run the application. As you scroll up with the mouse wheel, the message "Up" will appear and "Down" will appear when you scroll down.

Note that the *Delta* property of the *MouseWheelEventArgs* returns a value that specifies where the wheel is relative to where it was the last time the event fired. In other words, the *Delta* value is not an absolute value. Keep this in mind when you develop your apps. Instead, think of the *Delta* as being a negative value when you roll the wheel toward yourself and a positive value when you roll it away from yourself.

Using the *CheckBox* Control

Now that you've looked at how to use the *Content* property and how to use mouse events, you're ready for a tour of some of the other controls. You'll start with the *CheckBox* control. You may already be familiar with check box controls, where users select either yes or no by checking or unchecking the check box.

The typical check box control consists of text with a little box to the left. With Silverlight, you aren't limited to this form. *CheckBox* is a content control, meaning you can define the content of the check box to be anything you like. For simplicity, this section sticks to a typical check box form, but you should experiment with changing the content in a way similar to how you altered the *Button* control's contents earlier in this chapter.

Explore using the *CheckBox* control

1. Create a new Silverlight application and call it **SbSCh2_4**.

2. Add a *CheckBox* control to MainPage.xaml.

3. Add a *TextBlock* control to MainPage.xaml.

4. Select the *CheckBox* control and use the Properties window to find the *Checked* event. Double-click the *Checked* event to add an event handler for the event.

5. Visual Web Developer will open the Code window, which will now contain a stub event handler for the *Checked* event. This event will fire whenever the user checks the box. For this example, add a line of code to the event handler that sets the value of the *TextBlock* to the value of the *CheckBox* whenever the user checks it. Here's the full event-handler code:

```
private void checkBox1_Checked(object sender, RoutedEventArgs e)
{
    textBlock1.Text = checkBox1.IsChecked.ToString();
}
```

6. Now run the application. When you check the check box, you'll see that the *TextBlock* contains "true." If you then uncheck the box, nothing happens. That's because the event only fires when the check box is checked, not when it's unchecked.

7. To trap the event when the check box is unchecked, double-click on the *Unchecked* event on the Events tab of the Properties window. This will create an event handler stub for *checkBox1_Unchecked* and open the Code window. Edit the code to look like this:

```
private void checkBox1_Unchecked(object sender, RoutedEventArgs e)
{
    textBlock1.Text = checkBox1.IsChecked.ToString();
}
```

8. Press F5 to run the application. You can now see that the *TextBlock* changes its value both when you check and when you uncheck the check box.

> **Further Exploration** Experiment with how the *Clicked* event works with the *CheckBox* control. You can use the *Clicked* event to handle both the checked and unchecked states by trapping clicks—this might save you a little code. Because the *CheckBox* is a special type of button, many of the aspects of the *Button* control also apply—such as *ClickMode*.

Using the *RadioButton* Control

The *RadioButton* control is similar to the *CheckBox*, but rather than functioning individually, radio buttons are used in a group to let users select a single option from among two or more. You specify the group that a *RadioButton* belongs to using its *GroupName* property. If you don't set the *GroupName* property, then all the radio buttons on the same panel will be considered to be in the same group.

Don't worry, this isn't as complex as it sounds. You can see just how straightforward the *RadioButton* control really is by going through the following process.

Use the *RadioButton* control

1. Create a new Silverlight application and call it **SbSCh2_5**.

2. Add eight *RadioButton* controls. Double-click the *RadioButton* in the Toolbox eight times to add the controls.

3. Go into the XAML and change the *Content* property of each instance from
RadioButton to **Option 1**, **Option 2**, and so on, as shown here:

```
<Grid x:Name="LayoutRoot" Background="White">
    <RadioButton Content="Option 1" Height="16" HorizontalAlignment="Left"
                 Margin="10,10,0,0" Name="radioButton1"
                 VerticalAlignment="Top" Width="120" />
    <RadioButton Content="Option 2" Height="16" HorizontalAlignment="Left"
                 Margin="10,36,0,0" Name="radioButton2"
                 VerticalAlignment="Top" Width="120" />
...
    <RadioButton Content="Option 8" Height="16" HorizontalAlignment="Left"
                 Margin="10,192,0,0" Name="radioButton8"
                 VerticalAlignment="Top" Width="120" />
</Grid>
```

4. Press F5 to run the application. You'll see the eight radio buttons on the screen. Notice
that you can select only one at a time.

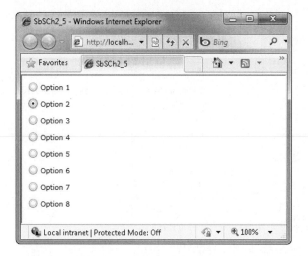

5. Stop the application and edit the XAML again. Change Option 5 through Option 8
to read **Option A** through **Option D**, respectively, and give each of these options a
GroupName property with the value **Letters**, as shown here:

```
<Grid x:Name="LayoutRoot" Background="White">
    <RadioButton Content="Option 1" Height="16" HorizontalAlignment="Left"
                 Margin="10,10,0,0" Name="radioButton1"
                 VerticalAlignment="Top" Width="120" />
```

```
...




        <RadioButton Content="Option C" GroupName="Letters" Height="16"
                    HorizontalAlignment="Left" Margin="10,166,0,0"
                    Name="radioButton7"
                    VerticalAlignment="Top" Width="120" />
        <RadioButton Content="Option D" GroupName="Letters" Height="16"
                    HorizontalAlignment="Left" Margin="10,192,0,0"
                    Name="radioButton8" VerticalAlignment="Top" Width="120" />
    </Grid>
```

6. Press F5 to run the application. This time you'll find that you can select two options—
   one of the options 1 through 4 and one of the options A through D. This is because
   these are now considered separate option groups due to the "Letters" *GroupName* you
   added.

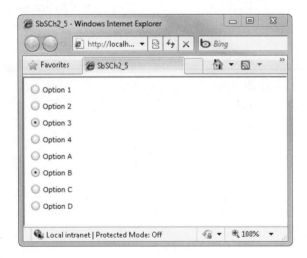

Like the *CheckBox*, the *RadioButton* is a special type of button. With that in mind, everything
you learned about the *Button* control—such as setting content, using the *Click* event, and
setting the *ClickMode*—all apply to the *RadioButton* too!

Using the *TextBox* Control

The *TextBox* is a simple control used for text entry. It can handle single-line and multiple-line
entry and even international character sets that require Unicode. Quite intuitively, the control
exposes its text programmatically through the *Text* property.

To explore some of the facets of using the *TextBox* control, you'll first look at how you can retrieve the text that a user typed in.

Use the *TextBox* control

1. Create a new Silverlight application and call it **SbSCh2_6**.

2. Add a *TextBox* control, a *TextBlock* control, and a *Button* to MainPage.xaml.

3. Double-click the *Button* to add a *Click* event handler and add the following code:

    ```
    textBlock1.Text = textBox1.Text;
    ```

4. Run the application and type something into the text input box. Press the button and you'll see that the application reads the text from the *TextBox* and loads it into the *TextBlock*.

5. Next, try visiting a site with international text. Copy the text and then place your cursor in the text input box in your Silverlight application. Press Ctrl+V to paste the text into the text box. When you press the button, you'll see that the text was copied from the *TextBox* into the *TextBlock*.

You've now created an application that demonstrates how to read the *Text* property of the *TextBox*.

Further Exploration As an exercise, see if you can move the data in the other direction, changing the application so that when you press the button, you set the *Text* in the *TextBox* instead of reading it.

So far, you've used a single-line *TextBox*, but it is common for an application to require a *TextBox* control that supports multiple lines (sometimes called a *TextArea*). Fortunately, making the *TextBox* control accept multiple text lines is very easy to do in Silverlight. Here's the procedure.

Configure a *TextBox* to accept multiple lines

1. Go back to MainPage.xaml in the designer tool and select the *TextBox* control. To make it a multi-line control, you only need to do two things. First, you must set the *AcceptsReturn* property to **true**.

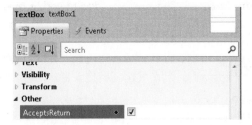

2. Next, enlarge the *TextBox* vertically so it can hold multiple lines of text.

3. Now press F5 to run your application. You'll see that the text input area accepts multiple lines. Easy, right?

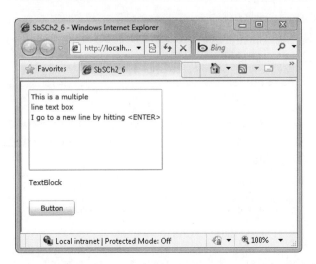

4. The final step in exploring this control is to understand how the *TextChanged* event works. The event is incredibly useful because it fires every time the content of the *TextBox* changes. You can use the event handler to capture keystrokes, perform validation, or do a number of other things.

5. Stop the application. Select the *TextBox* in the designer, and find the *TextChanged* event on the Events tab of the Properties window. Double-click it to add a *TextChanged* event handler.

6. Add the following code to the *TextChanged* event handler:

```
textBlock1.Text = textBox1.Text;
```

7. Run the application and start typing in the text box. You'll see that your keystrokes are being captured and sent to the *TextBlock*. This time you don't need to press the button to cause the "copy" to occur.

Using the *Image* Control

Earlier, you used the *Image* control to provide content for a *Button* control. However, the *Image* control is capable of much more than just rendering images. Here's a short application that explores these additional capabilities.

Use the *Image* control

1. Create a new Silverlight project called **SbSCh2_7**. Add an *Image* control to the MainPage.xaml by double-clicking the *Image* control in the Toolbox.

2. Find the *Image* control's *Source* property and use it to select a .jpg image to load into the control. You should see the image rendered on the design surface.

    To change *how* Silverlight renders the picture, find the *Stretch* property. You can set it to the following values:

    - **None**   This will load the image into the *Image* control with no stretching. If the *Image* control is 100 × 100 and the picture is 1000 x 1000, only the top 100 × 100 pixels will be rendered.

    - **Fill**   The image will be stretched (or crushed) to fit in the *Image* control.

    - **Uniform**   The image will be stretched to the best possible fill without changing its aspect ratio.

    - **UniformToFill**   The image will be stretched without changing its aspect ratio. It will be sized so that the entire *Image* control is painted over—but it may be cropped.

3. Add another three *Image* controls to your design surface. Give them the same source image as the first one, but set the *Stretch* property for each *Image* control to a different value. You'll see results similar to those shown here. Can you guess which image has which *Stretch* setting?

Using the *ComboBox* Control

A *ComboBox* control presents a list of selectable items where only one item at a time is visible. A user can click the control to open a scrollable menu of possible options.

In this section, you'll create an application that uses the *ComboBox* control.

Use the *ComboBox* control

1. Create a new Silverlight application and name it **SbSCh2_8**.

2. Double-click the *ComboBox* control in the Toolbox to add a new ComboBox to MainPage.xaml.

3. Find the control's *Items* property. You'll see it is a *Collection* and there's a caret button indicating that you have to press the button to set the property.

4. Press the button and the Collection Editor will appear. As a Silverlight developer, you will probably use this editor often.

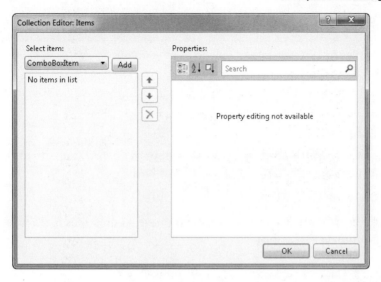

5. You can use this editor to edit any collection. Right now, you're editing an item type called *ComboBoxItem*. Click the Add button three times to add three *ComboBoxItem* instances to the *ComboBox* control.

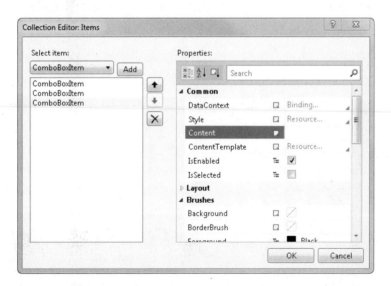

ComboBoxItem controls are *Content* controls, which means you can build rich menus that contain a lot more than just text. For this example, you'll use text to keep things simple, but after you've learned how to use the *ComboBox*, you can experiment with creating more sophisticated content.

> **Tip** Review the Button section earlier in this chapter for some hints.

6. Select the first *ComboBoxItem* in the list, and set its *Content* property to **Dog**. Set the second item's content to **Cat**, and the third to **Bird**.

7. Click OK to exit the Collection Editor.

8. Press F5 to execute the application. You now have a ComboBox that will let you pick your favorite type of animal.

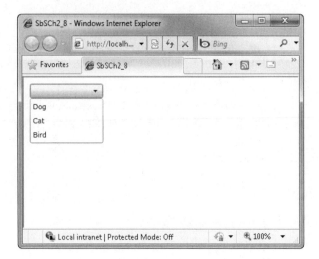

9. Now you'll find out how you can use code to discover which item a user has selected. Stop the application and add a new *TextBlock* to the design surface.

10. Select the *ComboBox* and find its *SelectionChanged* event. Double-click it to add a new event handler.

11. Your code window will open showing the *comboBox1_SelectionChanged* event handler stub. Add the following two lines to the event handler:

```
ComboBoxItem theItem = comboBox1.SelectedItem as ComboBoxItem;
textBlock1.Text = theItem.Content.ToString();
```

12. The first line takes the *SelectedItem* property of the *ComboBox*, which returns a *ComboBoxItem*, and assigns that to the variable *theItem*.

13. The second line then loads the *Content* property ("Dog," "Cat," or "Bird") of *theItem* into the *TextBlock*.

14. Press F5 to execute the application and select an animal.

Using the *ListBox* Control

The *ListBox* control is very similar to the *ComboBox*—except that the list doesn't require a user action to unveil the options. The *ListBox* control usually shows all the items that can be selected (limited, of course, by the size of the control). Hidden elements are usually available using a scrollbar. From a programming viewpoint, you'll see that the *ListBox* is very similar to the *ComboBox* that you've just explored.

Use the *ListBox* control

1. Create a new Silverlight project called **SbSCh2_9**.

2. Double-click the *ListBox* control to add a new *ListBox* to the design surface.

3. Find the *Items* collection. Click the Caret button to open the Collection Editor. You'll see it's the same editor you used for working with the *ComboBox*, except that this time you're adding *ListBoxItem* controls.

4. Press the Add button three times to add three *ListBoxItems*.

5. Call these Dog, Cat, and Bird by setting the *Content* property appropriately.

6. Click OK to exit the Collection Editor.

7. Now add a *TextBlock* control to the design.

8. Find the *SelectionChanged* event in the Events tab of the Properties window. Double-click it to create an event handler and the Code window will open.

9. Edit the *listBox1_SelectionChanged* to include the following code:

```
ListBoxItem theItem = listBox1.SelectedItem as ListBoxItem;
textBlock1.Text = theItem.Content.ToString();
```

Click F5 to run the application. When you select an item from the list, the *TextBlock* will change to display the text of the item you selected from the list.

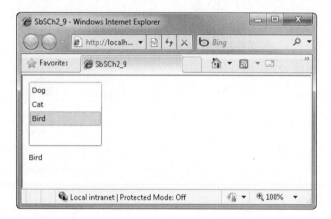

As you can see, the process is almost identical to what you did for the sample using the *ComboBox* control. This demonstrates some of the power of Silverlight—its control model is well designed, allowing you to learn skills that can be applied to a number of other areas.

Key Points

- Many Silverlight controls are *Content* controls. This powerful and flexible solution enables rich and creative ways to render controls. For example, buttons can be customized with XAML to become picture buttons without you needing to create a new type of *Button* control. And lists can be graphical, rather than containing just text items.

- In addition to *Property* types, many Silverlight controls share the same *Event* model. So, for example, once you've learned how to use the mouse with one control, you've essentially learned how to use it with many of the other controls.

- Some types of controls use *Collections* to store a number of items of data. For example, all the items in a *ListBox* or a *ComboBox* are a collection. Each item in a collection is an individual object in and of itself, containing a rich set of properties and events.

- You use common tools to define the collections, and the code to manage them is nearly identical. Many of the skills you learn to work with one control in Silverlight will be transferrable to other tasks.

Chapter 3
Layout and Styling

After completing this chapter, you will be able to:

- Use the *Canvas*, *Grid*, and *StackPanel* layout controls.
- Customize the look and feel of your controls with styling.
- Define templates that support a consistent look and feel.

In Chapter 2, "Silverlight Controls," you learned how many of the default controls in Microsoft Silverlight work. You saw how controls have many properties and events in common, so that learning how to use them for one control gives you a solid foundation for using them with other controls. You also saw how many Silverlight controls are *Content* controls, which can contain any content, giving you the ability to go beyond simple gray buttons or list items.

In this chapter, you'll first take a look at the controls used for layout, making it easier for you to have consistent user interfaces when the user resizes the window. Then you will examine styles and templates that let you set a consistent look and feel across all your controls.

Using the Canvas Control

The Canvas control is perhaps the simplest of the layout controls. It provides a free space on which you can paint controls wherever you like. You perform the layout by manipulating the *Canvas.Left* and *Canvas.Top* properties of your controls. Note that the *Canvas* control doesn't provide automatic layout. This short example illustrates how to lay out controls on a *Canvas*.

Lay out controls on the Canvas

1. Create a new Silverlight application and name it **SbSCh3_1**.
2. Look in the XAML editor, and you'll see that the root control that Silverlight gives you is a *Grid*.

```
<Grid x:Name="LayoutRoot" Background="White">

</Grid>
```

3. Change the Grid XAML to a *Canvas* control. This is as simple as changing the word "Grid" in the opening and closing tags to "Canvas."

```
<Canvas x:Name="LayoutRoot" Background="White">

</Canvas>
```

4. Add three buttons to the design surface by double-clicking *Button* in the Toolbox three times. Visual Web Developer will lay out these buttons for you, one on top of the other. The interesting thing here is *how* they are laid out. Take a look at the XAML and you'll see that Visual Web Developer performed the layout by setting the *Canvas.Left* and *Canvas.Top* properties of the controls.

```
<Canvas x:Name="LayoutRoot" Background="White">
    <Button Canvas.Left="10" Canvas.Top="10" Content="Button"
            Height="23" Name="button1" Width="75" />
    <Button Canvas.Left="10" Canvas.Top="43" Content="Button"
            Height="23" Name="button2" Width="75" />
    <Button Canvas.Left="10" Canvas.Top="76" Content="Button"
            Height="23" Name="button3" Width="75" />
</Canvas>
```

Properties such as *Canvas.Left* and *Canvas.Top* are special properties in Silverlight called attached Properties, meaning they are used to store a value associated with a property defined on the containing parent element, thus they can be used to define the layout of the control relative to its parent. In this case, the position that these properties define isn't the position of the button relative to the top left of the screen, but to the top left of the Canvas that contains the Button control.

5. Change the *Canvas.Left* property of the second Button to **20**, and for the third button, change it to **40**. This will cause the locations of the Buttons to change.

Even though controls are laid out on a *Canvas* control, you can use these properties to place them anywhere on the screen. Since positioning the controls *requires* using attached properties, manipulating them in code is a little different than the dot syntax that you've seen before.

6. Double-click the first button to generate a *Click* event handler.

You would expect to write code that looks something like this:

```
button2.Canvas.Top = 60
```

But when you try to type the code, IntelliSense will show you that such code isn't possible. This occurs because attached properties in Silverlight require a slightly different syntax: the *SetValue* and *GetValue* methods.

To set the value of the property, you use a dependency property, which is just a way of providing a reference to the parent property. So, for example, you refer to the Canvas.Top value using the *Canvas.TopProperty* dependency property. Revise the code so it uses the *SetValue* method and refers to the *Canvas.Top* value using a dependency property:

```
button2.SetValue(Canvas.TopProperty, 60.0);
```

Note that you use the value **60.0**, and not 60. This is because the Top and Left attached properties are double values. If you use 60, Silverlight will think you are setting it as an integer value and you'll get a run-time error. Rather than creating a new double value and loading it with 60, a handy shortcut is just to write **60.0**.

7. Press F5 to run the application and then click the top button. You'll see that the second button jumps to its new location.

Using the *Grid* Control

Using a Grid for layout takes control placement to the next level, letting you define your screen as an invisible grid of cells. These cells can have different heights and widths, allowing an automatic layout mechanism in which controls snap to the boundaries of the cells they occupy.

Place controls on the Grid

1. Create a new Silverlight project called **SbSCh3_2**.

2. The default layout root control is a Grid. Select the Grid and then look at the Properties window. You'll see properties for *ColumnDefinitions* and *RowDefinitions*. You should recognize the caret button to the right, which was discussed in previous chapters. This opens the now-familiar Collection Editor.

3. Click the caret button to the right of the *ColumnDefinitions* property to open the Collection Editor and edit the Grid columns.

4. Press the Add button four times to create four columns.

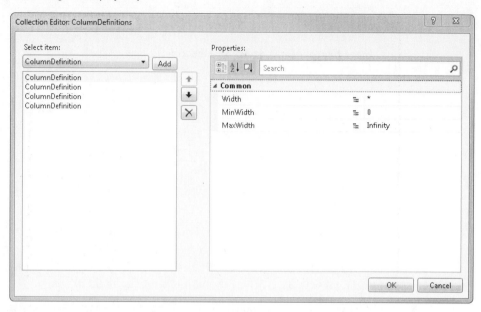

The columns have three properties that define their minimum, maximum, and current widths. Remember that, as your user resizes the application, you'll want your application to respond appropriately, and the Grid control supports effective resizing operations. The MinWidth and MaxWidth properties are pretty self-explanatory. Silverlight will not render the column any narrower than the MinWidth or wider than the MaxWidth. You can set the Width property at run time to fix a column at that width, or set it to an asterisk (*) to make the column width flexible. The asterisk is the default value.

Right now, there are four columns in your project, each with its Width property set to an asterisk, meaning Silverlight will divide the total width of the grid evenly between the columns with each taking 25 percent. If you had set one column to 100 pixels wide and set the other 3 to asterisk, then the one column would take up 100 pixels, while the other 3 columns split up the remaining width of the grid evenly.

5. Press OK to exit the Collection Editor.

6. Repeat the process for the RowDefinition to add three rows.

7. Because the default grid is 400 × 300 and you've added 4 columns and 3 rows, you'll now see twelve 100 × 100 cells in the designer.

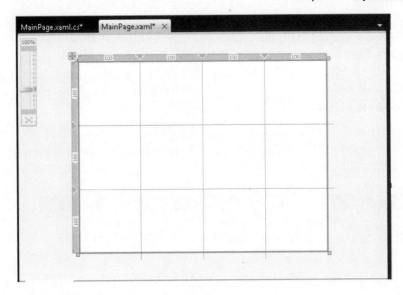

8. In addition to setting column widths and heights numerically, you can drag the column and row lines in the designer to resize columns or rows visually. Try changing the grid so that you have two narrow columns at the edges and narrow rows at the top and bottom.

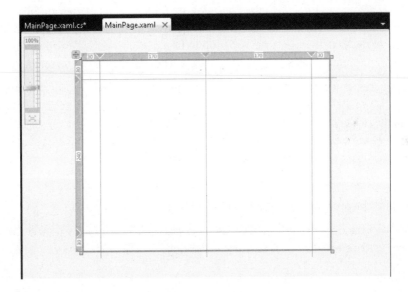

9. So far, you've placed controls by double-clicking them in the Toolbox. This time, instead of double-clicking, drag the control from the Toolbox onto the design surface. You'll notice that as you drag the control over the Grid, it highlights the cells, indicating which cell will contain the control when you drop it. Also note that when you drop the control into a cell, the drop location determines the control's Margin, meaning where the control sits in the cell relative to the cell's edges.

10. Drag three buttons onto the grid. Put two of them in the large central cells and one in the small upper-left cell. Note that the design interface shows margin guides after you drop the controls on the surface.

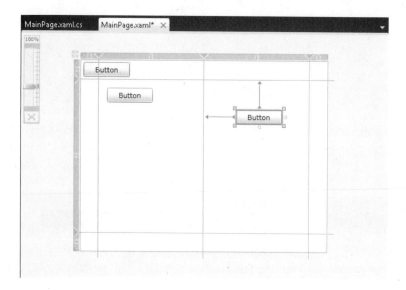

11. Press F5 to run the application and resize the window. As you resize the window, you'll see that the buttons are laid out according to their sizes and locations within the grid cells.

Using the Grid control gives you terrific control over the layout. With well-defined columns and rows, you can build a layout that will react effectively to practically any screen size.

Using the *StackPanel* Layout

You saw the *StackPanel* control briefly in Chapter 2 when you laid out a number of items within a *Content* control. StackPanel lets you create horizontal or vertical stacks of contained content. This section explores the StackPanel control in a little more detail so you can see how it works and how to use it in your applications.

Configure StackPanel controls

1. Create a new Silverlight project and call it **SbSCh3_3**.

2. Double-click StackPanel in the Toolbox to add a StackPanel control to the design surface.

3. Double-click the Button control three times to add three Buttons to the design surface.

4. Add another StackPanel to the design surface by double-clicking StackPanel in the Toolbox again.

5. Double-click the Button control three more times to add three additional buttons.

   You'll probably see a screen in which some of the later Buttons you added aren't fully visible. You'll see only the outline of those controls. Don't worry if that happens—you'll see what's going on in a moment.

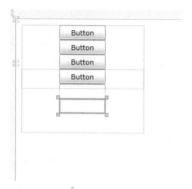

6. Take a look at the XAML code and you might begin to see why the UI looks the way it does. The first StackPanel contains the first three Buttons as well as the second StackPanel. This internal StackPanel contains the next three Buttons.

```xml
<StackPanel Height="100" HorizontalAlignment="Left"
        Margin="10,10,0,0" Name="stackPanel1"
        VerticalAlignment="Top" Width="200">
    <Button Content="Button" Height="23" Name="button1" Width="75" />
    <Button Content="Button" Height="23" Name="button2" Width="75" />
    <Button Content="Button" Height="23" Name="button3" Width="75" />
    <StackPanel Height="100" Name="stackPanel2" Width="200">
        <Button Content="Button" Height="23" Name="button4" Width="75" />
        <Button Content="Button" Height="23" Name="button5" Width="75" />
        <Button Content="Button" Height="23" Name="button6" Width="75" />
    </StackPanel>
</StackPanel>
```

7. Look carefully at the XAML. The Height property of the first StackPanel is 100. Since each Button is 23 pixels tall, you might expect to see 4 Buttons (4 * 23 is 96, which is less than 100). But because the second StackPanel contains the rest of the Buttons, all of which lie within the first StackPanel, the designer crops out those Buttons and shows you that with the ghosted outline of the missing controls.

8. Now change the Orientation property of the second StackPanel to Horizontal, and set its Height property to 25 to be consistent with the Orientation property.

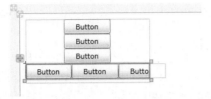

Now the buttons become visible. The first StackPanel is 100 pixels high, giving enough space to show the internal StackPanel and its three horizontally-oriented buttons.

Using these layout controls in your Silverlight application lets you create dynamic applications that can adjust seamlessly to varying screen and window sizes. And, in turn, this will give your users the best possible experience.

Styles and Templates

As you saw earlier, Silverlight controls are highly customizable because they are Content controls. You can define exactly how you want them to appear by using the Control.Content property.

Look at this code example from Chapter 2:

```
<Button Height="148" HorizontalAlignment="Left" Margin="10,10,0,0"
        Name="button1" VerticalAlignment="Top" Width="205">
    <Button.Content>
        <Image Height="95" HorizontalAlignment="Left"
            Name="image1" Stretch="Fill"
            VerticalAlignment="Top" Width="156"
            Source="/SbSCh2_2;component/Images/front-logo.jpg" />
    </Button.Content>
</Button>
```

This shows how you can easily make a Button a picture Button by overriding the default content with custom XAML. As you can imagine, building visually exciting Buttons can require quite a lot of XAML that may include animations, transitions, and more.

So what happens if you have 20 Buttons like this? That's a lot of XAML for Silverlight to parse through, and it could really slow down your Silverlight applications.

To solve such problems, you can use styles, which allow you to define the XAML for the content of your controls once and then apply the defined style to as many controls as you like. This reduces the size of your application by avoiding repetitive XAML and improves performance, because Silverlight will need to parse the XAML only once to determine how to render it.

Style a button with XAML

1. Create a new Silverlight project called SbSCh3_4.

2. Add a Button control to your design surface by double-clicking Button in the Toolbox.

3. Add a StackPanel control to your design surface and make sure that its orientation is set to Vertical.

4. Add an Image control to your design surface by double-clicking Image in the Toolbox. Make sure the image is added as a child of the StackPanel. If it isn't, you can just drag it over the StackPanel and drop it there. To ensure you did this correctly, you can check the XAML view to make sure the Image tag is nested inside the StackPanel tags.

5. Now set the Source property of the Image control. Use the dialog box to upload an image to your project.

6. Add a new TextBlock to your design surface and make it a child of the StackPanel.

7. Set the Text property of the TextBlock to Fancy Books.

8. Change the Font property of the TextBlock to something other than the default setting. The following screenshot uses Georgia font at 20 points.

9. Take a look at the XAML for your Button. The Content attribute will be set to "Button". Delete this attribute completely.

10. Add a full closing tag to the button. Instead of using /> at the end of the line, you should use the standard > and place </Button> at the end of the line. Your code should look something like this:

```
<Button ... HorizontalAlignment="Left" ... >
</Button>
```

11. Now add a <Button.Content></Button.Content> section to the Button, so that it looks like this:

```
<Button HorizontalAlignment="Left" ... >
    <Button.Content>
    </Button.Content>
</Button>
```

12. Cut the entire StackPanel XAML and paste it within the <Button.Content> tags. Don't worry if you can't see the content. If you don't see the content, it is probably due to the Margin property on the StackPanel being set. You can just delete the entire attribute.

13. Resize the Button so you can see its content.

14. Select the Button and use the copy (Ctrl+C) and paste (Ctrl+V) commands to make a few instances of the Button on your page. Take a look at how quickly your XAML document has grown and how much XAML is repeated across the page. Note that when you look at the design, you'll see only one button because they've all been laid out on top of each other.

15. Delete the duplicate Buttons so that you're back to just one.

16. To create a style for a container, you use something called a Setter and apply it to the control template. You create styles in the Resources section of your XAML. If you look at the root node of your XAML, you'll see that it's called a UserControl. Find the Grid node declaration and above it type <UserControl.Resources></UserControl.Resources>.

17. You define your styles within the <UserControl.Resources> tags. In this case, you'll define a style called PictureButton. Add the Style tags so your code looks like this:

```
<UserControl.Resources>
    <Style x:Key="PictureButton" TargetType="Button">
    </Style>
</UserControl.Resources>
```

18. You can now define a Setter to set properties as part of the template and enter the Value of the Setter using a ControlTemplate. Here's what your XAML should look like:

```xaml
<UserControl.Resources>
    <Style x:Key="PictureButton" TargetType="Button">
        <Setter Property="Template">
            <Setter.Value>
                <ControlTemplate TargetType="Button">

                </ControlTemplate>
            </Setter.Value>
        </Setter>
    </Style>
</UserControl.Resources>
```

19. At this point, the style defines a template that you can apply to controls when you want them to look alike. The template simply defines the look—your other code defines the Button and its content. So, following the example of the Fancy Books picture button from earlier, your style and template will look like this. Notice that the Button definition is placed inside the <ControlTemplate> tags.

```xaml
<UserControl.Resources>
    <Style x:Key="PictureButton" TargetType="Button">
        <Setter Property="Template">
            <Setter.Value>
                <ControlTemplate TargetType="Button">
                    <Button>
                        <Button.Content>
                            <StackPanel Height="100" HorizontalAlignment="Left"
                                Name="stackPanel1" VerticalAlignment="Top"
                                Width="200">
                                <Image Height="70" Name="image1" Stretch="Fill"
                                    Width="200"
                                    Source="/SbSCh3_4;component/Images/logo_sbo.jpg" />
                                <TextBlock Height="23" Name="textBlock1" Text="Fancy Books"
                                    Width="120" FontFamily="Georgia" FontSize="20" />
                            </StackPanel>
                        </Button.Content>
                    </Button>
                </ControlTemplate>
            </Setter.Value>
        </Setter>
    </Style>
</UserControl.Resources>
```

20. To create a button that uses this style and template, you simply set the Style property of a Button to the resource. You do this using the following syntax:

```
<Button Style="{StaticResource PictureButton}" Height="100" Width="200" />
```

21. You could also define the Height and Width in the template if you'd rather not include them in the Button tag.

22. Now, if you cut and paste your Button declaration so your application has four identical buttons, you'll see that you only need four lines of XAML to define them!

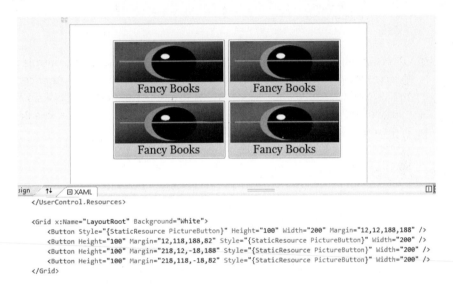

```
sign  ↑↓  ⊞ XAML                                          ⊡
    </UserControl.Resources>

    <Grid x:Name="LayoutRoot" Background="White">
        <Button Style="{StaticResource PictureButton}" Height="100" Width="200" Margin="12,12,188,188" />
        <Button Height="100" Margin="12,118,188,82" Style="{StaticResource PictureButton}" Width="200" />
        <Button Height="100" Margin="218,12,-18,188" Style="{StaticResource PictureButton}" Width="200" />
        <Button Height="100" Margin="218,118,-18,82" Style="{StaticResource PictureButton}" Width="200" />
    </Grid>
```

Key Points

- Using the layout controls, you can control how UI elements are rendered, including how they automatically flow when users change the window size.

- The Canvas control offers a completely definable surface on which you can place controls wherever you like.

- The Grid control lets you define a grid with cells that contain controls, letting you control the layout through fixed and dynamic column and row sizes.

■ You can use the StackPanel control to stack controls either vertically or horizontally, automatically laying them out according to the height of the control.

■ When using content controls in Silverlight, you can fine-tune exactly how you want any control to appear. This expands the volume of XAML used in your UI definition and can lead to maintenance and performance problems. To avoid such problems, you can use styles to define how controls should appear and templates to specify the parts of the control that will define the style.

Chapter 4
Data and RIA Services

After completing this chapter, you will be able to:

- Build a database using Visual Web Developer 2010 Express.

- Create an RIA Service that exposes the database's data.

- Connect to, view, and edit the data using a Silverlight client that contains a *DataGrid*.

Understanding RIA Services

RIA Services, sometimes called Windows Communication Foundation (WCF) RIA Services, are designed to simplify the development of multi-tier solutions with a rich presentation tier. The presentation layer does not have to be built using Microsoft Silverlight, but this book focuses exclusively on using Silverlight as the interface to an RIA Services-based application.

In the next section, you'll see how you can use Microsoft Visual Web Developer Express and Microsoft SQL Server to build a database. If you haven't installed SQL Server yet, go back to Chapter 1, "Introducing Silverlight," to see how you can install a SQL Server instance using Microsoft Web Platform Installer (Web PI).

The next section shows how to build the server project that provides the marshaling layer between the Silverlight client and the SQL Server database. You've already been using server projects in this book, but only for deploying the Silverlight application. In this section, you'll learn to expand the basic server project into a service tier for your application.

The third section will cover connecting your Silverlight client application to the data via the services tier, taking advantage of the methods that RIA Services tools provide.

Build a Database with Visual Web Developer Express

In this section, you'll see how to use Visual Web Developer Express to build a database that runs on the SQL Server engine. But first there are a number of steps you should follow to ensure that your SQL Server database is running and that Visual Web Developer can connect to it.

Prepare SQL Server

1. Ensure that SQL Server is running. If you followed the instructions in Chapter 1 for in-stalling SQL Server, you'll see a SQL Server entry on your Windows Start menu. Open this and you'll see a folder called Configuration Tools. In this folder you'll find the SQL Server Configuration Manager.

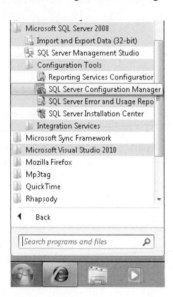

2. Open the SQL Server Configuration Manager and you'll see a list of installed SQL Server items on the left side. Make sure SQL Server Services is selected and you'll see the different services and the running state of each on the right. Make sure SQL Server (SQLEXPRESS) is running.

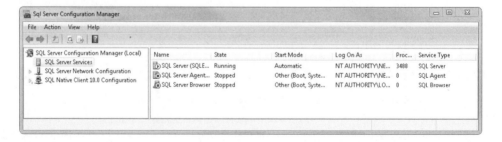

3. If it is not running, select SQL Server (SQLEXPRESS) and press the Start Service button on the toolbar.

4. You'll also need to make sure that Named Pipes are configured, as this is the mechanism that Visual Web Developer uses to connect to the database. On the left side, select SQL Server Network Configuration and you'll see the item Protocols for SQLEXPRESS on the right side. Double-click this and you'll see the list of protocols.

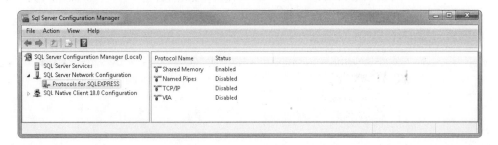

5. If Named Pipes are already enabled, you can skip the rest of this section. Otherwise, double-click this entry and you'll get the configuration dialog box. Set the Enabled field to **Yes** and click OK.

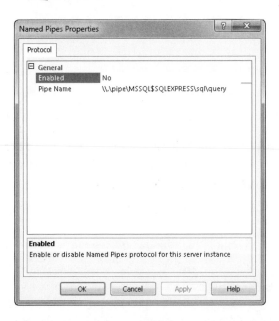

6. You'll get a warning that the changes will be saved but won't take effect until you stop and restart the service. To do this, select SQL Server Services on the left side of the screen and then select SQL Server (SQLEXPRESS) on the right side. Press the Stop button, wait for the service to stop, and then press the Start button to complete the restart operation.

You're now ready to use the SQL Service within Visual Web Developer.

Using SQL Server Within Visual Web Developer

Visual Web Developer provides tools for interacting with databases right in the development environment. In this section, you'll see how to create a simple database of contacts that will provide the data for your Silverlight application.

Build the application

1. Create a new Silverlight application called SbSCh4_1. Be sure to select the Enable .NET RIA Services check box in the New Silverlight Application dialog box.

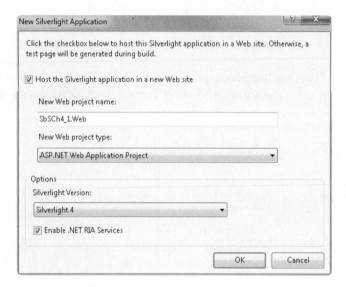

2. The Server element of your application will be called SbSCh4_1.Web. Select that item in Solution Explorer, right-click it, and select New Item from the Add menu. The Add New Item dialog box is displayed.

3. Select Data from the Installed Templates list and you'll see the list of available templates.

4. Select SQL Server Database from the list and name it Friendslist.mdf.

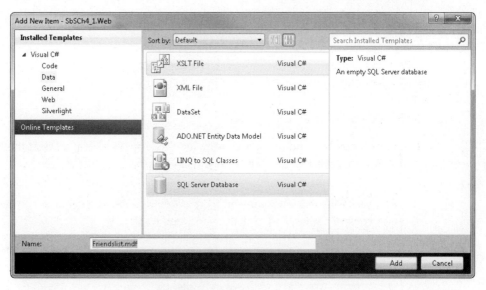

5. Click Add to add the database. You'll get a warning that asks if you want to add the content to the App_Data folder in your site. Click Yes to close the dialog box and accept the App_Data location.

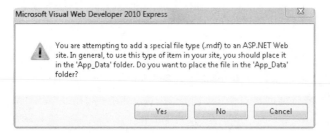

Visual Web Developer will create an App_Data folder that contains the Friendslist.mdf file. The new folder will appear in Solution Explorer.

6. Double-click the Friendslist.mdf file to open the Database Explorer window. Select the Tables item, right-click it, and select Add New Table.

7. The New Table editor will open in the design area. You can use this to create columns, enter column names, and select the appropriate data types. Add four database columns as shown in the screenshot: id, FirstName, LastName, and Phone. Be sure to enter the data types correctly.

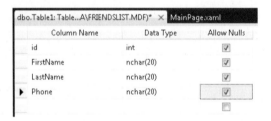

8. The id field functions as a unique identifier for each friend. To achieve this you'll need to do three things, and then save your changes:

   a. Clear the Allow Nulls check box because you don't want to allow any null values in this column.

   b. Configure the id field as an identity field. To do this, select the id field and then locate the Identity Specification row in the Column Properties pane at the bottom of the screen. Set the (Is Identity) field to Yes.

   c. Ensure that the id row is set to be the primary key. Right click on it and select the Set Primary Key option. You'll see a small key icon appear beside the id field.

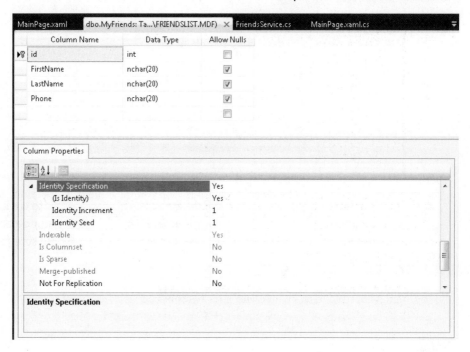

9. You will be asked to enter a name for the Table. Name it MyFriends and click OK.

10. Visual Web Developer will create a MyFriends table, which will appear in the Tables folder in Database Explorer. Right-click the new table and select Show Table Data. You'll see a spreadsheet-like interface into which you can enter data. The id field is read-only because you specified it as an identity field. To create some data, simply type several names and phone numbers into the appropriate fields.

MyFriends: Query(...\FRIENDSLIST.MDF) ✕	dbo.MyFriends: Ta...\FRIENDSLIST.MDF)		
id	FirstName	LastName	Phone
1	Laurence	Moroney	4251111111
2	Rebecca	Moroney	4252222222
3	Bucky	Moroney	4253333333
▶* NULL	NULL	NULL	NULL

◄◄ ◄ | 4   of 4 | ▶ ▶◄ ▶▪ | ⊛ | Cell is Read Only.

You now have a simple database that has been configured and contains some sample data. In the next section, you'll see how to expose this to your Silverlight application via WCF RIA Services.

Create an RIA Services Server Project

This section shows the steps involved in providing a pathway between the data and your Silverlight application via a server project. Remember, in a real-world scenario, the data will be hosted on a server and the Silverlight application will be running in a browser on the client. Therefore, you need a reliable mechanism for managing data being passed between the server and the client. RIA Services makes it easy to manage this data. First, you'll create an ADO.NET Entity Data Model and then you'll create a domain data service.

ADO.NET Entity Data Model

An ADO.NET Entity Data Model consists of a set of classes whose properties map to the tables and fields in a database, making it easy to work with data. Here's how to create the model.

Create the model

1. First, you need to add an ADO.NET Entity Data Model to your solution. Select the SbSCh4_1.web project in Solution Explorer, right-click it, and select the New Item option from the Add menu.

2. In the Add New Item dialog box, select Data and click ADO.NET Entity Data Model. Name the new model MyFriends.edmx.

3. Click the Add button and the Entity Data Model Wizard will open. You're going to create your data model from an existing database, so be sure to select Generate From
Database and then click Next.

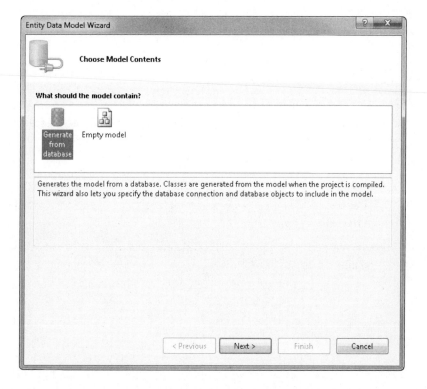

4. The next screen will ask which data connection you want to use to connect to your database. The default option should be Friendslist.mdf. Select it and make sure to select the Save Entity Connection Settings In Web.Config As check box. Keep the default name the wizard provides, which will be FriendslistEntities. Click Next to continue.

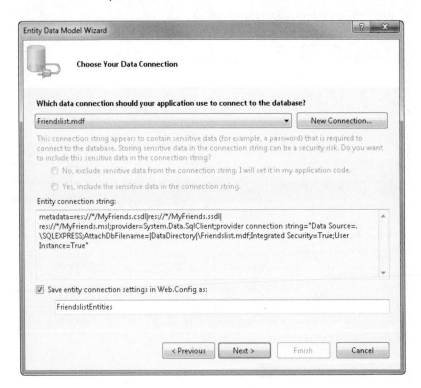

5. The Wizard will connect to your database and retrieve the details of your database. This might take a few minutes. When it's done, you'll see a list of objects in your database. Find and select the MyFriends table.

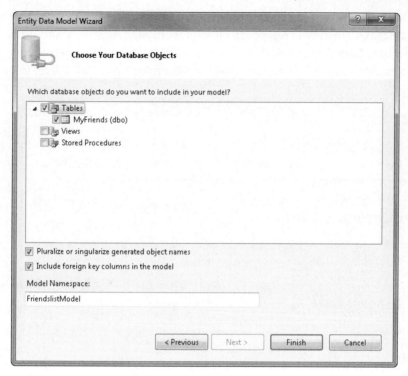

6. Click Finish and Visual Web Developer will create the Entity Data Model and load it into the designer.

7. At this point, you should build the solution, which allows Visual Web Developer to create the proxy classes that Silverlight will use. You can do this by right-clicking on the solution and choosing the Build Solution option. Now you'll create the Domain Service by performing the steps in the next section.

Create a Domain Service

Now that you have a model of your data entities, you can create a domain service that exposes them to your Silverlight client. You can also use the domain service to implement business logic. Here's the procedure.

Create a domain service

1. Select the SbSCh4_1.Web server project in Solution Explorer, right-click it, and select the New Item option from the Add menu.

2. From the Installed Templates list, select Web and then select the Domain Service Class template. Name it FriendsService.cs and click Add.

3. The Add New Domain Service Class dialog box will appear. This gives you a list of available entities around which you can create services. Make sure you select the check box next to the MyFriend class and ensure that the Enable Client Access check box is also selected.

Visual Web Developer will create the FriendsService.cs domain service class.

4. Build the solution before continuing.

Create the Silverlight Client

You've created a database, and a data model that allows you to program against that database, and a domain service that exposes the model. Now you are ready to create a Silverlight client that communicates to the database through the service and the model.

Build a Silverlight client

1. In Solution Explorer, make sure you're using the client project called SbSCh4_1 and open the MainPage.xaml file in the designer.

2. Drag a DataGrid control from the Toolbox onto MainPage.xaml. Change its Name property to FriendsGrid.

3. Make sure that the AutoGenerateColumns property of the grid is set to True.

4. Open the MainPage.xaml.cs code-behind page.

5. At the top of the code window, add the following "using" statements code:

```
Using System.ServiceModel.DomainServices.Client;
using SbSCh4_1.Web;
```

6. The connection to the domain service is done through a Context. The RIA Services framework creates a FriendsContext class based on the fact that your database was called Friends. You'll need to add a private class-level variable which is an instance of this:

```
private FriendsContext _friendsContext = new FriendsContext();
```

7. The concept of loading data from the service is embodied in the LoadOperation class, which will use the MyFriend data type. Remember that when you created the model, you called it MyFriends. RIA Services uses this to define a MyFriend data type. Create another class-level variable to hold an instance of LoadOperation<MyFriend>, like so:

```
private LoadOperation<MyFriend> loadOp;
```

8. Next, in the MainPage() constructor, you need to initialize the LoadOperation by calling a query within the context that connects you to the service.

```
loadOp = this._friendsContext.Load(this._friendsContext.GetMyFriendsQuery());
```

9. Loading is an asynchronous operation. When the operation completes, the Completed event will fire. Using the following syntax, you can specify which function to call when the Completed event fires:

```
loadOp.Completed += new EventHandler(loadOp_Completed);
```

10. After the load is complete, the loadOp instance will contain the data. You access data in the collection by using its Entities class, and you can bind the DataGrid to a collection by using its ItemsSource property. Here's what the loadOp_Completed event handler should look like:

```
voidloadOp_Completed(object sender, EventArgs e)
        {
FriendsGrid.ItemsSource = loadOp.Entities;
        }
```

11. As a checkpoint, here's the complete code for MainPage.xaml.cs. Make sure your code matches and then press F5 to compile and run the application. You should see the data rendered in the grid.

```
using System;
using System.Collections.Generic;
using System.Linq;
using System.Net;
using System.Windows;
using System.Windows.Controls;
using System.Windows.Documents;
using System.Windows.Input;
using System.Windows.Media;
using System.Windows.Media.Animation;
using System.Windows.Shapes;
Using System.ServiceModel.DomainServices.Client;
using SbSCh4_1.Web;

namespace SbSCh4_1
{
    public partial class MainPage : UserControl
    {
        private FriendsContext _friendsContext = new FriendsContext();
        private LoadOperation<MyFriend>loadOp;
        public MainPage()
        {
InitializeComponent();
loadOp =
                this._friendsContext.Load(this._friendsContext.
GetMyFriendsQuery());
loadOp.Completed += new EventHandler(loadOp_Completed);
        }
        void loadOp_Completed(object sender, EventArgs e)
        {
FriendsGrid.ItemsSource = loadOp.Entities;
        }
    }
}
```

12. So far, the application provides a read-only look at the data. But the DataGrid is capable of both display and editing. With very little extra work, you can transform the application so users can create, edit, and save changes to the data. To start, add a Button control to MainPage.xaml by double-clicking Button in the Toolbar.

13. Next, double-click the Button on the design surface. Visual Web Developer will create a button1_Clickevent handler and stub code. Add the following lines of code to the event handler. This code detects whether any data has changed in the data context bound to the grid. If so, then the user has changed something, and you need to submit the changes back to the database via RIA Services.

```
if (_friendsContext.HasChanges)
                 _friendsContext.SubmitChanges();
```

14. Press F5 to start the application. Change the data in a field and then click the Button. The application will write the changed data to the database.

15. Stop the application and take a look at Database Explorer in Visual Web Developer. Open the Tables node, right-click MyFriends, and select Show Table Data.

    You'll see the latest view of your database containing the changes you made to the data!

id	FirstName	LastName	Phone
1	Laurence	qwe	4251111111
2	Rebecca	qwet	4252222222
3	Bucky	12311j2h3j	4253333333
* NULL	NULL	NULL	NULL

Key Points

- You learned how to use databases with Silverlight and how to bind to data.

- RIA Services offer a simple way to expose data to Web clients through Silverlight.

- You explored the Visual Web Developer tools you use to work with SQL Server and learned how to create a table, define its columns, and add data.

- The ADO.NET Data Model can be used as the basis of a Domain Service class.

- RIA Services provides proxy classes that you can use from Silverlight to communicate with the Domain Service classes.

- You built a working data-entry application that uses the Silverlight DataGrid control to view, edit, and update data.

Chapter 5
Rich Imaging

In this chapter, you'll learn how to:

- Use Deep Zoom Composer to build high resolution, bandwidth friendly images.

- Combine images into smooth, zoomable panoramas.

- Build Silverlight applications that control Deep Zoom programmatically.

- Use Photosynth to create interactive 3-D images.

- Build Photosynth-based applications with Silverlight and JavaScript.

Imaging in Silverlight

In Chapter 2, "Silverlight Controls," you saw how you can use the *Image* control to render .jpg and .png images on your Silverlight design surface. This is a useful and powerful capability, but only scratches the surface of what you can do with imaging on the Web in Silverlight.

Consider a picture taken by a digital camera. Large pictures that are 5 or 6 megabytes or even bigger are common. A typical high-resolution photo may be 3,000 to 4,000 pixels across, but rendered on a screen that is only 1,024 pixels across. It's not effective to put such a picture on the Web—either the viewer will have to do a lot of scrolling to see all the detail or the image will have to be resized to fit on the screen.

Unfortunately, specifying an image size in HTML doesn't completely solve the problem. When you do that, the browser will render the image at the reduced size, but will still download the full image. This results in a 5 or 6 megabyte download to display something that is effectively only a few hundred pixels wide. The workaround, of course, is to resize the image prior to uploading it. To resize an image, you typically use some sort of image editing application to generate a smaller version of the image, and then you can use that file on your page.

But what if you could have the best of both worlds? What if you could render the image in a small space, but have the full image fidelity available, and still only download a small amount of information?

Silverlight Deep Zoom allows you to do just this. The Deep Zoom tools create several versions of your image at different resolutions and cut each image up into tiles. Then, the user can decide the level of detail she wants to see, zooming in and out. The application, in turn, will download and render the appropriate tiles. This is similar to the way online maps work.

Users don't download each individual picture of every street in the world—they only download the specific areas they're viewing.

Photosynth is another rich imaging technology that analyzes a set of pictures for overlapping content. It can stitch the pictures together to create a panorama automatically. It can even create a 3-D model of a scene or location using the pictures. Users can then explore this 3-D world, zooming in and out of the picture details using the same technology found in Silverlight Deep Zoom.

With that background, the next section shows how you can build sites that use the rich, bandwidth friendly imaging technologies in Silverlight.

Using Deep Zoom with Silverlight

In this section you'll explore Deep Zoom in Silverlight. You'll first see how to obtain, install, and configure Deep Zoom Composer. You'll step through the process of building a Deep Zoom picture and a Deep Zoom collection. Then you'll see how to use the *MultiScaleImage* control to build applications, as well as learn how to program against collections.

Getting Started with Deep Zoom Composer

Deep Zoom Composer is a free tool from Microsoft. You'll find a link to the latest download available at *http://www.silverlight.net/learn/quickstarts/deepzoom/*.

In this section, you'll step through the process of creating a Deep Zoom of a single image. You'll need to download and install the application before continuing.

Create a new Photosynth project

1. Launch Deep Zoom Composer. On the introduction screen, select New Project...

2. In the New Project dialog box, name your project SbSCh5_1. The default location for your project will be under your Documents folder.

3. Click OK and you'll be taken to the main Deep Zoom design surface. It's blank for right now, but note the three-part process through which the tool will guide you.

4. The process begins at the Import stage. On the right side of the screen, you'll see a button named Add Image. Press the Add Image button and you'll get a standard "File Open" dialog box. Select an image, and Deep Zoom Composer will add it to the design surface. Although you can add multiple images to the designer, this example uses only one image, so the next step is to compose the image.

5. Press the Compose button at the top of the screen. You'll see the Compose view, with thumbnails of any images you've added placed at the bottom of the screen. Right now you should have only one image, so your screen should look something like the one shown here.

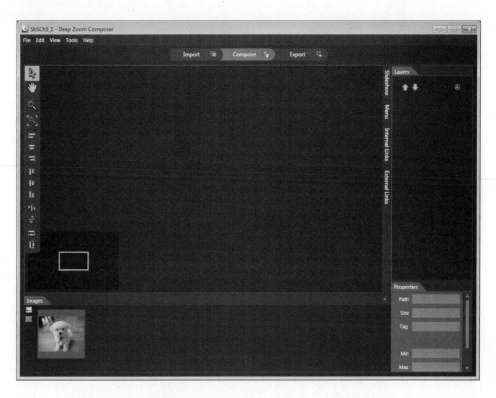

6. Drag the image from its thumbnail at the bottom to the main design surface. You can use the mouse wheel to zoom in and out of the picture while the preview window at the lower left indicates the portion of the image visible in the main window.

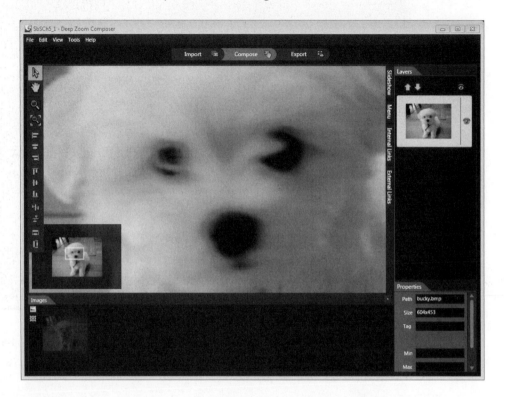

7. You can use tools in Deep Zoom Composer to align multiple images and provide clickable links within images. You'll explore these features a little later. For now, just use this single image.

8. Now click the Export tab at the top of the screen to begin the export process. When you click the Export tab, you'll see a Silverlight Deep Zoom control that you can use to zoom in and out of the picture, similar to the way users will interact with the image online. Of course, the Export tab also lets you export your creation so the rest of the world can see it.

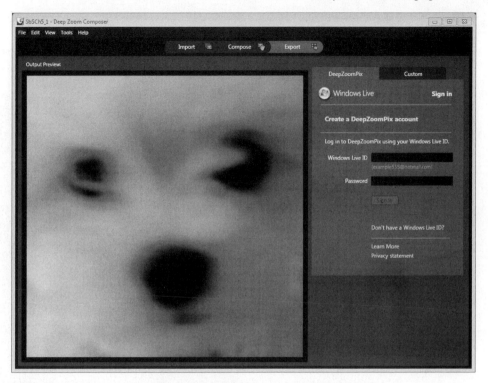

9. The default is to export to a DeepZoomPix account. However, this service has been discontinued and will be removed in the next version of Deep Zoom Composer. So you'll need to click the Custom tab.

10. The Output Type section at the top of the tab offers three options. You can export only the images, both the images and a Silverlight Deep Zoom experience, or the images with an AJAX experience. For this exercise, accept the default settings on the Custom tab, give the project a name, and click the Export button.

11. When the Export process completes, you'll be given the option to preview the application in your browser, view the image folder, or learn more. The View Project Folder option will be grayed out because the template that you selected in the previous step was one that didn't include the source. You'll see more about that in the next section.

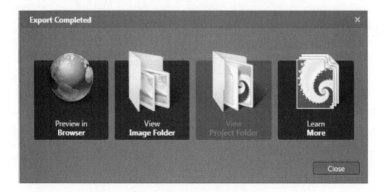

12. Select the Preview In Browser option. Your browser will launch and open a site that contains a Silverlight-based viewer for the Deep Zoom content.

13. You can now zoom in and out of the image with a smooth, animated experience. Experiment with the zoom features and note how different the interaction is from interaction with images using a standard in-browser approach.

You've just seen a straightforward approach to building a Deep Zoom image for Silverlight using a single image. In the next section, you'll see more sophisticated uses of Deep Zoom Composer, including the ability to manage multiple pictures and add clickable hotspots.

Note Yes, that's a real dog. His name is Bucky and he's a handful.

Building Deep Zoom Image Collections

You can use Deep Zoom Composer on a large number of images, which it calls a collection. When dealing with a collection of images, Deep Zoom Composer provides tools for navigating around the collection. Silverlight also offers an API that allows you to manage each individual image within the collection from code.

In this section, you'll explore how you can use Deep Zoom Composer to arrange images at different zoom levels, as well as how you can add internal links between images and external links to Web sites.

Work with multiple images

1. Start Deep Zoom Composer and create a new project called **SbSCh5_2**.

2. Click the Add Image button on the Import tab and add several new images. You can use the same dialog box to select multiple images.

3. Click the Compose tab. You'll see the images across the bottom of the screen.

4. Select one of the images and drag it to the design surface.

5. Use the mouse to zoom in on the image just a little and then place another image beside it. The new image will be at a different zoom level than the first image.

6. Zoom in and out to place the rest of the images.

7. Even though the three pictures at the bottom right look small, they are actually high-resolution images. Notice how Deep Zoom Composer places images at different zoom levels.

8. Click the Export tab. Export your project as discussed in the previous example, and Deep Zoom ComposerDZC will create a Deep Zoom composition for you.

The resulting multi-image experience is similar to the one created with only one image, but you can improve it by adding some functionality to the individual images.

Add links to your project

1. Return to the Compose tab. Find the Area tool on the Images pane and select it to add a new area to the composition.

2. Deep Zoom Composer will add a gray area to your composition. You can size this area and place it anywhere on the image.

3. Right-click the gray area and select Add Internal Link from the pop-up menu. You'll see a dialog box showing the different pictures in the composition. Select an image from this dialog box and click OK.

4. Deep Zoom Composer will create the internal link. When you view the final composition, clicking the specified area (the eye in this example), Silverlight will zoom to the linked image that you just selected.

5. Now define an external link. Add and position another area the same way you did earlier.

6. This time, right-click and select Add External Link.

7. You'll see the External Links Management dialog box. This lets you add a link between a selected area on an image and an external URL. The first time you use this feature, no existing URLs will be available in its list, so you'll have to create a new one. This is done quite easily.

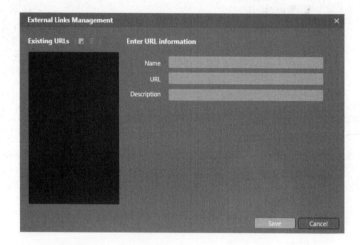

8. Click the Page icon at the top of the list. When you create a new URL, you can give it a short name, specify a URL to launch when a user clicks the specified area, and provide a description. Fill in these fields as shown in this screenshot and click Save.

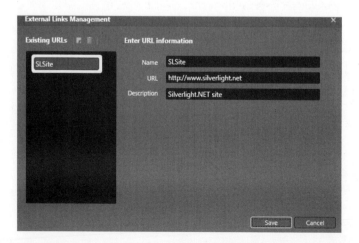

9. Click the Export tab and export the project as discussed earlier. When you view the project, the areas will not be marked visibly. When a user hovers over an area, the Silverlight application will display a hotspot and outline. This indicates the area is clickable.

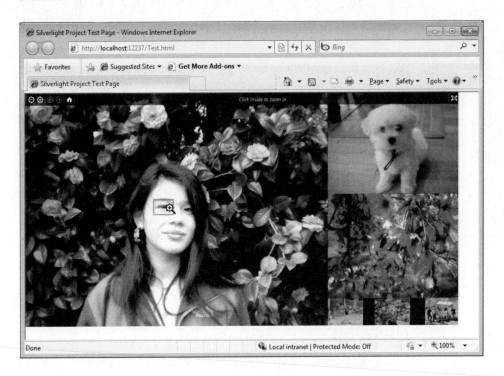

Tip Clicking an Internal link will cause Silverlight to jump to the linked image, zooming in so it will fill the current screen area. By default, Deep Zoom Composer creates a default internal link over each image to give you a quick zoom to that image. Clicking an External link, on the other hand, spawns a new browser instance that opens the external URL.

Programming with Deep Zoom

So far, you've seen the Deep Zoom Composer tool and the viewer application that lets you preview Deep Zoom compositions. But you probably want to know how you can program these projects yourself.

So in this section, you'll explore programming with Deep Zoom in Silverlight. You'll still use Deep Zoom Composer to create the image tiles, but you'll consume them through a Silverlight application of your own, which will show you the basics of how to program the MultiScaleImage control.

Program a Deep Zoom project

1. Use Deep Zoom Composer to create a new project and name it **SbSCh5_3**.

2. Add two images and position them side by side.

3. Click the Export tab and select the template Empty Project + Source.

4. When the export completes, click View Project Folder. This will open Windows Explorer and display the contents of the project folder.

5. Double-click the DeepZoomProject.sln file to open the project in Visual Web Developer Express. Because Deep Zoom Composer outputs the source code in an older format (Microsoft Visual Studio 2008), Visual Web Developer will display a dialog box that asks whether you want to convert the project. Click through each dialog box to finish the wizard.

6. Using Solution Explorer, locate and open the project's MainPage.xaml file. Open the XAML view and add a *MultiScaleImage* control as a child of the *Grid* element like this:

```
<Grid x:Name="LayoutRoot" Background="White">
 <MultiScaleImage Width="400" Height="400"
          Source="GeneratedImages/dzc_output.xml">
 </MultiScaleImage>
 </Grid>
```

7. The *Source* attribute of the control will be flagged with a warning. You don't need to worry about this. The warning occurs because the XAML resides in the Silverlight portion of the project, but the path that the *Source* attribute references resides elsewhere.

That path is in the Web part of the project, so Silverlight will see it properly at run time even though it doesn't see the path at design time.

8. Press F5 to run the application. When you run the application, you'll see that Silverlight renders the images, but you won't be able to interact with them yet. You'll see how to enable image interaction in the next steps.

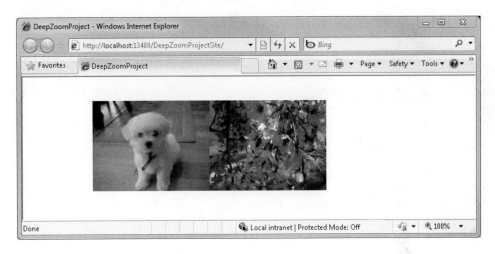

When you close the browser, Visual Web Developer takes you out of debug mode. Make sure you're viewing the XAML view, and then follow these steps to enable image interaction in the application.

Enable image interaction

1. Due to the *Source* attribute warning described a moment ago, Visual Web Developer will not allow you to drag controls onto the design surface. Delete the Source attribute from the MultiScaleImage tag. Also, at this point it's good to give the *MultiScaleImage* control a name. To do this, add an *x:Name* attribute and set its value to *msi*, like so:

```
<Grid x:Name="LayoutRoot" Background="White">
<MultiScaleImage Width="400" Height="400"
            x:Name="msi"></MultiScaleImage>
</Grid>
```

2. Drag two StackPanel controls into the XAML view. Edit the code so that it looks like this:

```
<Grid x:Name="LayoutRoot" Background="White">
<MultiScaleImage Width="400" Height="400"
x:Name="msi"></MultiScaleImage>
<StackPanel><StackPanel></StackPanel></StackPanel>
</Grid>
```

3. Add *Orientation* parameters to the *StackPanel* controls, setting the first *StackPanel* so its *Orientation* is Vertical and the second so its *Orientation* is Horizontal.

```
<Grid x:Name="LayoutRoot" Background="White">
<MultiScaleImage Width="400" Height="400"
            x:Name="msi"></MultiScaleImage>
<StackPanel Orientation="Vertical">
<StackPanel Orientation="Horizontal"></StackPanel>
</StackPanel>
</Grid>
```

4. Move the *MultiScaleImage* control so that it is a child of the first *StackPanel* (the Vertical one).

```
<Grid x:Name="LayoutRoot" Background="White">
<StackPanel Orientation="Vertical">
<MultiScaleImage Width="400" Height="400"
x:Name="msi"></MultiScaleImage>
<StackPanel Orientation="Horizontal"></StackPanel>
</StackPanel>
</Grid>
```

5. Add four buttons to the horizontal StackPanel. Name them **btnLeft**, **btnRight**, **btnUp**, and **btnDown**. Set their Content attribute values accordingly—to **Left**, **Right**, **Up**, and **Down**.

```
<Grid x:Name="LayoutRoot" Background="White">
<StackPanel Orientation="Vertical">
<MultiScaleImage Width="400" Height="400"
            x:Name="msi"></MultiScaleImage>
<StackPanel Orientation="Horizontal">
<Button x:Name="btnLeft" Content="Left"></Button>
<Button x:Name="btnRight" Content="Right"></Button>
<Button x:Name="btnUp" Content="Up"></Button>
<Button x:Name="btnDown" Content="Down"></Button>
</StackPanel>
</StackPanel>
</Grid>
```

6. Now switch to the code view and open MainPage.xaml.cs. First, you'll need to add some code to set the image source of the *MultiScaleImage* control so it will render at run time. (Remember, you removed it from the XAML to avoid the error, so you need to add it back in here.) In C#, this is easy. Just create a Uri object and point it at the location of the XML. Now you can use the *Uri* object to initialize a new *DeepZoomImageTileSource* instance. Set the *MultiScaleImage* control's *Source* property to this new *DeepZoomImageTileSource* and you're done.

It's simpler than it might sound. In fact, you can do all this in the *MainPage()* constructor. Here's the code:

```
Uri uri = new Uri("GeneratedImages/dzc_output.xml", UriKind.RelativeOrAbsolute);
msi.Source = new DeepZoomImageTileSource(uri);
```

7. You can also add *Click* event handlers (or any event handler) in code, rather than specifying them in the XAML. As an example, type **btnUp.Click +=**, and you'll see a hint asking if you want to create the default event handler. Press the Tab key to finish the statement, and then press it again to create the event handler. This is a great shortcut! The event declaration should look like this:

```
btnUp.Click += new RoutedEventHandler(btnUp_Click);
```

8. The newly created event handler will look something like this:

```
voidbtnUp_Click(object sender, RoutedEventArgs e)
    {
        throw new NotImplementedException();
    }
```

Note It's important that you understand how the MultiScaleImage control works. You specify the part of the composition that you are presently viewing with the ViewPortOrigin property, which tells you which part of the image is at the top left hand side of the control. When you first load an image, the ViewPortOrigin is set to 0,0. In other words, the top left corner of the control is also the top left corner of the image. To manipulate the view, you simply change the ViewPortOrigin point. Note that the values for the origin are between 0 and 1, where 0 is the top (or left) of each axis and 1 is the bottom or right of the axis, where the axis is either the width or height of the picture. Thus, to move the zoomed area up in the image, you change the Y value of the ViewPointOrigin coordinate by adding to it.

9. Now you can add some code to the event handler. Place this code into the *btnUp_Click* handler:

```
voidbtnUp_Click(object sender, RoutedEventArgs e)
        {
                Point o = msi.ViewportOrigin;
o.Y += 0.1;
msi.ViewportOrigin = o;
        }
```

10. As an exercise, implement appropriate Click events for the other three buttons. To move left and right, manipulate the *X* property of the *Point*.

11. Now go back and add two new buttons, called *btnIn* and *btnOut*. You'll use these to zoom in and out of the image.

12. Add a *Click* handler for the *btnIn* button in the same way as you did for *btnUp*—by specifying it in the *MainPage()* constructor function.

13. Add a class-level variable—under the class declaration, but above the *MainPage()* function—to keep track of the zoom factor:

```
double zoom = 1.0;
```

14. VWDE will create a *btnIn_Click* function. To zoom into the scene, you multiply the current zoom factor by a value greater than 1. To zoom out, you multiply it by a value less than 1. You then call the *ZoomAboutLogicalPoint* function, passing it the new zoom factor and a point on the image to use as the center of your zoom. As an example, the following code will zoom in, using the origin as the zoom center point:

```
voidbtnIn_Click(object sender, RoutedEventArgs e)
        {
                zoom *= 1.3;
msi.ZoomAboutLogicalPoint(zoom,
msi.ViewportOrigin.X, msi.ViewportOrigin.Y);
        }
```

15. Now you can run your application. Pressing the In button will zoom into the image. As an exercise, try implementing zoom out functionality in the same way.

Note When you use Deep Zoom Composer, if you choose to export using the Deep Zoom Classic + Source template, you'll get a full Visual Studio solution that contains all the code you need to provide a full Deep Zoom experience. This includes mouse and mouse wheel control so users can pan and zoom around your image using a mouse.

Using Photosynth with Silverlight

Photosynth is a technology that allows you to take a number of pictures of the same scene from different angles and stitch them together into a 3-D simulation of that scene. Imagine you are standing in a room. You take a photograph of the door, then turn a little to the left and take another photograph. You'll likely have part of the door in the second photograph. Photosynth can detect that overlap and stitch the images together.

The end result will provide an experience that simulates standing in the room. As the user pans around the scene, Photosynth figures out the best picture to render and transforms that picture so it will approximate what users would see if they were standing in the room!

The following image is an example of a Photosynth project created with photos taken at a little league game, with the photographer (me) standing close to first base.

The scene is composed from a number of images—notice where the light and color levels appear to be different. As you move around the scene, the application highlights the outlines of the images. Clicking will center the scene on the image you clicked, so you can effectively move around the scene and explore it. The more photos used for a project, the more immersive the project will be.

You can zoom in and out of the images just like you can with Deep Zoom. The images themselves are processed by a server at *http://www.photosynth.net*, but you can add a Silverlight-based Viewer control for these images to your own applications.

Create a Photosynth

Before you begin, you'll need a bunch of pictures of the same scene. If you don't have any, just take out a digital camera and shoot some. The easiest way to begin is to stay in the same spot, and take a number of overlapping pictures as you rotate through about 180 degrees.

Note how the images overlap. Both images show the slightly different views of the lines on the floor, the outline of the window, and the chair at the front. Photosynth uses these overlapping features when it calculates the 3-D scene to determine the camera's point of view.

Also, if you don't have one already, you'll need to sign up for a Windows Live ID. You can do this at *http://www.live.com*. You'll need this to sign into *http://www.photosynth.net* to create and upload your pictures.

Install the Photosynth Creation Tool

After you've signed into Photosynth, you'll see the home page, which contains a number of Photosynths (called "synths" for short) already showing. At the top of the screen you'll see a Create link.

Install the Photosynth creator

1. Click the Create link. This will take you to *http://photosynth.net/create.aspx*. If you don't already have the Photosynth creation control, you'll see an Install Photosynth button in the center of the screen.

2. Click the Install Photosynth button. After a moment, you'll see the Photosynth file download. Click the Run button to download and install Photosynth.

3. The control will download and install. Note that this is not the Photosynth viewer, which is implemented in Silverlight. This is the creator, which is a Windows application used for authoring Photosynths. Your end users do not need this application to view your compositions—all they need is Silverlight.

4. Follow the install wizard's instructions to install the creator tool.

5. When you're done, revisit *http://photosynth.net/create.aspx*. This time, you'll see a Create A Synth button in the center of the screen.

Use the Synth Creator

Now that you have installed the creator, you can create a new synth by clicking on the create button found at *http://photosynth.net/create.aspx*. In this section, you'll step through the procedure to create your own synth.

Create a new synth

1. Go to *http://photosynth.net/create.aspx* and click the Create button.

2. Photosynth will ask you to sign in. Use your Live ID and password.

3. After signing in, you'll see the Create Synth dialog box. Click the Add Photos button and select all the pictures you want to add to the project. When you're done, your window should look something like the one shown here.

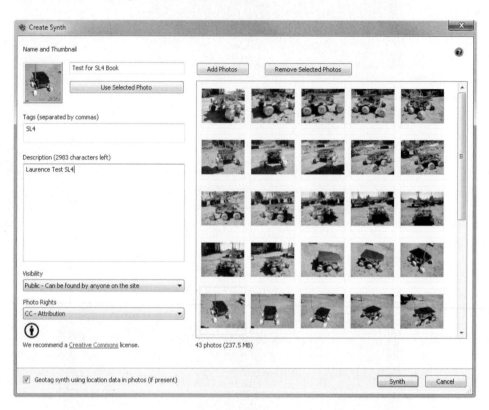

4. Give your composition a name. Add some tags to your image. And set the description, visibility, and photo rights appropriately. After you complete those fields, the Synth button will be enabled.

 Note You must select at least 3 photos to be in your synth.

5. Press the Synth button, and Photosynth will start uploading and processing your synth. This can take a few minutes.

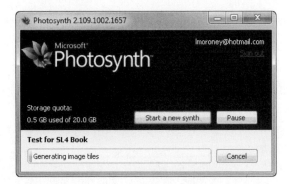

6. When the synth generation process is complete, you'll be able to view the synth by clicking the View button. This button will appear in place of the Cancel button after your upload completes successfully. You've now created your very first Photosynth! Well done!

7. To Add a Highlight (for a shortcut to a particular image), select the Highlights tab seen in the upper right. Then use the Photosynth viewer to navigate to a picture you want to highlight and click Add Highlight. The following image shows a Photosynth project with several highlights already added.

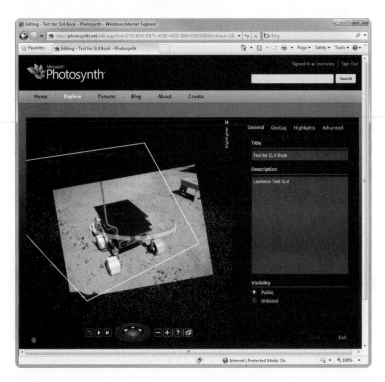

8. When you're done, click the Save button. You're now ready to share your synth with the world.

Sharing Your Synths

Sharing your synths is a straightforward operation. People can either discover them at Photosynth.net, using the tags you specified when you created the synth, or you can create an Embed link to share a Photosynth on your Web site or blog. The procedure for both is essentially the same.

Share your synths online

1. Go to *http://photosynth.net* and sign in.

2. Click your name at the top of the screen (where the link reads "Signed in as:<Your Name>").

3. Click Synths at the top of the screen.

4. You'll see all the synths you've created. Select the one that you want to share.

5. At the bottom of the synth, you'll see some icons that let you copy the embed code, copy the sharing code, or even add the synth as a favorite to your browser. The Embed link gives you the HTML code required for an IFrame that references a page containing the Photosynth viewer initialized with your synth. You can paste this HTML directly into a Web page.

6. The Share icon creates a direct URI to the viewer for this synth. Thus, you could copy the generated URI directly into an instant message or e-mail message.

7. Click the Share icon and copy the text. It should look something like this:

```
http://photosynth.net/view.aspx?cid=d7de4242-db75-4cbe-ae09-
100908205b0d&m=false&i=0:0:20&c=1.00941:-0.546529:-0.0530795&z=
177.390922003041&d=-1.99872539837712:-1.04816317761388:-0.530711994658234&p=
0:0&t=Falseasd
```

8. Note the *CID=* parameter in the preceding URI. The *CID* is a unique GUID that identifies this specific synth.

Important Keep a copy of this URI. You'll need the CID in the next section, where you'll create a custom page that embeds the Silverlight viewer. Embedding the viewer eliminates the need to use an IFrame. The CID is used by the JavaScript API to let you build an application around a synth.

Building a Photosynth Web Application

Microsoft provides a JavaScript library that allows you to interact with the Photosynth viewer using the Silverlight Browser Bridge interface. You can find documentation for the JavaScript Photosynth API at *http://photosynth.net/api/docs/default.html*.

Note This book was written against version 0.1 of the Photosynth JavaScript API libraries. Future updates to it may require changes to your applications.

This section shows you how to use the Photosynth viewer on your own page (without an IFrame) and provides a simple example of using the JavaScript Photosynth API to retrieve some details from the images within your synth. These are some of the same techniques used to build the popular Stargate Universe Photosynth, which you can view at *http://stargate. mgm.com/photosynth/index.html*.

Use the API to build a Web application

1. Launch Visual Web Developer and select New Web Site from the File menu.

2. Choose the Empty Web Site template from the New Web Site dialog box.

3. Name the new application **SbSPSDemo**.

4. Visual Web Developer will create a new solution for you. Add a new HTML file named **index.htm** to the solution.

5. In the new index.htm file, edit the *head* tag, adding references to the Photosynth JavaScript API libraries, as shown in the following code:

```
<head>
<title>Photosynth Test</title>
<script type="text/javascript"
src="http://photosynth.net/api/Silverlight.js" >
</script>
<script type="text/javascript"
src="http://photosynth.net/api/Microsoft.Photosynth.js" >
</script>
</head>
```

6. Edit the *body* tag to create two *div* layers: one to hold your synth and one to hold information about your synth. Note that the *onload* attribute of the following body tag is set to *bodyLoaded();*:

```
<body onload="bodyLoaded();">
<div id="pslayer" style="position: absolute; width: 742px; height: 501px; left:
13px; top: 56px"></div>
<div id="detailslayer" style="position: absolute; width: 273px; height: 496px;
left: 766px; top: 52px">TEST</div>
</body>
```

7. Now the *bodyLoaded* function will execute immediately after your page loads. This function will load your synth using the JavaScript API. To do this, you must follow these three steps:

   a. Initialize a new *Microsoft.Photosynth.Viewer* with the name of a layer (a *div*) on your page. You created a *div* named *pslayer* for this purpose in the preceding step.

   b. Set up the load parameters for the player, which include the GUID for your synth. If you don't still have the GUID for your synth, review the previous section to get it. Otherwise, you can help yourself to a GUID for one of the thousands of synths that are already on *Photosynth.net*.

   c. Initialize the viewer with the parameters. That's it!

8. Here's the code for the *bodyLoaded* function. Remember to put this between the head tags in your HTML.

```
<script type="text/javascript">
    function bodyLoaded() {
var SYNTH = "d7de4242-db75-4cbe-ae09-100908205b0d";
        viewer = new Microsoft.Photosynth.Viewer("pslayer");
varloadParameters = new
        Microsoft.Photosynth.Viewer.LoadParameters(SYNTH,"",false,false);
viewer.loadCollectionAsync(loadParameters);
    }
</script>
```

9. Press F5, and you'll see a page with your synth and the word "Test" to its right. This is because the other layer (the *div* named *detailslayer*) was initialized with the word Test.

It's worth spending some time experimenting with this API. One useful feature is that the Photosynth API can provide the ID of the image currently being viewed. The ID is useful in some applications because it can be used to obtain context-sensitive data about the synth. For example, if you explore the Stargate Universe synths, you'll notice that the page updates based on the image you are looking at.

The Stargate Universe synths frequently contain Easter eggs that you will discover only by exploring the synths. The next example walks you through how this works.

Add Easter eggs

1. Whenever the user moves to a new image, Photosynth fires the *moveToImageCompleted* event. To handle that event, the first thing you need to do is edit the *bodyLoaded()* function to set up an event handler. Name the handler **ImageMoved**. Now add the following to the bottom of the *bodyLoaded()* function:

```
viewer.moveToImageCompleted = ImageMoved;
```

2. Next you need to write the event handler, which is fairly straightforward. Here's a sample event handler that renders the ID of the image currently being viewed in the details layer:

```
functionImageMoved(sender) {
        id = viewer.getSelectedImageId();
document.getElementById("detailslayer").innerHTML = id;
    }
```

3. Press F5 to run the application, and browse around your synth. As you move from image to image, you'll see the ID number of the current image appear in the detailslayer on the right side.

4. To extend the display to be more meaningful, you need to write code that checks the ID of the image and assigns HTML to it. Because there could be many images, you might approach the problem by having a large case statement create different HTML snippets for different IDs. Alternatively, if you want to be able to handle huge lists of image IDs, you could make a service call to a database, sending it the ID, getting the HTML back, and rendering that HTML in the details layer. It's really up to you—this quick tutorial simply illustrated the basics. You can take time to explore the rest, including the samples at *http://photosynth.net/api/docs/default.html*.

For your convenience, here's the full HTML:

```
<html xmlns="http://www.w3.org/1999/xhtml">
<head>
<meta content="text/html; charset=utf-8" http-equiv="Content-Type" />
<title>Photosynth Test</title>
<script type="text/javascript"
src="http://photosynth.net/api/Silverlight.js" ></script>
<script type="text/javascript"
src="http://photosynth.net/api/Microsoft.Photosynth.js" ></script>
<script type="text/javascript">
    function bodyLoaded() {
var SYNTH = "d7de4242-db75-4cbe-ae09-100908205b0d";
        viewer = new Microsoft.Photosynth.Viewer("pslayer");
varloadParameters = new Microsoft.Photosynth.Viewer.LoadParameters(
SYNTH, "", false, false);
viewer.moveToImageCompleted = ImageMoved;
viewer.loadCollectionAsync(loadParameters);
    }
    function ImageMoved(sender) {
        id = viewer.getSelectedImageId();
document.getElementById("detailslayer").innerHTML = id;
    }
</script>
</head>
<body onload="bodyLoaded();">
```

```
<div id="pslayer" style="position: absolute;
width: 742px; height: 501px; left: 13px; top: 56px">
</div>

<div id="detailslayer" style="position: absolute;
width: 273px; height: 496px; left: 766px; top: 52px">
Test
</div>
</html>
```

Key Points

- You explored some of the rich imaging capabilities supported by Silverlight and experimented with the Deep Zoom and Photosynth technologies.

- You used Deep Zoom Composer to build Deep Zoom projects without writing any code.

- You learned how to create a Deep Zoom image, as well as a Deep Zoom collection that has multiple images and provides a context for moving around within the composition.

- You learned how to write code for the *MultiScaleImage* control that Silverlight uses to render Deep Zoom images and collections.

- You were introduced to Photosynth, and saw how to create your own Photosynth compositions.

- You explored the Photosynth API and saw how you can use it to create Photosynth-based applications.

Chapter 6
Media, Webcams, and Video

After completing this chapter, you will be able to:

- Use the Silverlight *MediaElement* control.

- Build a video player application in Silverlight.

- Use markers in video to trigger activity.

- Access your webcam using Silverlight.

Media in Silverlight

One of the most important uses for Microsoft Silverlight on the Web is to enable cross-platform multimedia. To accomplish this, Silverlight supports the *MediaElement* control.

In this section, you'll look at *MediaElement* in detail and you will have a chance to build a simple media player that supports progressive download and playback of videos. In addition, you'll learn how to paint surfaces with the video brush, which enables interesting graphic effects.

The *MediaElement* control supports the following video formats:

- **WMV1**   Windows Media Video 7

- **WMV2**   Windows Media Video 8

- **WMV3**   Windows Media Video 9

- **WMVA**   Windows Media Video Advanced Profile, non-VC-1

- **WMVC1**   Windows Media Video Advanced Profile, VC-1

- **H.264**   Video encoded in the popular H.264 format (introduced in Silverlight 3)

It also supports the following audio formats:

- **WMA7**   Windows Media Audio 7

- **WMA8**   Windows Media Audio 8

- **WMA9**   Windows Media Audio 9

- **MP3**   ISO MPEG Layer 3

And it supports these audio specifications:

- Mono or stereo

- Sampling frequencies from 8 to 48 kHz

- Bit rates from 8 to 320 KB/s

- Variable bit rate audio

In addition, the *MediaElement* control also supports Advanced Stream Redirector (ASX) playlists, as well as the *HTTP*, *HTTPS*, and *MMS* protocols.

MediaElement supports live and on-demand streaming from a Windows Media Server. If the URI specifies the *MMS* protocol, streaming is enabled. Otherwise, Silverlight will download and play back the file by using progressive download. This is when Silverlight downloads just enough of the file to fill a playback buffer and plays the buffered media while downloading the rest of the file.

If the protocol specifies the *HTTP* or *HTTPS* protocols, the reverse happens. The *MediaElement* control first tries to progressively download the file. If that fails, the control then attempts to stream the file.

Using the *MediaElement* Control

In this section you'll build a Silverlight application that uses the *MediaElement* control to play video. This will demonstrate just how easy it is to build video applications with Silverlight.

You can use any video file that meets the criteria listed in the preceding section. Windows ships with a number of sample videos you can use. You can also use the sports.wmv video that is available on the download site for this book. Note that the screenshots in this section come from that video.

Create a Silverlight application

1. Create a new Silverlight project and name it **SbSCh6_1**.

2. Locate *MediaElement* in the All Silverlight Controls section of the Toolbox and double-click it to add the control to your design surface.

3. Right-click the SbSCh6_1 project and select Add Existing Item. Find the video file that you want to use and add it to your project.

4. Select the video in Solution Explorer. In the Properties dialog box, you'll see an option to Copy To Output Directory. Make sure that this is set to **Copy Always**.

5. Set the Build Action to **Resource**.

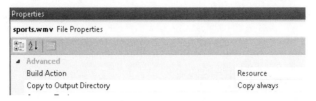

6. Press F5 to build and execute the application. You'll see a blank browser, but that's ok—the display is blank because you haven't set the *Source* property of the *MediaElement* yet. You can't set the *Source* until you've compiled the application, as the compile process turns the media file into a resource that Silverlight can access.

7. Go back to the designer, select the *MediaElement* control, and set its *Source* property to the name of your video file (for example, sports.wmv). When you set the *Source* properly, the property entry text box clears and the little black diamond beside the *Source* name fills in. If you set the *Source* incorrectly, you'll get an error message.

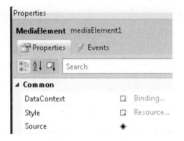

8. Press F5 to build and execute the application. This time, you'll see the video playing in your browser.

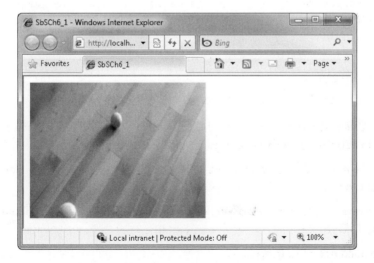

Easy, right? In the next section, you'll see how to add interactive functionality with Play, Pause, and Stop controls.

Controlling the Video Playback

In the previous section, you added a video to your page. In this section, you'll discover how to provide basic playback features by adding Play, Pause, and Stop controls.

Add controls to your Silverlight video project

1. If it isn't already open, open the SbSCh6_1 project that you created in the last section.

2. Add a StackPanel control, set its orientation to Vertical, and place the *MediaElement* control inside it.

```
<StackPanel Orientation="Vertical">
    <MediaElement ... />
</StackPanel>
```

3. Note that the *MediaElement* properties have been omitted from this code. Be sure you don't delete them when editing your code!

4. Add a StackPanel underneath the *MediaElement* and set its orientation to *Horizontal*. Add three *Button* controls to the *StackPanel*. From left to right, name them **bPlay**, **bPause**, and **bStop**.

```
<StackPanel Orientation="Vertical">
    <MediaElement ... />
    <StackPanel Orientation="Horizontal">
        <Button x:Name="bPlay" Content="Play"></Button>
        <Button x:Name="bPause" Content="Pause"></Button>
        <Button x:Name="bStop" Content="Stop"></Button>
    </StackPanel>
</StackPanel>
```

5. Double-click the Play button to create an event handler for its *Click* event. Edit the handler so it has the following code:

```
private void bPlay_Click(object sender, RoutedEventArgs e)
{
    mediaElement1.Play();
}
```

6. Repeat step 4 for the Pause and Stop buttons, but call them *mediaElement1.Pause()* and *mediaElement1.Stop()*, respectively.

When a user pauses playback by pressing Pause, pressing Pause a second time does nothing. This is because clicking the button simply calls the *Pause()* method again.

> **Exercise** Try adding a Boolean flag (*bPaused*) to your code that gets set when a user first pauses the video. Have it reset when the user clicks the Pause button a second time or when the user presses Play or Stop.

Showing Playback Position

In the previous sections, you built a video player and added play, pause, and stop buttons. But you may have noticed that when the video is playing, you have no way to know where you are in the video stream. In this section, you'll learn how to use a *Slider* control to show users their position in the video stream.

Add a position indicator

1. Open the SbSCh6_1 project that you've been working on thus far in this chapter.

2. Add a Slider control to your design surface. In the XAML, make sure that it's positioned below the *MediaElement* and above the horizontal *StackPanel*. This will place it between the video and the control buttons.

```xaml
<StackPanel Orientation="Vertical">
  <MediaElement ... />
  <Slider Height="23" Name="slider1" Maximum="100" Value="0" />
  <StackPanel Orientation="Horizontal">
    <Button x:Name="bPlay" Content="Play" Click="bPlay_Click"></Button>
    <Button x:Name="bPause" Content="Pause" Click="bPause_Click"></Button>
    <Button x:Name="bStop" Content="Stop" Click="bStop_Click"></Button>
  </StackPanel>
</StackPanel>
```

The Slider control allows users to set a value between some minimum and maximum value by sliding a thumb along a track. The control is also useful for showing status, which is how you'll use it here. To do this, you set the *Maximum* property value to the length of the video. As the video plays, you'll periodically set the Value to the current position in the video, which will move the thumb some distance along the track, thus providing a visual update of the current position.

3. The *MediaOpened* event fires after the *MediaElement* has finished opening the video. Only then can you query the control to discover the length of the video. So you need to set up an event handler for the *MediaOpened* event. Find the *MediaElement* in the designer, switch to the Events tab, and create a new event handler by double-clicking the *MediaOpened* entry.

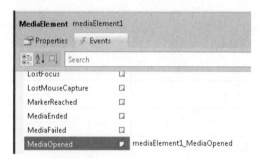

4. In the MediaOpened event handler, add code to set the maximum value of the slider to the length of the video (in seconds), which you can get from the *mediaElement1.NaturalDuration.TimeSpan.TotalSeconds* property.

```
void mediaElement1_MediaOpened(object sender, RoutedEventArgs e)
{
    slider1.Maximum = mediaElement1.NaturalDuration.TimeSpan.TotalSeconds;
}
```

5. You need to update the Value of the slider at a regular interval, which will move the thumb across the track as the video plays. To do this, you need a timer. In Silverlight, you accomplish this with a *DispatcherTimer* object from the System.Windows.Threading namespace. The following code creates an instance of a *DispatcherTimer* and gives it a one-second interval. Place the following code in your *MainPage()* constructor:

```
System.Windows.Threading.DispatcherTimer vidTimer =
    new System.Windows.Threading.DispatcherTimer();
vidTimer.Interval = new TimeSpan(0, 0, 0, 1);
```

6. Whenever the timer ticks, it raises a Tick event. So you also need to set up a *Tick* event handler. You'll see the handler code in a moment. For now, just declare the handler:

```
vidTimer.Tick += new EventHandler(vidTimer_Tick);
```

7. To start the timer, call its *Start()* method.

```
vidTimer.Start();
```

8. Now all you need to do is update the position of the slider based on the current play-back position of the video within the *Tick* event that you created in step 6. Here's the code:

```
void vidTimer_Tick(object sender, EventArgs e)
{
    slider1.Value = mediaElement1.Position.Seconds;
}
```

9. Press F5 to execute your application and you'll see that the slider position updates as the video plays, and that it stops when you pause the video.

10. The example you just created updates the slider every second, so you'll see the thumb make a little jump every second. For a smoother experience, you can set the interval to a smaller value, such as 100 milliseconds. If you do that, you also need to set the *Maximum* value to the *Ticks* property of the *NaturalDuration.TimeSpan* when the *MediaOpened* event fires, and set the slider Value to the *Ticks* property of the *MediaElement* whenever the timer *Tick* event fires. Go ahead and make these changes.

Setting the Playback Position with a Slider

Using the *MediaElement* properties to control the slider provides visual feedback about the current video position, but doesn't give users control over the video. However, the slider control allows you to drag the thumb and drop it somewhere else to change the slider's Value property. You can capitalize on the slider's capabilities to let users move the play position to a new spot and then watch the video from that position. And this requires just a little code.

Add slide to position capabilities

1. Select the slider and find the *ValueChanged* event setting in the Properties window. Double-click it to create a new event handler, which will probably be named *slider1_ValueChanged*.

   The *ValueChanged* event fires whenever the value of the slider changes. Thus far you have been changing the slider position at every timer tick, which causes this event to fire. That, however, creates a dilemma. When the timer changes the thumb position, you don't want to do anything. The thumb position will already be correct relative to the current play position of the video. But when a user moves the thumb, you want to change the video position so it matches the thumb position.

2. So how can you tell when the user has changed the slider *Value*, as opposed to when the timer tick code has changed it? The solution is actually very simple. When the timer's *Tick* event fires, the video position is at the same position as the thumb. If the user moves the thumb, then the thumb position will be at a different position, so all you need to do is check whether the thumb position differs from the current video position. When they're different, you move the play head to the position indicated by the value of the thumb. When they're the same, you do nothing. Here's the code:

```
private void slider1_ValueChanged(object sender,
    RoutedPropertyChangedEventArgs<double> e)
{
  if (slider1.Value != mediaElement1.Position.Ticks)
     mediaElement1.Position = new TimeSpan((long)slider1.Value);
}
```

3. Press F5 to execute the application. Now you can drag the slider's thumb and drop it into a new position and the video will rewind or fast forward to that position.

As you can see, it's not only easy to display video in Silverlight, but also takes little additional effort to provide a way for users to control the video playback position.

Using Video Markers in Silverlight

Many video formats support markers that have been encoded into the video at certain points in the timeline. For example, the sports.wmv video encodes a marker that describes the type of ball (such as baseball, soccer ball, or pointy football) that you see when it first appears in the video.

You can encode your own markers using a tool like Microsoft Expression Encoder, which is available as a free download from *http://www.microsoft.com/expression/products/Encoder_Overview.aspx*.

You can also dynamically add markers to a video stream at run time. This is very easy to do in Silverlight, and you'll see how to do this in a moment.

To continue, you'll need to use the sports.wmv file that you can download from the page for this book. If you want, you can use a different video as long as the video file has markers encoded into it. You can even use Expression Encoder to add markers to a video if you desire.

Use markers to update a TextBlock

1. Open the SbSCh6_1 project file. In the MainPage.xaml file, add a new *TextBlock* control to the horizontal *StackPanel* beneath the three Buttons. Name the *TextBlock* **lStatus** using the *Name* attribute.

2. Select the *MediaElement*, and find the *MarkerReached* event in the Properties window. Double-click it to create the *mediaElement1_MarkerReached* event handler.

3. The event handler takes a parameter of type TimeLineMarkerRoutedEventArgs. The *TimeLineMarkerRoutedEventArgs* parameter has a property called *Marker* that contains the metadata about the marker. A marker typically contains such metadata as the time when the marker fires and any text associated with the marker. Therefore, to render the text on screen, you can simply set the *Text* property of the *TextBlock* you created in step 2 to the text of the current marker, like so.

```
private void mediaElement1_MarkerReached(object sender,
TimelineMarkerRoutedEventArgs e)
{
  lStatus.Text = e.Marker.Text;
}
```

4. Press F5 to compile and execute your application. When you watch the video, you'll see the *TextBlock* update to show which ball you're looking at on the screen. Remember, you're only looking at the text for the markers that were pre-encoded into the video.

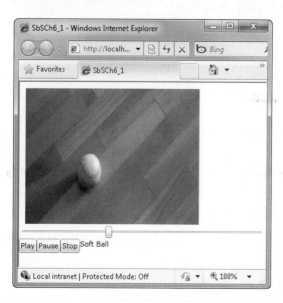

The markers collection in Silverlight is not read-only, meaning you can create markers dynamically at run time. Here's the procedure to add a marker.

Add a marker at run time

1. Because you are going to add the new marker after Silverlight opens the video, you need to find the *MediaOpened* event handler that you created earlier in this chapter (when you were setting the maximum value of the *Slider*).

2. Create a new instance of a *TimeLineMarker* class, like so:

```
TimelineMarker t = new TimelineMarker();
```

3. Set the *Text* for the new marker:

```
t.Text = "My dynamically added marker.";
```

4. Set the *Time* property of the marker to the offset from the beginning where you want the marker to be encoded. The following code sets the marker at the 22-second position in the video.

```
t.Time = new TimeSpan(0, 0, 22);
```

5. Add your marker to the *Markers* collection.

```
mediaElement1.Markers.Add(t);
```

Your *MediaOpened* event should now look like this:

```
void mediaElement1_MediaOpened(object sender, RoutedEventArgs e)
{
    slider1.Maximum = mediaElement1.NaturalDuration.TimeSpan.Ticks;
    TimelineMarker t = new TimelineMarker();
    t.Text = "My dynamically added marker.";
    t.Time = new TimeSpan(0, 0, 22);
    mediaElement1.Markers.Add(t);
}
```

6. Press F5 to compile and execute the application. You'll see that your marker causes the *TextBlock* to update at the 22-second mark.

Markers provide a way for you to add interactivity—pertinent bits of information, such as titles and names, or links to larger blocks of information that enhance the video. You can also use markers to raise events that allow you to change the UI. This is handy for having the UI interact with the video in creative ways.

Using Video as a Brush

In Silverlight, you can paint surfaces with a Brush. Silverlight offers a variety of *Brushes* for coloring objects, such as the *SolidColorBrush* used to fill an area. But you aren't limited to *Brushes* that paint surfaces with colors; you can also paint them with video.

Paint an area with video

1. Open the SbsCh6_1 project and set the Height attribute of your *MediaElement* to **0**.

2. Add an *Opacity="0"* attribute to your MediaElement.

3. Now add an *IsHitTestVisible="False"* attribute to your *MediaElement*. Here's the complete *MediaElement* declaration:

```
<MediaElement HorizontalAlignment="Left" Name="mediaElement1"
   VerticalAlignment="Top" Width="378" Source="sports.wmv"
   MediaOpened="mediaElement1_MediaOpened"
   MarkerReached="mediaElement1_MarkerReached" Opacity="0"
   IsHitTestVisible="False" Height="0" />
```

4. Add a new *TextBlock* control and set its *Text*, *FontSize*, and *FontWeight* properties like this:

```
<TextBlock Text="Video" FontSize="80" FontWeight="Bold">
</TextBlock>
```

5. You can paint the *TextBlock* with a *VideoBrush* by using its *Foreground* property. You simply point the *VideoBrush* at the *MediaElement* and Silverlight does the rest.

```
<TextBlock Text="Video" FontSize="80" FontWeight="Bold">
  <TextBlock.Foreground>
    <VideoBrush SourceName="mediaElement1"></VideoBrush>
  </TextBlock.Foreground>
</TextBlock>
```

6. Press F5 to compile and run the application. You'll see the word "Video" being painted with your video file.

Using a Webcam with Silverlight

A new feature in Silverlight 4 is the ability to use your webcam to capture and render video. In this section, you'll see how easy it is to do this.

Access a webcam from your application

1. Create a new Silverlight 4 project called **SbSCh6_2**.

2. Add a *StackPanel* containing a Rectangle named **cam** and a *Button* named **bStart**.

```
<Grid x:Name="LayoutRoot" Background="White">
  <StackPanel Orientation="Vertical">
    <Rectangle Height="200" Width="300" x:Name="cam" />
    <Button x:Name="bStart" Content="Start Webcam" Click="bStart_Click" />
  </StackPanel>
</Grid>
```

3. Due to Silverlight security requirements, a users must grant permission before you can use the camera from your code. You ask users to grant such permission programmatically by calling the *CaptureDeviceConfiguration.RequestDeviceAccess()* function. Double-click the *Button* to create a *Click* event handler and add the following code:

```
bool bOk = CaptureDeviceConfiguration.RequestDeviceAccess();
```

4. This code will display the following dialog box when a user runs your application and clicks the *Button*.

When a user answers Yes, the *RequestDeviceAccess* function returns true; otherwise it returns false. Note that if the user answers No, calls to the webcam will fail. The dialog box also displays the Web site that originated the request. In the case of this screenshot, my development machine (*http://localhost*) made the request.

5. When a user answers Yes, you need to create a new *CaptureSource* object initialized to the user's default video capture device.

```
CaptureSource cs = new CaptureSource
{
   VideoCaptureDevice = CaptureDeviceConfiguration.GetDefaultVideoCaptureDevice()
};
```

6. Now that you have a *CaptureSource* that is capturing video, you can create a *VideoBrush* from it. As you saw in the previous section, "Using Video as a Brush," a *VideoBrush* lets you paint video onto a surface. Here's the code:

```
VideoBrush vidBrush = new VideoBrush();
vidBrush.SetSource(cs);
```

7. Now that you have initialized the *VideoBrush,* you can fill the rectangle with it. All that's left to do is begin the capture. The end result will render your webcam on screen.

```
cam.Fill = vidBrush;
cs.Start();
```

8. Here's the complete *Click* event handler:

```
private void bStart_Click(object sender, RoutedEventArgs e)
{
  bool bOk = CaptureDeviceConfiguration.RequestDeviceAccess();
  if (bOk)
  {
    CaptureSource cs = new CaptureSource
    {
      VideoCaptureDevice = CaptureDeviceConfiguration.
GetDefaultVideoCaptureDevice()
    };
    VideoBrush vidBrush = new VideoBrush();
    vidBrush.SetSource(cs);
    cam.Fill = vidBrush;
    cs.Start();
  }
}
```

9. Press F5 to compile and run your application. When you press the Start Webcam button, you'll get the dialog box that asks for permission to access the camera and microphone. If you answer Yes, video from your webcam (if you have one) will paint the rectangle. The following screenshot shows a video stream from my webcam pointing at bobbleheads from my favorite baseball team—plus a special guest or two.

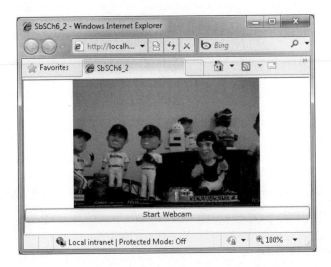

Key Points

- You explored the capabilities of the *MediaElement* control and learned how to use it with a source video file treated as a resource.

- You saw how to add interactive functionality to your videos, providing functional Play, Pause, and Stop buttons.

- You learned how to use a timer to track the current video position and to set the video position by using a *Slider* control.

- You were introduced to markers and saw how Silverlight can extract markers from a video stream and how you can add them dynamically at run time.

- You saw how to use the VideoBrush control to paint any surface (including text) with a video. And you even learned how to use *CaptureDevice* to capture webcam video and send it to a VideoBrush to paint a surface with live video.

Chapter 7
Transformation and Animation

After completing this chapter, you will be able to:

- Use transformations in Silverlight to manipulate objects.

- Define your own transformation using a *Matrix*.

- Use *PerspectiveTransform* to create a 3-D effect.

- Define animations in XAML code.

- Use key frames to fine-tune animation behavior.

- Use Easing to add real-life physics to your animations.

- Use Expression Blend to define an animation.

Transformations

In graphics terminology, a *transform* defines how points from one coordinate space should map to another. This mapping operation is typically described using a *transformation matrix*, which is a special mathematical construct that allows for simple mathematical conversion from one system to another.

Microsoft Silverlight XAML supports transformations for rotation, scaling, skewing, perspective, and translation, as well as a special transformation type that allows you to implement your own matrix, which you can use to combine transformations. Fortunately, Silverlight XAML abstracts transformations so you don't have to deal with the mathematics involved, and so this book will not go into detail about the mathematics.

In this chapter, you'll look at how to define transformations by using XAML with Silverlight in Visual Web Developer Express.

Exploring Transformations

You apply Transformations using the *RenderTransform* property of an object. In this section, you'll write the code to do each transform so you can see how each works. When you combine a transform with an animation (which you'll see later in this chapter), you can create some very powerful UI effects.

Remember that when you use a transform, you are not changing properties of an object. Instead, you are defining how the object is drawn. So, for example, if your object has a top of 0, and a left of 0, and you use *TranslateTransform* to move it to a new location, it will still have a top of 0 and a left of 0, despite where it moves to on the screen.

Using *RotateTransform*

RotateTransform allows you to rotate an element by a specified angle around a specified center point. You set the angle of rotation using the *Angle* property. It's value should be a number of degrees through which you want to rotate the item. Consider the horizontal vector pointing to the right to be 0 degrees, and rotation takes place *clockwise*, so the vertical vector pointing down is the result of a 90-degree rotation.

You set the center of transformation using the *CenterX* and *CenterY* properties to specify the coordinates of the pivot. These default to (0, 0), which makes the default rotation pivot the upper-left corner of the container.

Configure *RotateTransform* in an application

1. Create a new Silverlight application and name it **SbSCh7_1**.

2. Add a new *Rectangle* to the design surface by double -clicking the Rectangle tool in the Toolbox.

3. Change the closing rectangle tag from a default closing slash (/>) to a fully qualified closing tag. In other words, the closing tag should look like this: *</Rectangle>*.

4. Between the *<Rectangle>* tags, add a *<Rectangle.RenderTransform>* tag. Visual Web Explorer will automatically generate the closing tag.

5. Between the *<Rectangle.RenderTransform>* tags, add a *<RotateTransform>* tag.

6. Set the attributes of *RotateTransform*. You can do this directly (by typing **Angle="45"**). Alternatively, you can place your pointer on the *<RotateTransform>* tag, click within it, and set the attribute values in the Properties window. Set the *Angle* value to **45**.

As you set the property, Visual Web Developer renders the transform in the design window.

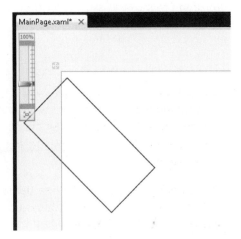

7. Here's what your code should look like:

```
<Rectangle Height="100" HorizontalAlignment="Left" Name="rectangle1"
    Stroke="Black" StrokeThickness="1" VerticalAlignment="Top" Width="200">
  <Rectangle.RenderTransform>
    <RotateTransform Angle="45"></RotateTransform>
  </Rectangle.RenderTransform>
</Rectangle>
```

8. You'll notice that the default point of rotation is the top-left corner of the rectangle. To change the point of rotation, set the *CenterX* and *CenterY* properties. These define the center of rotation—effectively, the point around which the object will rotate. So if your rectangle's dimensions are 200 x 100, as in this example, and you set *CenterX* to **200** and *CenterY* to **100**, the rectangle will rotate around its bottom right-hand corner.

```
<Rectangle Height="100" HorizontalAlignment="Left" Name="rectangle1"
    Stroke="Black" StrokeThickness="1" VerticalAlignment="Top" Width="200">
  <Rectangle.RenderTransform>
    <RotateTransform Angle="45" CenterY="100" CenterX="200"></RotateTransform>
  </Rectangle.RenderTransform>
</Rectangle>
```

9. Just as before, Visual Web Developer will display the results in the designer window, so you won't need to run the application to see how it looks.

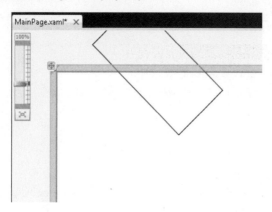

Using *ScaleTransform*

You use the *ScaleTransform* property to change the size of an object based on the horizontal axis, the vertical axis, or both axes.

When scaling an object, you need to specify at least one of the axes along which you want to scale and by how much you want to scale against that axis. You use the *ScaleX* property to scale the object on the horizontal axis (the X axis) and the *ScaleY* property to scale the object on the vertical axis (the Y axis).

Both *ScaleX* and *ScaleY* are double values—they represent the value by which you multiply the object's current size on the specified axis. Values greater than 1 will stretch the object by that multiple. For example, a *ScaleX* value of 2 will double the size of the object horizontally. Values less than 1 but greater than 0 will shrink the object. Setting *ScaleX* to 0.5, for instance, will reduce the size of the object by half horizontally.

Define a *ScaleTransform*

1. Open the SbSCh7_1 project you just created.

2. Delete the *RotateTransform* tags on your Rectangle, replacing them with a <ScaleTransform> tag.

3. Take a look at the Properties window and you'll see the *CenterX, CenterY, ScaleX,* and *ScaleY* properties.

4. Set the *ScaleX* property to **1.5** and the Rectangle's width grows by 50 percent.

5. Set the *ScaleY* property to **.5** and the Rectangle's height will be reduced by 50 percent.

6. Like with *RotateTransform*, *ScaleTransform* lets specify the point around which you want to scale the object using the *CenterX* and *CenterY* properties.

Using *TranslateTransform*

A *translation* is a type of transform that moves an object in a 2-D plane from one position to another. You create a translation by setting up vectors that define the object's motion along its X and Y axes. These are set using the *X* and *Y* properties on the transform. For example, to move an item two units horizontally to the right, you set the *X* property to *2*. To move it to the left, you use a negative value, such as -2. Similarly, to move an object vertically, you use the *Y* property. Positive *Y* values cause the object to move down the screen, whereas negative *Y* values move it up.

Add *TranslateTransform* to your application

1. Open the SbSCh7_1 project.

2. Delete the *ScaleTransform* tags and replace them with a *<TranslateTransform>* tag.

3. Select the *<TranslateTransform>* tag and you'll see that you can set *X* and *Y* values in the Properties window.

4. Set the *X* value to 100 and the *Y* value to 50.

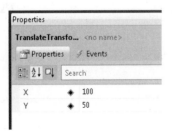

In the designer window, the rectangle will immediately move to the new location.

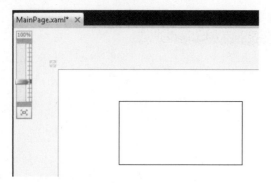

As mentioned earlier, the top and left coordinates of the rectangle are still 0, 0. Silverlight treats the rectangle as if it were still at that original location, but renders it at the translated location.

Using *SkewTransform*

Skewing an object involves shifting it in a progressive, uniform manner along an axis. For example, skewing a square or rectangle turns it into a parallelogram. This visual effect is very useful in creating the illusion of depth on a 2-D surface.

You can apply a skew at a specified angle on either the X or Y axis and apply the skew around a center point. These skews can be combined, allowing you to skew on both axes at the same time.

Skew an object

1. Open the SbSCh7_1 project.

2. Delete the *TranslateTransform* tags and replace them with a *<SkewTransform>* tag.

3. Place your cursor in the *SkewTransform* tag and you'll be able to set the *AngleX*, *AngleY*, *CenterX*, and *CenterY* properties of the *SkewTransform* in the Properties window.

4. Set the *AngleX* property to **45** and you'll see a left-leaning parallelogram in the designer window.

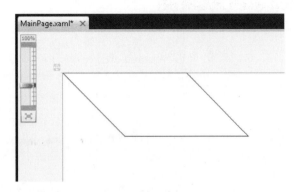

5. Now change *AngleX* back to **0** and set *AngleY* to **45**. You'll see that the Rectangle is now skewed along the Y axis.

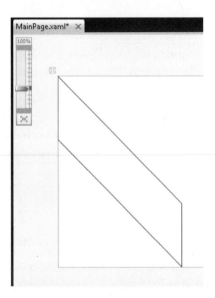

6. As you've already seen, the *CenterX* and *CenterY* properties let you define the center point of the skew. As you can see from these examples, the default center point of 0, 0 shows that the skew is defined from the object's top left corner.

You should spend a little time experimenting with the *CenterX* and *CenterY* property values to see how they affect the *SkewTransform*.

Using *MatrixTransform*

All transformations, at their core, are performed by multiplying the coordinate space of the object by a transformation matrix. Each of the transforms you've seen so far in this chapter is a well-known and well-defined transform.

Matrix mathematics and how transforms are implemented are beyond the scope of this book, but for the sake of syntactic completeness, you'll explore how to define them in Silverlight XAML.

Note that the matrix used in *MatrixTransform* is an *affine* matrix, which means the bottom row of the matrix is always set to (0 0 1). As such, you set only the first two rows. You set the values by using the transform's *Matrix* property, which takes a string containing the first two rows of values separated by spaces or commas.

If you understand the Matrix transformations that define computer graphics, you can use this transform to define the first and second rows of your affine matrix.

Add *MatrixTransform* to your application

1. Open the SbSCh7_1 project.

2. Delete the *SkewTransform* tags and replace them with a *<MatrixTransform>* tag.

3. You'll see that the only property you can enter is the *Matrix* property. It defaults to *Identity*, which is the special name for a matrix that defines no change. (It corresponds to the value 1, 0, 0, 1, 0, 0.)

4. Set the Matrix property to **1, 0, 0, 2, 0, 0** and the height of the rectangle will change.

5. Now set the Matrix to **1, 0, 1, 2, 0, 1** and you'll see changes in both the height and the skew of the object. You've combined transforms. If you understand the matrix mathematics behind graphics transforms, you can use this type of transform to define your own transforms.

Combining Transforms

For those who don't understand matrix mathematics that well—don't worry, you're not alone—Silverlight provides the ability to combine transforms without having to crunch numbers. To do this, you use the *<TransformGroup>* tag, which allows you to stack multiple transforms within it.

Combine transforms inside *TransformGroup*

1. Open the SbSCh7_1 project.

2. Delete the *MatrixTransform* tags and replace them with a *<TransformGroup>* tag.

3. Within *TransformGroup*, add a *ScaleTransform* and set its *ScaleX* property to **1.5** and its *ScaleY* property to **.5**.

4. Now, also within *TransformGroup*, add a *SkewTransform* with its *AngleX* property set to **30**.

5. Within *TransformGroup*, add a *RotateTransform* with its *Angle* set to **45**.

6. Finally, within *TransformGroup*, add a *TranslateTransform* and set its *X* property to **50**.

7. Your code should now look like this:

```
<Rectangle Height="100" HorizontalAlignment="Left"
    Name="rectangle1" Stroke="Black" StrokeThickness="1"
    VerticalAlignment="Top" Width="200">
  <Rectangle.RenderTransform>
    <TransformGroup>
      <ScaleTransform ScaleX="1.5" ScaleY=".5"></ScaleTransform>
      <SkewTransform AngleX="30"></SkewTransform>
      <RotateTransform Angle="45"></RotateTransform>
      <TranslateTransform X="50"></TranslateTransform>
    </TransformGroup>
  </Rectangle.RenderTransform>
</Rectangle>
```

8. As you add the transforms, the designer updates the rendering of the Rectangle. When you're done, you'll see that the Rectangle has been simultaneously scaled, skewed, rotated, and translated.

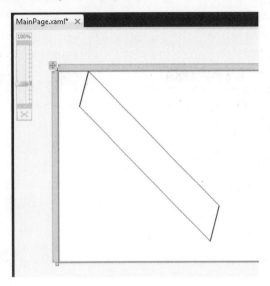

Using *PerspectiveTransform*

Perspective transforms, in a nutshell, are transforms that can be applied to XAML elements to simulate rotating them in a 3-D space. Note that a perspective transform isn't true 3-D—it lacks 3-D mesh models, shading, hidden line removal, and so on. Nonetheless, it's good for simulating 3-D effects with XAML.

Imagine the screen to be a 3-D space with the X axis going left to right, the Y axis going up and down and the Z axis representing the depth that goes in and out of the screen (away from you and toward you). If you want to rotate the image so that it appears to be in 3-D, with the perspective being that the left of the image is towards the back of the screen and the right of the image is in the forefront of the screen, you would rotate the image around the Y axis. Similarly, if you want to rotate the image so that the top or bottom of the image is towards the back of the screen and the rest is in the forefront, then you'd rotate around the X axis.

At first, you might expect to rotate around the Z axis, but that's the depth or in/out plane. A rotation on the Z axis, in 3-D space, would just change the angle at which you're viewing the picture.

A perspective transform is a little different than the transforms you've already explored. It is a *Projection* transform, and not a *Render* transform. The difference is that this transform isn't based on a mathematical matrix calculation that changes the coordinate space. Instead, it's based on code built into Silverlight to render the content based on 3-D calculations. As such, it's handled a little differently, and it happens only at run time. This means you won't see changes made to perspective transforms within the designer. You'll have to run your application to see the results.

Explore perspective transforms

1. Create a new Silverlight project and name it **SbSCh7_2**.

2. Add a new *Image* control to the design surface.

3. Set the *Source* property of *Image*. Choose any picture you like.

4. In the XAML view, edit the closing *Image* tag to remove the closing slash so that it is a fully qualified closing tag, like so: *</Image>*.

5. Add an *<Image.Projection>* tag.

6. Within the *<Image.Projection>* tag, add a *<PlaneProjection>* tag.

7. As discussed earlier, if you want to rotate the image so its left side is toward the back of the screen plane, and the right is in the forefront of the screen plane, you want to rotate the image around the Y axis. To do this, set the *RotationY* attribute of the *PlaneProjection*. Set the *RotationY* value to **30**.

8. Your code should look like this.

```
<Image Height="278" HorizontalAlignment="Left" Name="image1"
    Stretch="Fill" VerticalAlignment="Top" Width="200"
    Source="/SbSCh7_2;component/Images/fw.jpg" >
  <Image.Projection>
    <PlaneProjection RotationY="30"></PlaneProjection>
  </Image.Projection>
</Image>
```

Note that the value of the *Source* attribute on your *Image* tag might be different.

9. Press F5 to run your application. You'll see the image displayed in 3-D space.

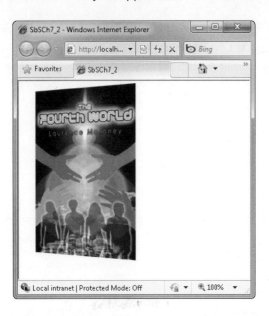

10. To make it look as if the image is tilted, set the *RotationX* property. Positive values will tilt the image toward you and negative ones tilt it away from you. So, for example, set *RotationX* to **-30**. This will tilt the top of the image back away from you.

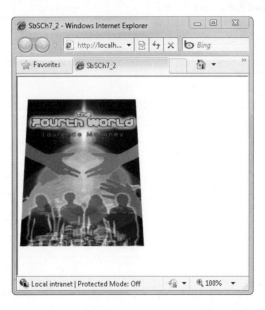

11. You can combine the two, so a *RotationX* of -30 and a *RotationY* of 30 will give you a result like this:

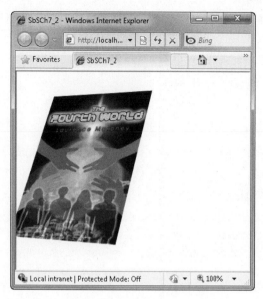

12. When using an Image like this, Silverlight treats the image as if it were transparent. Thus, if you rotate the image far enough so that you are looking at the backside of it, you'll see the inverse of the image, as if you were looking through it from the back. To see this, set its rotation to a value greater than 90. For example, set *RotationY* to **135** (and remove *RotationX* if you are using it). Notice in the following screenshot that the text on the image is inverted because you are viewing the image from the backside.

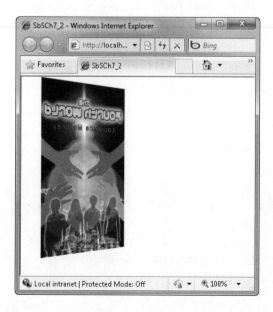

You can combine a perspective transform with the *RenderTransform* types that you used earlier. Just add both sets of tags (*<Image.Projection>* and *<Image.RenderTransform>* for an *Image*) as children of the control. Experiment with this to see the different results you can produce.

Animation

With animation, you can bring your creations to life by changing the attributes of your objects, such as their color, size, opacity, and other properties. This can be done over time, in response to user actions, or both.

In XAML, you animate an item by changing one or more of its properties over time. To define this time, you use a timeline. For example, to move an item across the screen in five seconds, you would specify a five-second timeline that animates the *Canvas.Left* property from zero to the width of the screen.

Creating an Animation

Visual Web Developer does not provide tools for defining animations. However, Microsoft does offer some powerful tools that you can use for this. If you want to build animations using tools, download and experiment with Microsoft Expression Blend. This application allows you to set up timelines and visually test them.

In this section, however, you're going to write the code by hand. After the first couple of times it isn't difficult!

Create an animation step by step

1. Open the SbSCh7_2 project you created in the previous section.

2. Edit *Image.Projection* to give your *PlaneProjection* an *x:Name* attribute and value. You need to give the projection a name so you can refer to it when you define the animation. Set the *RotationY* property value to 0 to create a starting position with no rotation.

```
<Image.Projection>
  <PlaneProjection x:Name="prj"  RotationY="0"></PlaneProjection>
</Image.Projection>
```

3. You can define a trigger to start your animation. One trigger could be when Silverlight first loads the control. To start the animation using that trigger, you need to define a sibling of the *<Image.Projection>* tag called *Image.Triggers*. This should contain an

<EventTrigger> tag. The event should be triggered when the *Image* loads, which you specify using the *RoutedEvent* attribute, like so:

```
<Image.Triggers>
  <EventTrigger RoutedEvent="Image.Loaded">
  </EventTrigger>
</Image.Triggers>
```

4. You define animations using a storyboard. So add a *<BeginStoryBoard>* tag and place a *<Storyboard>* definition within it.

```
<Image.Triggers>
  <EventTrigger RoutedEvent="Image.Loaded">
    <BeginStoryboard>
      <Storyboard>
      </Storyboard>
    </BeginStoryboard>
  </EventTrigger>
</Image.Triggers>
```

5. Now you need to define the parameters of the animation. There are a number of animation options. In this example, you'll use *DoubleAnimation*, which changes a numeric value over time. This works in the application you're building because *RotationY* is a numeric value. So place the following code between the *<Storyboard>* tags:

```
<DoubleAnimation Storyboard.TargetName="prj"
    Storyboard.TargetProperty="RotationY" From="0" To="360"
    Duration="0:0:10" RepeatBehavior="Forever" AutoReverse="True">
</DoubleAnimation>
```

6. Press F5 to execute the application and you'll see your image rotate around the Y axis. Then, once done, it will turn around and rotate back in the other direction before repeating.

Here's why it acts in this way. First, you set the *TargetName* of the *Storyboard* to prj, which is the name that you gave the Projection. You then set the *TargetProperty* of the *Storyboard* to *RotationY*, which is the property that you want to change over time. The *From* and *To* values are the starting and ending points of the animation. Thus, you are starting from a rotation of 0 and ending at a rotation of 360. The *Duration* sets the total amount of time that you want the animation to take, defined in hours, minutes, and seconds. In this case, the *Duration* is set to 10 seconds, so the image is going to rotate by 36 degrees each second. *RepeatBehavior* determines what should happen at the end of the animation. It's set to *Forever* which means the animation will just keep running. Finally, the *AutoReverse* property is set to *true*. This means that as the animation repeats, it will reverse direction each time. So, the first time, the value animates from 0 to 360. The second time it reverses from 360 to 0. The third time it animates from 0 to 360 again. And so on.

This example built a *DoubleAnimation*. You should investigate building similar animations using *ColorAnimation* and *PointAnimation*. These allow you to change color definitions and point spaces over time respectively.

Understanding Key Frames

As you just saw, a *DoubleAnimation* changes a double value over time. For example, the earlier rotation example moved a *double* value from 0 to 360 over 10 seconds, incrementing by 36 each second. This is an example of *linear interpolation*, which means that the rate of change is constant.

To tweak this behavior, you can define the transition by using a set of milestones called *key frames*. To change the linear behavior of the animation from the starting property to the ending property, you insert one or more key frames. You can then define the style of animation that you want between the various key frames.

You define key frames by using *key times*, which are times specified relative to the start time of the animation that specify the end time of the key frame. So, imagine you need a nine-second animation with three evenly spaced key frames. You can specify the first key frame to end at 0:0:3, the second key frame to end at 0:0:6, and the third to end at 0:0:9. You do not specify the *length* of the key frame—instead, you specify the end time for each key frame.

Using a Linear Key Frame

As another example, suppose you want a *DoubleAnimation* to span half the range between 0 and 360. You want the animation to move very quickly in the first half and very slowly in the second half, requiring a 10-second total transition time. Because 180 is the midpoint between 0 and 360, you would define a key frame at point 180. You'd set the animation duration to 1 second between the start point and the midpoint, using a key time of 0:0:1. Then you would set a duration of 9 seconds between the midpoint and the endpoint by using a second key time of 0:0:10. Now the item will zip across the screen to the midpoint and then crawl the rest of the way.

Add a key frame

1. Open your SbSCh7_2 project, and change the *<DoubleAnimation>* tag to **<DoubleAnimationUsingKeyFrames>**.

2. Delete the *From* and *To* attributes.

3. Add a child *<LinearDoubleKeyFrame>* tag, and set its *KeyTime* property to **0:0:1** and its *Value* to **180**.

4. Add another *<LinearDoubleKeyFrame>*, setting its *KeyTime* to **0:0:10** and its *Value* to **360**.

5. Your XAML should look like this:

```
<Storyboard>
   <DoubleAnimationUsingKeyFrames Storyboard.TargetName="prj" Storyboard.
TargetProperty="RotationY" Duration="0:0:10" RepeatBehavior="Forever"
AutoReverse="True">
     <LinearDoubleKeyFrame KeyTime="0:0:1" Value="180"></LinearDoubleKeyFrame>
     <LinearDoubleKeyFrame KeyTime="0:0:10" Value="360"></LinearDoubleKeyFrame>
   </DoubleAnimationUsingKeyFrames>
</Storyboard>
```

6. Press F5 to run your application. You'll see that Silverlight takes 1 second to animate the value to 180 and then 9 seconds to take it the rest of the way to 360.

Using a Discrete Key Frame

A Linear key frame moved the value smoothly over time. If you want the value to jump to the desired value at the desired time, you use a *Discrete* key frame. When animating a *Double* value, use *DiscreteDoubleKeyFrame*.

To see this in action, simply remove the *<LinearDoubleKeyFrame>* tag from the preceding example and replace it with a *<DiscreteDoubleKeyFrame>* tag.

Here's the code:

```
<Storyboard>
   <DoubleAnimationUsingKeyFrames Storyboard.TargetName="prj"
       Storyboard.TargetProperty="RotationY" Duration="0:0:10"
       RepeatBehavior="Forever" AutoReverse="True">
     <DiscreteDoubleKeyFrame KeyTime="0:0:1" Value="180"></DiscreteDoubleKeyFrame>
     <DiscreteDoubleKeyFrame KeyTime="0:0:10" Value="360"></
DiscreteDoubleKeyFrame>
   </DoubleAnimationUsingKeyFrames>
</Storyboard>
```

When you run the application, you'll see that after 1 second the image flips, and then after 10 seconds it flips back.

Using a Spline Key Frame

To change the property from one value to another using a curved value that provides for acceleration and deceleration, you use a spline key frame. To do this, you first define a quadratic Bezier curve. Subsequently, Silverlight determines the speed of the property as it moves from one value to another using a parallel projection of that curve.

If that is hard to visualize, consider the following scenario: The sun is right overhead and you hit a baseball into the outfield. Watch the shadow of the ball. As it climbs into the air, the movement of the shadow appears to accelerate. As it reaches its apex, the shadow's speed of movement decelerates. Finally, as the ball falls, the shadow's speed accelerates again until it hits the ground.

Imagine that your animation in this case is the ball's shadow and the spline is the path of the baseball. You define the spline—the trajectory of the baseball in this example—using *KeySpline*. *KeySpline* defines control points for a quadratic Bezier curve, which is a type of curve that's defined by drawing between a number of points. It is normalized so that the first point of the curve is at zero and the second at one. For a parabolic arc, which is the trajectory the baseball would follow, *KeySpline* will contain two comma-separated normalized values.

For a curve similar to the arc of the baseball, you define *KeySpline* as **0.3,0 0.6,1**. This defines the first point of the curve at (0.3, 0) and the second point at (0.6, 1). The result is that the animation accelerates quickly until approximately one-third of the movement is complete. It then moves at a uniform speed until approximately two-thirds of the trajectory is reached. Finally, it accelerates for the remainder of the animated flight, simulating the ball's fall to earth.

Using this knowledge of spline key frames, you can make the rotation animation feel a little more organic using *KeySpline*.

Here's the code:

```
<Storyboard>
  <DoubleAnimationUsingKeyFrames Storyboard.TargetName="prj"
      Storyboard.TargetProperty="RotationY" Duration="0:0:10"
      RepeatBehavior="Forever" AutoReverse="True">
    <SplineDoubleKeyFrame KeyTime="0:0:10"
        KeySpline="0.3,0 0.6,1" Value="360"></SplineDoubleKeyFrame>
  </DoubleAnimationUsingKeyFrames>
</Storyboard>
```

Animation Easing

Easing functions let you create and use a variety of specialized animation effects, including bounce or spring effects. Silverlight ships with a number of built-in easing functions in the *System.Windows.Media.Animation* namespace.

Using animation easing functions makes it a lot easier to animate your objects so they mimic realistic behavior—without having to figure out the physics of them for yourself.

So, for example, if you want your animation to provide a realistic bounce, you can either do the physics yourself and program the behavior manually or you can use the built-in bounce easing function, which you access using the *EasingFunction* child of the *Animation* tag.

Add a bounce effect

1. Open the SbSCh7_2 project.

2. Delete everything inside the *<Storyboard></Storyboard>* tags.

3. Add a new *DoubleAnimation*, setting its *TargetName* to **prj**, its *TargetProperty* to **RotationY**, its *Duration* to **0:0:10**, its *From* property to **0**, and its *To* property to **360**.

4. Do not set the *RepeatBehavior* or *AutoReverse* properties.

5. Your code should look like this:

```
<Storyboard>
  <DoubleAnimation Storyboard.TargetName="prj"
      Storyboard.TargetProperty="RotationY" Duration="0:0:10" From="0"
To="360">
  </DoubleAnimation>
</Storyboard>
```

6. Add a *<DoubleAnimation.EasingFunction>* tag as a child of *DoubleAnimation*.

```
<Storyboard>
  <DoubleAnimation Storyboard.TargetName="prj"
      Storyboard.TargetProperty="RotationY" Duration="0:0:10" From="0"
To="360">
    <DoubleAnimation.EasingFunction>
    </DoubleAnimation.EasingFunction>
  </DoubleAnimation>
</Storyboard>
```

7. You can define the easing behavior within this tag. To make your animation bounce, use the *BounceEase* declaration. Here's an example that specifies that the animation should bounce four times at the end:

```
<BounceEase Bounces="4" EasingMode="EaseOut" Bounciness="2"></BounceEase>
```

The *Bounces* attribute specifies four bounces. The *EasingMode* specifies when the easing behavior should occur—*EaseOut* causes it to occur at the end of the animation. For the *Bounciness* attribute, think about balls made of different materials. A softball is thick and dense, so if you drop it on the ground it will have a very low bounce. A rubber ball, on the other hand, will bounce much higher. You change the material of the bounce by specifying *Bounciness*. The higher the number, the bouncier the object will be.

8. Press F5 to run your application. You'll see the image rotate through 360 degrees. At the end of the animation, the rotation will bounce back through 180 degrees. It will then go back to the end and bounce back through 90 degrees, and so on.

Other Easing Functions

You'll find the built-in easing functions in the *System.Windows.Media.Animation* namespace. In the following descriptions, the descriptions are based on the *EaseIn* mode. You can deduce the *EaseOut* and *EaseInOut* effects from these descriptions. Although this text describes them briefly, the differences between the different ease modes can be subtle. It's best to experiment with them to get the best results.

The Easing functions are:

- **BackEase**   This moves the animation backwards a little before continuing. It's a little bit like starting a car on a hill—you roll back a little before moving forward.

- **BounceEase**   As you saw in the sample code, this creates a bouncing effect.

- **CircleEase**   This accelerates the animation based on a circular function, where the initial acceleration is slower and the later acceleration faster.

- **CubicEase**   This is similar to *CircleEase*, but based on a cubic formula where time causes a slower acceleration in the beginning of the animation and a more rapid acceleration towards the end.

- **ElasticEase**   This is similar to *BounceEase* in that it oscillates the value until the objects comes to a rest.

- **ExponentialEase**   This is similar to *CircleEase* and *CubicEase* in that it causes an exponential acceleration from one value to the next.

- **PowerEase**   This causes an exponential acceleration where the value of the ease is proportional to the power of the elapsed time.

- **QuadraticEase**   This is very similar to *CubicEase* except that the value is based on the square of the time.

- **QuarticEase**   This is similar to *QuadraticEase* and *CubicEase*, but here the value is based on time to the power of four.

- **QuinticEase**   This is similar to *QuadraticEase*, *CubicEase*, and *QuarticEase*. This time, however, the value is based on the time to the power of five.

- **SineEase**   This changes the value along a sine wave.

Note that these are classes, so each has its own properties that you can use to configure and fine-tune it. So, for example, if you inspect the *BounceEase* class, you'll see that it has properties for the number of bounces that it will provide and the Bouncinessof the animation (the variation in value bounds as it changes direction). When you use one of the ease classes, be sure to check out the API documentation for that class (available at *http://msdn.microsoft.com/en-us/library/cc189019(VS.96).aspx#easing_functions*) to make sure you get its implementation just right.

Defining Animation with Expression Blend

You can define animations graphically in Expression Blend, which will then generate the XAML to perform the animation. This lets you build different types of animations automatically.

In this section, you'll go through the process of building a simple animation by using Expression Blend.

Build an animation

1. Launch Expression Blend, specify that you want to create a new Silverlight 3 Application + Website, and name it **SbSCh7_3**.

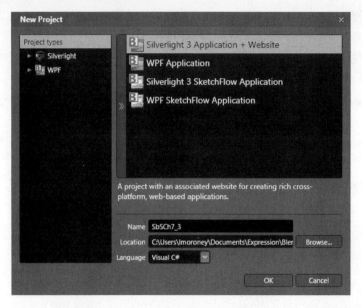

2. Select the Ellipse tool from the toolbar on the left and use it to draw an ellipse on the screen. Fill the ellipse with a solid color.

3. On the Window menu, select the Animation workspace. This will give you the tools to graphically design timelines. When you edit the properties that you want changed using the visual editor, Expression Blend generates the XAML code for the animation.

4. At the bottom of the screen, you can see the Objects And Timeline panel. This allows you to add a timeline and then visually add key frames. To add a new timeline, click the plus (+) button in the Objects And Timeline panel.

5. When you click the + button, you'll get a dialog box asking for the *Name* property of the Storyboard that you are about to create. Leave it set to the default name, **Storyboard1**.

6. The Objects And Timeline panel will change to show the timeline associated with the Storyboard you just created. The yellow vertical line (set to time zero, by default) shows the current time. Drag this to the four-second point and press the Record Keyframe button, which looks like an egg with a little plus sign (+) beside it. It's right below the Back button on the timeline's shuttle controls.

You'll see a little mark on the timeline that indicates the key frame has been recorded in that location.

7. Now do something to the ellipse. Drag it to a different spot on the screen, change the color or size, or alter any of its other properties. Do this while you are still in the animation workspace mode and while the yellow timeline is on the keyframe at the four-second mark.

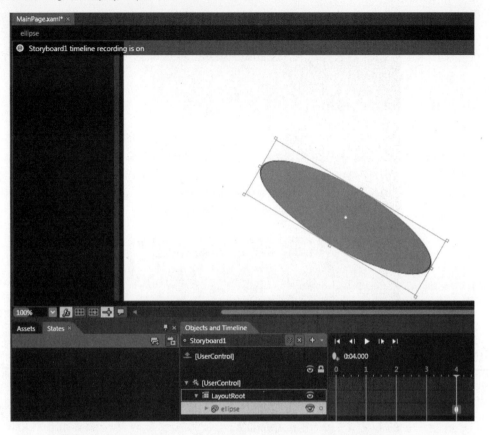

8. Drag the yellow timeline marker around, and you'll see a preview of how the animation will look at any point in time. For example, in the preceding screenshot, the ellipse has been moved from one position to another, rotated, and changed to green. Dragging the yellow bar to the two second point shows the halfway point along that change, accurately reflecting its position, rotation, and color at that point in time.

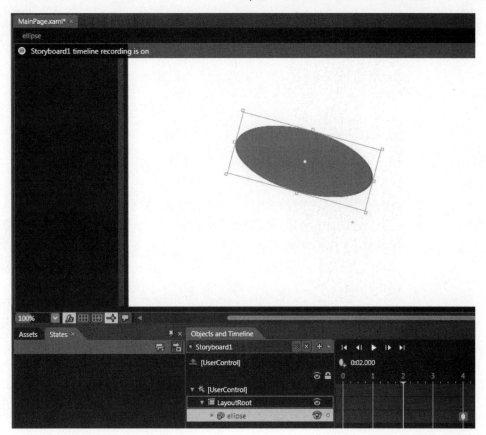

You can fine-tune your animation by using the controls at the top, allowing you to play the animation and skip through it frame by frame. You can also add other key frames and control how the animation should look at those key frames. Meanwhile, Expression Blend calculates all the XAML code for you.

Additionally, you can use Expression Blend to define splines and all the other attributes of an animation. A detailed look at using Expression Blend is beyond the scope of this book, but you can find numerous resources online at *http://www.microsoft.com/ Expression*.

Key Points

- Transformations are based on either the Render or the Projection of an element.

- You used the *Rotate, Scale, Translate, Skew,* and *Matrix* rendering transforms and learned how to combine them into a single transform.

- The *PerspectiveTransform, is a* projection transform that you can use to simulate 3-D effects by rotating 2-D objects in a 3-D space.

- You discovered how animation works in Silverlight by defining a Storyboard that changes a property over time.

- You used key frames to define how property changes occur at set times.

- You experimented with easing to see how it lets you easily apply lifelike physics effects to objects in your animations.

- You took a brief tour of the features Expression Blend offers for defining animations in a graphical UI.

Chapter 8
Building Desktop Applications

After completing this chapter, you will be able to:

- Install and run applications outside of the browser.
- Detect when an application has been updated.
- Detect network connectivity and availability.
- Use isolated storage.
- Determine when an application requires Elevated Trust.
- Interoperate with COM.
- Use the *NotificationWindow* class.

Running Applications Outside of the Browser

With version 3 of Microsoft Silverlight, Microsoft introduced the concept of *out of browser* applications. An out-of browser application runs without requiring a browser other than for its initial installation. Silverlight 4 has enhanced this concept with updates that support Elevated Trust, COM interoperability, native file access, and more.

In this chapter, you'll take a tour of the out of browser features, and you'll learn how to develop applications that use them.

Build a simple application

1. Launch Visual Web Developer and create a new Silverlight project called **SbSCh8_1**.

2. Add a *Button* control to MainPage.xaml and create a *Click* event handler for it.

3. Edit the code for the *Click* handler to include a *MessageBox* command.

```
private void button1_Click(object sender, RoutedEventArgs e)
{
    MessageBox.Show("I'm a desktop application now!");
}
```

4. Right-click the SbSCh8_1 project in Solution Explorer and select Properties from the pop-up menu.

5. You'll see the Project Properties page. Select the Enable Running Application Out Of The Browser check box.

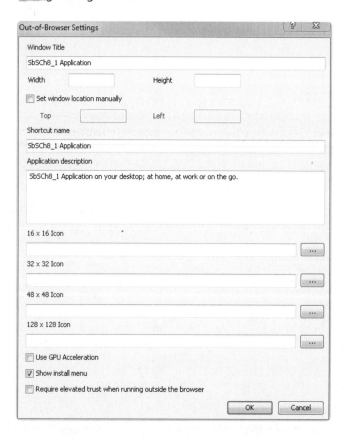

6. The Out of Browser Settings button will now be enabled. Click this button to open the settings dialog box.

7. You use this dialog box to configure everything necessary for enabling your application to run outside of the browser. For now, just familiarize yourself with the options and keep the default settings. Click OK to go back to the Project Properties page.

8. Save your application and press F5 to execute it.

9. You'll see that your application is still running *within* the browser. That's OK, you'll take it out of the browser in a moment. Click the button and to see the message box you programmed into the *Click* event.

10. Right-click any part of the Silverlight application. In the pop-up menu, you'll see an option to Install SbSCh8_1 Application Onto This Computer.

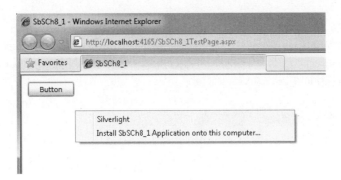

11. Select the install option. The installation dialog box will appear. Notice the icon on the left. You have not specified a custom icon for the application, so Silverlight will assign the default icon. This dialog box also indicates the name of the application and the location from which it is being installed, and gives users the option to add shortcuts to the Start menu and desktop.

    Note that you can change the default icon, specify an initial window size and position, and set other options using the Out of Browser Settings dialog box discussed in step 7.

12. Make sure the Desktop check box is selected and click OK.

13. Silverlight will add an icon to your desktop. Double-click the icon and the application will launch in its own window.

The default Window size may not be suitable for all applications—it certainly isn't for this one—so remember to set the desired default size and location using the Out of Browser Settings dialog box. The window is also resizable by the user, so bear that in mind when designing the user interface.

14. Applications may be uninstalled as easily as they are installed. Right-click the background of either the application running within its own window or the application running within the browser and you'll see the option to Remove This Application.

15. When you select the remove option, you'll be asked to confirm that you want to remove the application. Select Yes and Silverlight will delete the shortcuts from the Start menu and desktop, and the application will shut down.

Creating a Custom Install Link

In the previous example, the end user had to know to right-click in the running Silverlight application to reach the out of browser installation option. That probably isn't as intuitive as you might like. With Silverlight 4, you can access an API that allows you to create your own user interface that prompts users to install the application to the computer. However, for security reasons, users must still use the right-click menu as described in the previous section to remove the application.

Add an install button

1. Open your SbSCh8_1 project and add a new *Button* to the design surface.

2. Name the new *Button* **button2** and set its *Content* property to **Install**.

3. Set the *Visibility* property of the *Button* to **Collapsed**.

4. Double-click the button to create a *Click* handler and edit its code like so:

```
private void button2_Click(object sender, RoutedEventArgs e)
{
    Application.Current.Install();
}
```

As you might have guessed, this code installs the current application. At run time, it triggers the same installation interface as the default Silverlight UI you saw in the previous section.

5. Find the *MainPage()* constructor function and edit it to look like this:

```
public MainPage()
{
    InitializeComponent();
    if (Application.Current.InstallState != InstallState.Installed)
    {
        button2.Visibility = Visibility.Visible;
    }
}
```

This code checks the current install state of the application. When the application is not installed, the Install button is shown. (Remember that you set the default state of the *Button* to invisible by setting its *Visibility* to *Collapsed*).

6. Press F5 to run the application. You'll see that it now has an Install button. Note that if the application is already installed on your desktop, you won't see the Install button. If this is the case, uninstall the application and then run it again after the application is no longer installed.

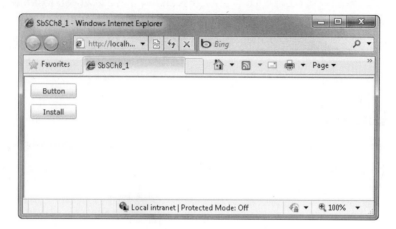

7. Click the Install button. You'll get the familiar Install Application dialog box.

8. Click OK and the application will install and run. When the application runs, the Install button will no longer be visible. This is because when the constructor code ran, it detected that the application is currently installed.

Note that in the browser, the Install button is still visible. Clicking it now will result in an error because the application is already installed. The error occurs because the installation code calls *Application.Current.Install()* to get it to install again. In a real application, you should put a *try...catch* clause around this code to avoid the error. Alternatively, you can just set the *Visibility* property of the button to *Collapsed* to hide it in the *Click* handler.

9. If you refresh the browser or run the application again, the Install button disappears because the code now detects that the application is currently installed.

Detecting Updates

It's pretty easy to imagine a scenario where your out of browser application is deployed to end users over the network and then updated on the server. Fortunately, it's easy for a Silverlight application on the client to detect that an update has been made and then update itself automatically.

Add support for automatic updates

1. If SbSCh8_1 is already installed on your computer, run the application and then remove it by right-clicking the window background and selecting the remove option.

2. Open Visual Web Developer and find the *MainPage()* constructor.

3. You need to add a declaration for an event handler that will check for updates and download any that are found. To do this, add the following code to the end of the *MainPage()* function:

```
Application.Current.CheckAndDownloadUpdateCompleted +=
new CheckAndDownloadUpdateCompletedEventHandler(
        Current_CheckAndDownloadUpdateCompleted);
```

4. If you're using IntelliSense, Visual Web Developer will have created the event handler function for you. You'll revisit that in a moment. For now, you need to add one more line of code in the *MainPage()* function that checks for an update and downloads it if one is available.

```
Application.Current.CheckAndDownloadUpdateAsync();
```

5. Your *MainPage()* function should now look like this:

```
public MainPage()
{
  InitializeComponent();
  if (Application.Current.InstallState != InstallState.Installed)
  {
    button2.Visibility = Visibility.Visible;
  }
  Application.Current.CheckAndDownloadUpdateCompleted +=
    new CheckAndDownloadUpdateCompletedEventHandler(
            Current_CheckAndDownloadUpdateCompleted);
  Application.Current.CheckAndDownloadUpdateAsync();
}
```

When you launch the application out of the browser, this code checks the server to see whether a newer version is available. If so, it will download the newer version and call the *CheckAndDownloadUpdateCompleted* handler when it is done.

6. At this point, it makes sense to inform the user that he should restart for the latest version. Note that you don't have to do this. Because the latest version is already on the user's machine, it will run the next time the user launches the application. However, it's a good practice to inform users, so the following steps will add a notification.

7. First, because you'll be using a *ChildWindow*, you'll need to add a reference to *System.Windows.Controls*.

   a. In Solution Explorer, right-click the References item in your SbSCh8_1 project.

   b. Select Add Reference and the Add Reference dialog box will appear.

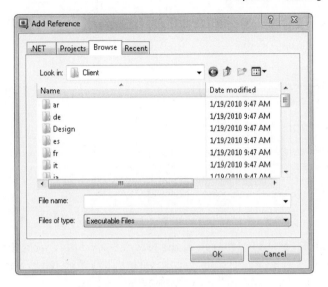

c. Select the Browse tab and locate the System.Windows.Controls DLL in the Silverlight SDK. (It should be located in a directory named something like *C:\ Program Files\Microsoft SDKs\Silverlight\v4.0\Libraries\Client\System.Windows. Controls.dll.*)

d. Select the System.Windows.Controls DLL and click OK to add the reference.

8. Now add the following code to the *CheckAndDownloadUpdateCompleted* event handler:

```
void Current_CheckAndDownloadUpdateCompleted(object sender,
    CheckAndDownloadUpdateCompletedEventArgs e)
{
  if (e.UpdateAvailable)
  {
    ChildWindow cw = new ChildWindow();
    cw.Title = "This application has been updated.";
    cw.Content = "A new version of this application has been downloaded and
installed. Please restart to get the new version.";
    cw.Show();
  }
}
```

9. Press F5 to run the application so you can test to ensure that the changes work properly.

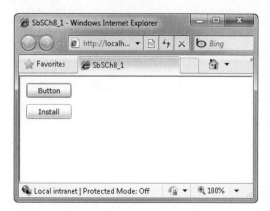

10. Click the Install button and you'll see the install dialog box.

11. Select the Desktop and Start Menu options and click OK. The application is now installed on your computer.

12. Shut down both the browser version of the application and the stand-alone version that launched when you installed it.

13. Open Visual Web Developer and add a new *TextBlock* to the application. Set its text to **This is a new Version!**.

14. Press F5 to build and run the application. You'll see the first button, but not the second button because the application is already installed. More importantly, you'll see the new *TextBlock* that contains "This is a new Version!"

15. Find the icon on your desktop or on your Start menu to launch the out of browser version you just installed. Launch the application and, after a moment, the UI will become grayed out and Silverlight will render a message telling you that the application has been updated.

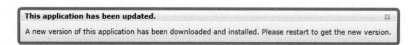

16. Close the application and then reopen it. You'll see that the new version is now installed with the new *TextBlock* being shown.

Detecting Out of Browser Status

So far, you've seen that writing the application is consistent whether it is running in the browser or as a stand-alone application. However, there are some scenarios where you might want to know if the application is currently running in or out of the browser, so Silverlight offers an API to detect this.

Detect where the application is running

1. Open the SbSCh8_1 application.

2. Change the *Content* property of the *TextBlock* to read **I am now running**.

3. Go to the *MainPage()* constructor function and add the following code after the existing code:

```
if (Application.Current.IsRunningOutOfBrowser)
  textBlock1.Text += " on your Computer";
else
  textBlock1.Text += " in your Browser";
```

4. If you are running in the browser, the code will add "in your Browser" to the end of the *TextBlock* text. Otherwise, it will add "on your Computer."

5. Press F5 to run the application. You'll see that the text reads, "I am now running in your Browser."

6. Double-click the SbSCh8_1 application on your desktop.

7. If you've been following along, you'll see the auto update UI that you added in the previous section. Close and then reopen the application as it instructs you to do. You'll now see the new code that detects you are running out of browser, displaying that fact with the message "I am now running on your Computer."

Detecting Network Connectivity and Availability

With an application that a user first encounters in the browser but that can be installed on the computer by using the out of browser functionality, it's important that you address the scenario in which the user launches the application from the desktop in a disconnected state. To do this, you'll need to know how to make your application detect whether it is online.

Detect network connectivity and availability

1. Open the SbSCh8_1 project.

2. Add a new *TextBlock* control by double-clicking TextBlock in the Toolbox. Name the new *TextBlock* **textBlock2**. Set its *Text* property to **I am now:**.

3. At the top of the MainPage.xaml.cs code file, you'll see a lot of *using* statements. This is where you define the namespaces your code is using in C#. Add the following line to the end of the *using* statement list:

```
using System.Net.NetworkInformation;
```

4. At the bottom of the *MainPage()* constructor, you need to set up an event handler that fires whenever a change in network conditions occurs. In Silverlight, the *NetworkChange* class gives you this functionality through the event called *NetworkAddressChanged*. To handle the event, type the following code:

```
NetworkChange.NetworkAddressChanged +=
    new NetworkAddressChangedEventHandler(NetworkChange_NetworkAddressChanged);
```

5. If you use IntelliSense, Visual Web Developer will create a stub event handler for you.

```
void NetworkChange_NetworkAddressChanged(object sender, EventArgs e)
{
}
```

6. The *NetworkAddressChanged* event fires whenever the network conditions change. Within the event handler, you can call the *GetIsNetworkAvailable* function on the *NetworkInterface* object to see whether you are online or offline, like so:

```
void NetworkChange_NetworkAddressChanged(object sender, EventArgs e)
{
  if (NetworkInterface.GetIsNetworkAvailable())
  {
    textBlock2.Text = "I am now: Online";
  }
  else
  {
    textBlock2.Text = "I am now: Offline";
  }
}
```

As shown, this application sets the *TextBlock* text only when network conditions *change*; it doesn't set the initial state of the application.

7. Press F5 to execute the application to see how well it works. The functionality you added works both in and out of the Browser. When the application starts, you'll see the label that you added earlier.

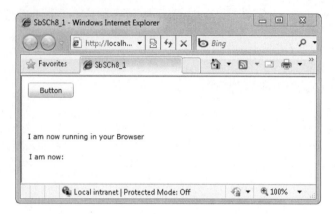

8. If you are on a wired-only connection, disconnect the network cable to see the effect of going offline. If you're on a wireless network, you'll need to follow the next few steps.

9. In Windows 7, open the Network And Sharing Center.

10. Select the Change Adapter Settings option on the left to display your network connections.

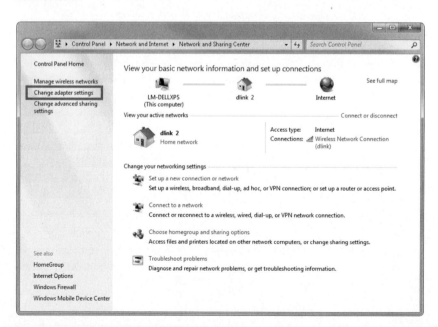

11. Right-click the Wireless Network Connection and you'll see the context menu.

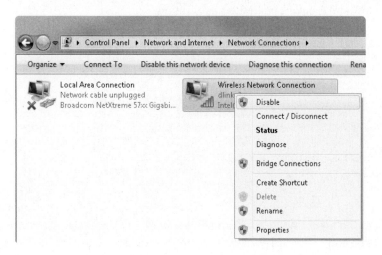

12. Select Disable from the context menu and the network connection will be disabled.

13. Now take a look at your application and you'll see that the UI has updated to read "I am now: Offline."

14. Re-enable your wireless connection by right-clicking it and selecting Enable from the context menu. As soon as the wireless connection reconnects, your application will change to say "I am now: Online."

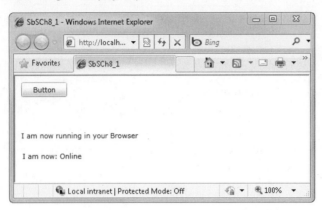

By having your applications detect their online or offline state, you can ensure that your applications respond accordingly. One common scenario is to have an application cache some of its most important data locally, using isolated storage, so the user can use this data when working offline. Then when the system is back online, the data is synchronized to the data on the network.

Using Isolated Storage

Isolated storage is so called because the data is isolated in an obscure set of directories and files on your hard drive. Silverlight assigns isolated storage space on a per-domain basis, reserving a default limit of 1 MB per domain. In other words, if you have several applications using the same domain, the total default limit for all of them is 1 MB. However, for each out of browser application, the default limit is raised to 25 MB. You can increase these limits, but it will require user approval to do so. In this section, you'll learn how to read from and write to isolated storage.

1. Create a new Silverlight application and name it **SbSCh8_2**.

2. Add a *TextBox*, a *TextBlock*, and two *Button* controls to the Mainpage.xaml file.

3. Name the first *Button* **button1** and change its *Content* property value to **Write**. Name the second *Button* **button2** and change its *Content* property value to **Read**.

4. Double-click each button to create a *Click* event handler for each.

5. Add the following code to the top of MainPage.xaml.cs, beneath the existing *using* statements:

```
using System.IO;
using System.IO.IsolatedStorage;
```

6. The *Write* button has an event handler named *button1_Click*. You want this event handler to take the text the user types into the *TextBox* and write it to isolated storage. Start by setting up an isolated storage file called **store**.

```
using (IsolatedStorageFile store =
        IsolatedStorageFile.GetUserStoreForApplication())
{
}
```

7. Now that you have a reference to an isolated storage file, create a new file in it using the *OpenFile* method. Here's how you can open a new file called **MyStore.Text**. Note This *OpenFile* call will create the file if it doesn't already exist.

```
store.OpenFile("MyStore.Text", FileMode.OpenOrCreate, FileAccess.Write)
```

8. You can pass this entire line of code to a *StreamWriter* to make it easy to write to the file.

```
using(StreamWriter sw = new StreamWriter(
        store.OpenFile("MyStore.Text", FileMode.OpenOrCreate, FileAccess.Write)))
{

}
```

9. Now that you have a *StreamWriter* object called *sw,* it's easy to write the content of textBox1 to it.

```
sw.WriteLine(textBox1.Text);
```

10. Here's the full *button1_Click* event handler:

```csharp
private void button1_Click(object sender, RoutedEventArgs e)
{
  using (IsolatedStorageFile store =
         IsolatedStorageFile.GetUserStoreForApplication())
  {
    using(StreamWriter sw = new StreamWriter(
        store.OpenFile("MyStore.Text", FileMode.OpenOrCreate, FileAccess Write)))
    {
      sw.WriteLine(textBox1.Text);
    }
  }
}
```

11. Now you can implement the code for *button2*. In this event handler, you want to read
back whatever was written into isolated storage and write it into the *TextBlock*. The
code for this click handler is very similar to what you just wrote, except this time the application is reading.

```csharp
private void button2_Click(object sender, RoutedEventArgs e)
{
  using (IsolatedStorageFile store =
         IsolatedStorageFile.GetUserStoreForApplication())
  {
    using(StreamReader sr = new StreamReader(
        store.OpenFile("MyStore.Text", FileMode.Open, FileAccess.Read)))
    {
      textBlock1.Text = sr.ReadToEnd();
    }
  }
}
```

12. Press F5 to run your application and you'll see the four controls.

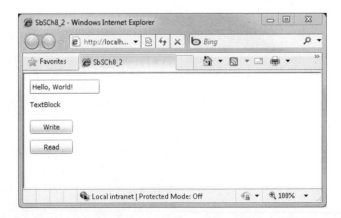

13. Type something into the *TextBox* and press the Write button and the application will write the text to isolated storage.

14. Press the Read button and the application will read the text from isolated storage and display it in the *TextBlock*.

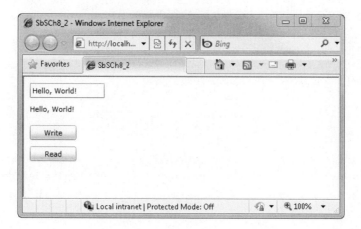

15. Take note of the address from which your application is running (check your browser's address field). For example, the following screen shows that the application is running from *http://localhost:10216*. You will likely have a similar address, but the port number (10216 in this case) might be different. That's fine—just remember which port number your application is using.

16. Right-click anywhere in your application and a pop-up menu will appear. It likely just contains the item "Silverlight." Select that, and you'll see the Microsoft Silverlight Configuration dialog box. Select the Application Storage tab and you'll see your Web site listed.

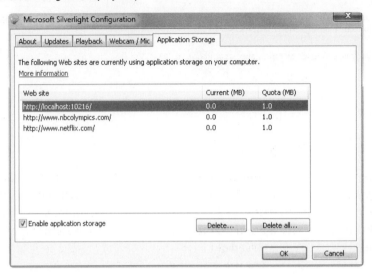

Note that this dialog box contains a check box that allows users to enable or disable isolated storage (the dialog box calls it Application Storage). Be sure to wrap plenty of error checking around any code you write that reads or writes to isolated storage, because there's every chance the user could have disabled it. You can detect whether isolated storage is enabled by using the *IsolatedStorageFile.IsEnabled* property.

Increasing Isolated Storage

As mentioned earlier, a domain has a maximum of 1 MB for isolated storage with an in-browser application and 25 MB for an out of browser application. The space available for isolated storage, however, can be increased. But the user has to allow it.

Increase the amount of isolated storage

1. Stop the application, and go to the *button1_Click* event handler. Find the line that reads:

```
using(StreamWriter sw = new StreamWriter(
```

Add the following code above that line:

```
Int64 newSpace = 2097152;
Int64 curSpace = store.AvailableFreeSpace;
if (curSpace < newSpace)
```

```
{
    if (!store.IncreaseQuotaTo(newSpace))
    {
        MessageBox.Show("Sorry, the user refused!");
    }
    else
    {
        MessageBox.Show("Your Isolated Storage is now 2Mb");
    }
}
```

This code checks the available free space in isolated storage. When the free space is less than *newSpace* (2097152 bytes or 2 MB), the code calls the *IncreaseQuotaTo()* method. In this case, it tries to increase the quota to 2 MB. The attempt causes Silverlight to raise a dialog box that asks the end user for permission to increase isolated storage space. If the user answers yes, Silverlight increases the quota and the code displays a *MessageBox* that reflects the new size. If the user answers no, the quota stays the same.

2. Press F5 to execute the application. This time, when you click the Write button, you'll see a dialog box that asks if you want to increase the size of available storage.

3. Click No, and you'll see the "Sorry the user refused!" message box, and you'll be returned to your application.

4. Press the Write button again and this time click Yes. Now you'll see the message that says your isolated storage is now 2 MB and you'll be returned to the application.

5. Right-click the application and open the Silverlight configuration dialog box. Take a look at the isolated storage tab. You'll see that your quota is now 2 MB.

This describes just about everything you need to know about isolated storage and how to use it in your applications. You can now take advantage of this incredibly useful technology to provide productive experiences both online and offline.

Enabling Elevated Trusted Mode

Out of browser applications in Silverlight allow you to use *Elevated Trust*, which provides a way to break out of the security sandbox restrictions Silverlight typically imposes. These typical restrictions include, for example, limited access to the file system. Elevated Trust takes you a little beyond what isolated storage offers, letting your application access a limited set of directories, including the My Documents, My Music, My Pictures, and My Videos folders.

Enable Elevated Trust

1. Create a new Silverlight project called **SbSCh8_3**.

2. Add a *Button*, a *TextBlock*, and an *Image* control to your design surface.

3. In Solution Explorer, right-click the project and select Properties.

4. On the Silverlight tab, select the Enable Running Application Out Of The Browser check box and then click the Out of Browser Settings button.

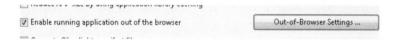

5. In the Out Of Browser Settings dialog box, make sure that the Require Elevated Trust When Running Outside The Browser check box is selected and click OK.

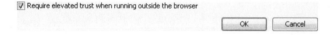

6. Double-click the button to create a *button1_Click* event handler and type the following code into the event handler:

```
private void button1_Click(object sender, RoutedEventArgs e)
{
  if (Application.Current.HasElevatedPermissions)
  {
    string myPics =
         Environment.GetFolderPath(Environment.SpecialFolder.MyPictures);
    textBlock1.Text = myPics;
  }
}
```

7. Run the application and right-click the window background to install the application to your computer. You'll notice that the install dialog box is a little different from what you have seen before—that's because this is a trusted application. When the out of browser version launches, click the button, and you'll see where Silverlight believes your My Pictures directory resides.

8. Close the desktop application. If the browser application is still open, use it to remove the application from your computer (by right-clicking the application and selecting the remove option). If it isn't running, run the application again and make sure you remove the out of browser version.

9. Place a picture file in that directory and make sure you know the name of the picture. The following code sample uses a picture called bucky.jpg that has been placed in the C:\Users\lmoroney\Pictures directory.

10. Update your *button1_Click* event handler so it has code that reads a picture called bucky.jpg from the My Pictures directory and loads it into the image control. If your image has a different name, be sure to change the name in the code.

```
private void button1_Click(object sender, RoutedEventArgs e)
{
    if (Application.Current.HasElevatedPermissions)
    {
        string myPics =
            Environment.GetFolderPath(Environment.SpecialFolder.MyPictures);
        textBlock1.Text = myPics;
        string myLoc = myPics + "\\bucky.jpg";
        StreamReader streamReader = new StreamReader(myLoc);
        Stream stream = streamReader.BaseStream;
        BitmapImage m = new BitmapImage();
        m.SetSource(stream);
        image1.Source = m;
    }
}
```

11. Make sure you add the following lines to the top of your code.

```
using System.IO;
using System.Windows.Media.Imaging;
```

12. Press F5 to execute your application. Right-click the background and install the application to your computer.

13. Press the button in the application and the application will load the image from your hard drive and render it using the *Image* control.

File system access is only one of the benefits of running with Elevated Trust. There are many more benefits, including better network access and support for Component Object Model (COM) interoperability. Going through all the benefits in detail is beyond the scope of this book.

Debugging Out of Browser Applications

You may be used to debugging Silverlight applications running within the browser, but it's just as easy to debug applications that run outside the browser. This is particularly useful for cases where you're building and testing functionality that only works out of the browser, such as when you need to use Elevated Trust.

Set up out of browser debugging

1. Open your SbSCh8_3 application.

2. If it isn't already installed as an out of browser application, run it and install the application to your desktop. Then close the application and return to Visual Web Developer.

3. Right-click the project item in Solution Explorer and select Properties from the pop-up menu.

4. Select the Debug tab.

5. Make sure that the Installed Out Of Browser Application option is selected.

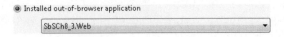

◉ Installed out-of-browser application

> SbSCh8_3.Web ▼

6. Go back to Solution Explorer and right-click the SbSCh8_3 project again. This time, click the Set As Startup Project option.

7. Set a breakpoint on any of the lines of code in the *button1_Click* event. You can do this by placing the cursor on that line and pressing F9.

8. Press F5 and the out of browser version of the application will execute.

9. Click the button. Visual Web Developer will stop executing the program at the line with the breakpoint. You can now step through the code and inspect your variables.

```
24    private void button1_Click(object sender, RoutedEventArgs e)
25    {
26        if (Application.Current.HasElevatedPermissions)
27        {
28            string myPics = Environment.GetFolderPath(Environment.SpecialFolder.MyPictures);
29            textBlock1.Text = myPics;
30            string myLoc = myPics + "\\bucky.jpg";
31            StreamReader streamReader = new StreamReader(myLoc);
32            Stream stream = streamReader.BaseStream;
33            BitmapImage m = new BitmapImage();
34            m.SetSource(stream);
35            image1.Source = m;
```

Interoperating with COM

An out of browser application running with Elevated Trust can do a lot more than just access files. One of these extras is the ability to interoperate with other Windows applications or components through a Windows technology known as COM.

Perform COM interop

1. Create a new application called **SbSCh8_4**.

2. Add a *Button* to the design surface.

3. Use the Project Properties to configure the application, allowing it to run out of browser with elevated permissions.

4. Execute the application and right-click the background to install it as an out of browser application. Close the application and return to Visual Web Developer. You have to run the application and install it as an out of browser application before you can set it up for debugging.

5. Use the Project Properties to set the application up to allow debugging from Visual Web Developer.

6. Find the References folder in SbSCh8_4 and right-click it to add a new reference.

7. On the Browser tab, browse to the SDK folder that contains Microsoft.CSharp.Dll (it will look something like C:\Program Files\Microsoft SDKs\Silverlight\v4.0\Libraries\Client). This will give you some of the C# version 4.0 features, such as the *dynamic* keyword that you need for COM interop within Silverlight.

8. Double-click the *Button* in the designer to create a *Click* event handler.

9. At the top of the MainPage.xaml.cs code window, add the following line of code:

```
using System.Windows.Interop;
```

Note that some versions of the Silverlight pre-release bits use this line of code instead. If you're having trouble with the code in this section, try the following *using* statement instead:

```
using System.Runtime.InteropServices.Automation
```

10. Now go to the *button1_Click* event handler and add the following code:

```
private void button1_Click(object sender, RoutedEventArgs e)
{
    if (App.Current.IsRunningOutOfBrowser && AutomationFactory.IsAvailable)
    {
        dynamic excel = AutomationFactory.CreateObject("Excel.Application");
        excel.Workbooks.Add();
        excel.Cells[1, 1] = "Top Cell";
        excel.Cells[1, 2] = "Next Cell";
        excel.Visible = true;
    }
}
```

This code uses the *AutomationFactory* object to create an object of type *Excel.Application*, and then adds a workbook, adds text values to two cells, and displays the Microsoft Excel application.

Note that if you are new to COM programming, this is how you create and program COM objects. You'll have to check MSDN or other COM development references to understand the options that are available for any other type of COM object. In this case, the object that references the Excel application is a *dynamic* type, which means that its properties, methods, and events aren't known until it is instantiated at run time (sometimes called late binding). It also means that IntelliSense will not work when you are developing with dynamic objects, so you'll have to understand the underlying COM API.

11. Press F5 to run the application.

12. Press the button and the COM Interop will work its magic. It might take a few seconds, but Excel will fire up and populate the cells as specified.

Using Notification Windows

Another nice addition in Silverlight 4 is the notification window. You've probably seen these when using other applications. In Microsoft Outlook, for example, when a new e-mail message arrives, a little pop-up window in the system tray informs you of the new message. These pop-up windows are sometimes nicknamed "toast" because they pop up like a slice of toast.

Silverlight makes it easy to implement notifications in your applications. Here you'll update the previous example to give you a toast window when the Excel workbook is ready.

Add a notification to your application

1. Open the SbSCh8_4 project.

2. Go to the *button1_Click* event handler and add the following line of code underneath the *excel.Visible=true* line:

```
NotificationWindow notW = new NotificationWindow();
```

This code creates an instance of the *NotificationWindow* class. This class is a *Content* class, meaning you can load any XAML into it to style the notification window however you like. To keep things simple, this example loads only a simple *TextBlock* into the notification window. In real life, however, you can make notifications as simple or as complex as you like.

3. Here's the complete code to create and populate a simple notification window. Paste this into the *button1_Click* event handler:

```
NotificationWindow notW = new NotificationWindow();
notW.Height = 100;
notW.Width = 320;
TextBlock t = new TextBlock();
t.FontSize = 24.0;
t.Text = "Excel is ready!";
notW.Content = t;
notW.Show(2000);
```

4. Execute your application and press the button. After the Excel worksheet appears, you'll get the notification, which will disappear after two seconds. Note that you may need to remove the application from your desktop and then reinstall it from the browser to get this to work.

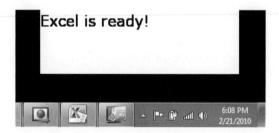

This simple example is a little ugly. But with a bit of creativity, you can create your own custom class that uses XAML and animation to define the look and feel of the notification window. You can then use a reference to this class as the *Content* property in your notification window, and you'll get the behavior you want!

Key Points

- You learned how to configure an application to run out of browser and how to define an install link for users.

- You saw how out of browser applications can self-detect updates and how they can notify the user that they've been updated.

- You learned how to detect out of browser status and how to detect network connectivity and availability.

- You saw how an out of browser application can use isolated storage to store information, and discovered how you can extend the default isolated storage size limits.

- You saw how Silverlight 4 and Elevated Trust let you go outside the security sandbox, and how you can use Elevated Trust to interact more deeply with the user's computer using COM.

- You learned how to debug applications as they run on the desktop.

- You discovered how to build and use notification windows that run in the system tray.

Chapter 9
Integrating with the Browser

After completing this chapter, you will be able to:

- Access Silverlight from HTML.
- Access HTML content from Silverlight.
- Integrate your application with external JavaScript APIs.
- Use the Silverlight *<object>* tag in HTML.

Web development today stands at a crossroads, with different camps evangelizing different philosophies about how you should develop for the Web. One side takes the position that the unenhanced browser is enough. You can do everything you want to do with clever JavaScript, Dynamic HTML, CSS, and AJAX programming.

The other side preaches that the browser was designed to render *documents* and not *applications*. Therefore, relying on the browser alone when building applications that have increasingly sophisticated requirements is like building a house of cards.

But there's a happy medium between the two camps when you use Microsoft Silverlight, which allows you to choose what technology to use. You may have already invested significant time and effort in building JavaScript-based APIs and don't want to throw them away and start again—but you may also be tempted by the performance improvements and richness that Silverlight can offer. Well, fear not! Silverlight has a browser bridge that makes it a first-class browser citizen. The browser bridge provides several possibilities including:

- The ability to expose any code compiled into a Microsoft .NET assembly to the browser and call it from JavaScript.
- The ability to access any JavaScript code in the browser from a .NET assembly and call it from your Silverlight application.

This chapter shows you how to work in each of these scenarios. To discover just how easy it is to interface with JavaScript from Silverlight, you'll work with the Microsoft Bing Maps API, which are JavaScript-based.

Bridging Silverlight and HTML

In this section you'll see how to create a simple Silverlight application controlled via the browser bridge from some HTML-based buttons and JavaScript.

Create the Silverlight application

1. Create a new Silverlight application called **SbSCh9_1**.

2. Right-click the SbSCh9_1 project in Solution Explorer and select Class from the Add menu.

3. The Silverlight Add New Item dialog box appears. Select Class from the dialog box, and name the class **CityData.cs**

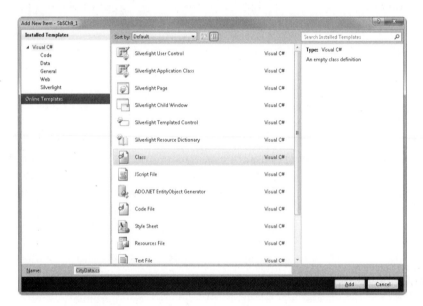

4. You now have a *CityData* class in the SbSCh9_1 namespace. Add three properties to the class by typing them in the code page for *CityData*, just below the class declaration, but before the constructor. They will use .NET *getter* and *setter* syntax, making your code shorter. Basically, you no longer need to write separate code for each property to create a private member variable representing the property along with code that exposes it using a member function. It's a really nice shortcut. Here's how to create the three properties (a string and two doubles) for the class:

```
public string CityName { get; set; }
public double Latitude { get; set; }
public double Longitude { get; set; }
```

5. Create a constructor that you will use to set the values of the three properties, making it easier for the developers. They can construct an instance of the class by using the city name, latitude, and longitude, instead of having to construct a class and then set each property. So, edit the constructor to accept three input parameters, and use them to initialize the three properties.

```csharp
public CityData(string strCityName, double nLatitude, double nLongitude)
{
   CityName = strCityName;
   Latitude = nLatitude;
   Longitude = nLongitude;
}
```

6. You now have a data class that can be used to manage cities. Here's what the full class listing will look like:

```csharp
using System;
using System.Net;
using System.Windows;
using System.Windows.Controls;
using System.Windows.Documents;
using System.Windows.Ink;
using System.Windows.Input;
using System.Windows.Media;
using System.Windows.Media.Animation;
using System.Windows.Shapes;

namespace SbSCh9_1
{
    public class CityData
    {
            public string CityName { get; set; }
            public double Latitude { get; set; }
            public double Longitude { get; set; }

            public CityData(string strCityName, double nLatitude,
                            double nLongitude)
            {
                CityName = strCityName;
                Latitude = nLatitude;
                Longitude = nLongitude;
            }
    }
}
```

7. Silverlight comes with a powerful but basic control called *ItemsControl* that lets you draw items on a page bound to a data source. That control is ideal for this application, which requires drawing a list of cities for a particular country on the Silverlight page. You specify the data binding using a *DataTemplate*, which in turn contains the controls that define how you want to draw the items on the page. Because this case requires drawing only text, a *TextBlock* is ideal. You don't know what text will be in the *TextBlock* until you actually run the application and get the data, so you define it using a binding. You already created a *CityData* class that exposed a property called *CityName*. To get a *TextBlock* to render the *CityName*, use a binding to that property, which looks like this:

```
<TextBlock FontSize="14" Height="30" Text="{Binding CityName}" ></TextBlock>
```

Your application doesn't yet know where the data is coming from, so if you run it in this state, Silverlight simply ignores the binding. As you build the application, however, the content will begin to take shape.

8. You need to tell the *ItemsControl* how to render the data, which you do with a data template. You saw an example of how to use a *TextBlock* in a data template, so here's the full code for an *ItemsControl* that renders data as a set of *TextBlock* controls bound to the *CityName* property. Add this code to your MainPage.xaml within the default Grid.

```
<ItemsControl x:Name="itmCities">
  <ItemsControl.ItemTemplate>
    <DataTemplate>
      <TextBlock FontSize="14" Height="30"
        Text="{Binding CityName}" ></TextBlock>
    </DataTemplate>
  </ItemsControl.ItemTemplate>
</ItemsControl>
```

9. You now have a way of presenting the data. But your application still isn't ready to be run. You need to create some data to display! The *ItemsControl* binds to classes that expose the *IEnumerable* interface. One such *IEnumerable* is the *List<>* class. This form of generics type-definition (<>) syntax is extremely useful—it basically lets you create a list that's restricted to containing any type. For example, to create a list containing only *CityData* objects, you can write *List<CityData>*. In your MainPage.xaml.cs file, create a function called *getCities* that accepts a string parameter identifying a country and returns a list of *CityData* objects (*List<CityData>*).

```
private List<CityData> getCities(string strCountry)
{

}
```

10. Based on the country passed in via the *strCountry* parameter, you need to generate a *List<CityData>* that contains the cities for that particular country and return it. Typically, you'd retrieve such values from a database. For demonstration purposes, this example hard codes three cities for each of three countries. Here's the full function:

```
private List<CityData> getCities(string strCountry)
        {
            List<CityData> ret = new List<CityData>();
            switch (strCountry)
            {
            case "france":
                {
                    ret.Add(new CityData("Paris", 48.87, 2.33));
                    ret.Add(new CityData("Lourdes", 43.1, 0.05));
                    ret.Add(new CityData("Toulouse", 43.6, 1.38));
                    break;
                }
            case "uk"":
                {
                    ret.Add(new CityData("London", 51.5, 0));
                    ret.Add(new CityData("Stratford-Upon-Avon",
                            52.3, -1.71));
                    ret.Add(new CityData("Edinburgh", 55.95, -3.16));
                    break;
                }
            case "germany":
                {
                    ret.Add(new CityData("Berlin", 52.52, 13.42));
                    ret.Add(new CityData("Munich", 48.13, 11.57));
                    ret.Add(new CityData("Hamburg", 53.58, 9.98));
                    break;
                }
            }
            return ret;
        }
```

At this point, you can probably see how much simpler the *CityData* class constructor that took three parameters for name, latitude, and longitude made the above code.

11. Now that you have a way to generate data, you need to bind this data to the *ItemsControl* control to render it. To prevent a lot of code duplication later, it's best to create a function that does this for you. The function *upDateCities* passes a country to *getCities*, gets the *List<CityData>* back, and then sets the *ItemsSource* property of the *ItemsControl* to that list.

```
public void upDateCities(string strCountry)
{
    List<CityData> myCities = getCities(strCountry);
    itmCities.ItemsSource = myCities;
}
```

12. You're almost ready to test the data and data binding, but there's one last thing to do: create a default binding. The best place to do this is in the *MainPage()* constructor so that when the page first renders, it will bind to some data. To do this, simply call the *upDateCities* function and hard-code a default country to pass in.

```
public MainPage()
{
    InitializeComponent();
    upDateCities("uk");
}
```

13. In Solution Explorer, in the SbSCh9_1.Web project, you'll find a file called SbSCh9_1 TestPage.html. Right-click it and select the Set As Start Page item from the pop-up menu.

14. Press F5 to execute the application. You'll see that, by default, the page renders three cities in the UK.

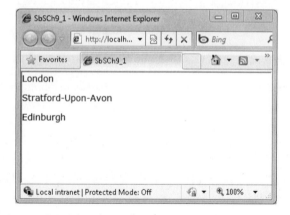

The Silverlight application is now complete, but it isn't yet bridged to HTML. You'll see how to do that in the next section.

Open the Browser Bridge

Now you'll see how to open the browser bridge to that application so that HTML and JavaScript code on the page can interact with it.

Build a bridge

1. To use the browser bridge, you need to include a reference to *System.Windows.Browser* in your code. So open MainPage.xaml.cs and add the following reference to the list of *using* statements at the top of the code page:

   ```
   using System.Windows.Browser;
   ```

2. You need to register the Silverlight application as scriptable to the browser after it loads, which you can do in the *Loaded* event for *MainPage*. You register a handler for this event within the *MainPage()* constructor like this:

   ```
   this.Loaded += new RoutedEventHandler(MainPage_Loaded);
   ```

3. You can now implement your *MainPage_Loaded* event handler, which will run after the page has loaded. To open the browser bridge and register Silverlight as a script-able object on the hosting HTML page, call the *RegisterScriptableObject* method on the *HtmlPage* class. Here's the *MainPage_Loaded* event that does this:

   ```
   void MainPage_Loaded(object sender, RoutedEventArgs e)
   {
       HtmlPage.RegisterScriptableObject("MySilverlightObject", this);
   }
   ```

   This code simply registers the Silverlight application as an object that can be scripted within the HTML page. The first parameter specifies a name. In this case, code running on the page will access your object as *MySilverlightObject*. The second parameter passes a reference to the object itself.

4. Now that code running on your HTML page can talk to Silverlight, it needs something to talk to. Earlier you wrote the *upDateCities* function that took in a country, retrieved the *List<CityData>* for the cities in that country, and then bound that *List<CityData>*

to the *ItemsControl*. Ideally, you would expose the *upDateCities* function to an external caller. And that is as easy as adding a *[ScriptableMember]* attribute to it.

```
[ScriptableMember]
public void upDateCities(string strCountry)
{
    List<CityData> myCities = getCities(strCountry);
    itmCities.ItemsSource = myCities;
}
```

At this point, your Silverlight application has opened its side of the browser bridge. You've registered it as an object that code running on the page can access, and exposed a method call. In the next section, you'll see how to call this method from JavaScript on your HTML page.

Using the Browser Bridge to Control the Silverlight Application

You've now written a Silverlight application that renders data from a number of datasets and a function that filters the data down based on a parameter. And you saw how to open the browser bridge to expose that function. In this section, you'll create HTML and JavaScript that uses the exposed function to change the state of the Silverlight application.

Call your application from JavaScript

1. Open the SbSCh9_1TestPage.html file. You'll find it in the SbSCh9_1.Web project within Solution Explorer.

```
Solution 'SbSCh9_1' (2 projects)
  SbSCh9_1
    ▷  Properties
    ▷  References
    ▷  App.xaml
       CityData.cs
    ▲  MainPage.xaml
          MainPage.xaml.cs
  SbSCh9_1.Web
    ▷  Properties
    ▷  References
    ▲  ClientBin
          SbSCh9_1.xap
       SbSCh9_1TestPage.aspx
       SbSCh9_1TestPage.html
       Silverlight.js
    ▷  Web.config
```

2. Find the *<object>* tag on the page that instantiates your Silverlight control. It should look something like this:

```
<object data="data:application/x-silverlight-2,"
  type="application/x-silverlight-2" width="100%" height="100%">
```

3. Add an *id* attribute to the *<object>* tag to give your Silverlight object a name. To access the application via the browser bridge, JavaScript will need to access the control, and for that it needs a name (an *id*) to refer to it by. The following code names it "slcontrol."

```
<object id="slControl" data="data:application/x-silverlight-2,"
type="application/x-silverlight-2" width="100%" height="100%">
```

4. Near the bottom of the HTML, right before the closing *</div>* tag, add some new code to define a simple UI, composed of a *<div>* that contains three buttons. In HTML you define buttons using an *<input>* tag.

```
<div style="position: absolute; width: 400px; height: 76px;  left: 0px;
top: 200px"
      id="JSLayer">

  <input id="bUK" type="button" value="uk"
         onclick="doCities('uk');" />
  <input id="bGermany" type="button" value="germany"
         onclick="doCities('germany');"/>
  <input id="bFrance" type="button" value="france"
         onclick="doCities('france');" />

</div>
```

5. Notice that each button defines an *onclick* event handler that calls a function named *doCities()*. In an HTML page, events are typically handled using JavaScript, so you need to add a new JavaScript function.

```
<script type="text/javascript">
  function doCities(country) {
  }
</script>
```

You already named the Silverlight control *slControl* and registered it as a scriptable object called *MySilverlightObject*. You also exposed the *upDateCities* function, which expects you to pass it a string. This JavaScript function will get a string, called *country*, so you will have all the pieces you need for talking to Silverlight.

6. First, create a JavaScript variable (*var*) to hold a reference to the control.

```
var slPlugin = document.getElementById("slControl");
```

7. Now that you have an object reference to the control, you can just call the Silverlight-based functionality on that!

```
slPlugin.content.MySilverlightObject.upDateCities(country);
```

8. Here's the full JavaScript function. If you're not too familiar with JavaScript, just make sure this code is within the *<head>* tag of your HTML page.

```
<script type="text/javascript">
  function doCities(country) {
    var slPlugin = document.getElementById("slControl");
    slPlugin.content.MySilverlightObject.upDateCities(country);
  }
</script>
```

9. You're almost ready to test this out. You've done everything that you need to do to call Silverlight via the bridge, but the automatically generated HTML page specifies that the Silverlight content will fill the page—so you'll never see your HTML UI. To solve that problem, look at the CSS code in the HTML page, and find the *#silverlightControlHost* setting. Change it to look like this:

```
#silverlightControlHost {
        height: 100px;
    width: 200px;
        text-align:center;
}
```

10. Press F5 to run your application. You'll see a similar UI to that from before, except, now you have three buttons at the bottom, reading "uk," "germany," and "france."

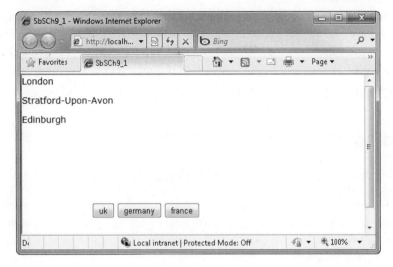

11. The Silverlight code defaults to show cities from the UK. If you press the France button, you'll see that the UI updates to display three cities from France.

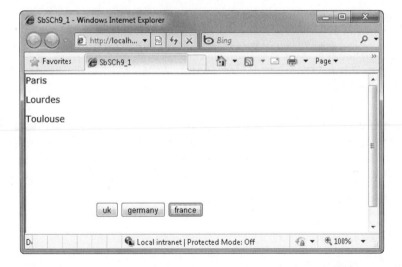

This example may be very simple, but it's showing off some very powerful functionality. The France button is an HTML input control on an HTML page. Pressing it causes a JavaScript function to execute. The JavaScript function finds the Silverlight control and queries its running application for a bridged object. It finds the bridged object, and calls a method that was exposed on this object. The method creates the data and binds it to an ItemsControl, which renders the data. You've manipulated .NET code running within the Silverlight object from JavaScript on the page. Because .NET code runs many times faster than JavaScript, you can build very powerful in-browser applications that can interface with existing JavaScript, HTML, and CSS solutions that you have already made.

Calling Browser Functions from Silverlight

You just saw how to create a Silverlight application that exposes functionality to JavaScript-based applications. In this section, you'll do the exact opposite: you'll use Silverlight to call JavaScript-based functionality that resides on the page. There are some excellent reasons why you might want to do this. Namely, huge amounts of functionality and APIs on the Internet have been designed to work with JavaScript and you can now take advantage of these from within Silverlight.

Integrate the Bing Maps API

This example uses Bing Maps, which exposes a JavaScript API for manipulating the map within the browser. You can learn more about the JavaScript API for Bing maps at the Bing Maps Interactive SDK (*http://www.microsoft.com/maps/isdk/ajax/*).

Use the Bing Maps API

1. Open the SbSCh9_1 project.

2. Add a *<script>* tag to access the JavaScript functions in the Bing Maps SDK. Make sure that you place the following script in the *<head>* section of your page.

   ```
   <script type="text/javascript"
     src="http://ecn.dev.virtualearth.net/mapcontrol/mapcontrol.ashx?v=6.2">
   </script>
   ```

3. Add a new *<div>* to the page. Put it immediately above the *<div>* that has the *id silverlightControlHost*.

   ```
   <div id='mapDiv' style="position: absolute; width: 443px;
       height 417px; z-index: 2; left: 301px; top 0px">
   </div>
   ```

> **Note** The long string in the *style* attribute is CSS code that specifies the dimensions of the map. You can manipulate these values to make the map bigger or smaller. The important thing to remember here is that the *id* of the *<div>* is *mapDiv*. You'll need that *id* in a moment.

4. Add a new JavaScript function to the page. Make sure that it's either within an existing *<script>* block or add a new *<script>* block to contain it. This function will use the Bing Maps API to get a new map and draw it within the *<div>* that you just created. Note that you pass *mapDiv* to the new *VEMap*. (Bing Maps are based on Virtual Earth technology, so you'll see the prefix "VE" a lot when using them.)

```
var map=null;

function GetMap() {
  map = new VEMap('mapDiv');
  map.LoadMap();
}
```

5. The last thing you need to do is call this function when the page loads. You can do this by adding an *onload* event handler to the page body. Find the *<body>* tag and edit it so the event calls the *GetMap()* function you just added, as shown here:

```
<body onload="GetMap();">
```

6. Now press F5 to run your application And the default Bing map will render.

Remember that Silverlight renders the city names. In the next section, you'll see how to call back out to the browser when a user clicks a city name, using the Bing API to move the map so it displays the selected city.

Control the JavaScript API from Silverlight

In this section, you'll see how to call out to JavaScript from Silverlight, in this case causing the map to move so it shows the city that has been clicked on.

Control JavaScript from your Silverlight application

1. Open the SbSCh9_1 application, and load the SbSCh9_1TestPage.html file.

2. Add a new JavaScript function to the page. This function will move the map to a named location. Bing maps are pretty smart—they know the names of locations, so you can tell the map to show you, for example, "London" and it will know where that is on the map. Here's the JavaScript *MoveMap()* function:

```
function MoveMap(where) {
    try {
        map.Find(null, where);
    }
    catch (e) {
        alert(e.message);
    }
}
```

3. With the *MoveMap()* function in place, to find London, you can now call *MoveMap("London")*.

4. Go back to your Silverlight application. When a user clicks the name of a city, you want to have the map show that city. In the Silverlight application, you rendered the city names using *TextBlock* controls within the *DataTemplate* of an *ItemsControl*. To handle a user clicking these *TextBlock* controls, you'll need an event handler.

5. Find the *<TextBlock>* tag in the MainPage.xaml file. Type **MouseLeftButtonUp=** and use IntelliSense to complete the attribute with *TextBlock_MouseLeftButtonUp*. Your XAML should look like this:

```
<TextBlock FontSize="14" Height="30" Text="{Binding CityName}"
    MouseLeftButtonUp="TextBlock_MouseLeftButtonUp"></TextBlock>
```

6. Switch to your code-behind file. If you used IntelliSense to create the *MouseLeftButtonUp* handler, you'll see the stub event handler in your code. If not, just type it in. It should look like this:

```
private void TextBlock_MouseLeftButtonUp(object sender, MouseButtonEventArgs e)
{

}
```

7. To build up this function, start by declaring a string to hold the city name.

```
string strCity = "";
```

8. Look at the event handler declaration. It takes two parameters: an object called *sender* and a *MouseButtonEventArgs* named *e*. The *sender* is a reference to the instance of the control that raised this event. Remember that because this is in an *ItemsControl*, lots of *TextBlock* instances may get generated at run time—one for each city you are binding to.

The *sender* parameter will be a reference to a specific *TextBlock* that raised the event (the one the user clicked), and that *TextBlock* will have a *Text* property containing the city name. So all you need to do is retrieve that text, which you do by telling Silverlight that *sender* is a *TextBlock* and then getting the *Text* property. Here's the code:

```
TextBlock clickedText = sender as TextBlock;
strCity = clickedText.Text;
```

9. At this point, you know the name of the city the user clicked. Now all you need to do is call the JavaScript function that you created earlier that moves the map to a specified city. That function was called *MoveMap*. You need to tell Silverlight which function to call and how to find it. In Silverlight, you use a *ScriptObject* to refer to a JavaScript function, and you find it by using the *HtmlPage.Window.GetProperty* method, passing it the name of the function you want to find.

```
ScriptObject sMoveMap = (ScriptObject)HtmlPage.Window.GetProperty("MoveMap");
```

10. To call this JavaScript function, you use the *InvokeSelf* method on the *ScriptObject* and pass it the parameters. In this case, you want to pass in the city name.

```
sMoveMap.InvokeSelf(strCity);
```

11. Here's the complete event handler that fires when a user clicks one of the *TextBlock* controls.

```
private void TextBlock_MouseLeftButtonUp(object sender, MouseButtonEventArgs e)
{
  string strCity = "";
  TextBlock clickedText = sender as TextBlock;
  strCity = clickedText.Text;
  ScriptObject sMoveMap = (ScriptObject)HtmlPage.Window.GetProperty("MoveMap");
  sMoveMap.InvokeSelf(strCity);
}
```

12. Press F5 to run the application.

13. Click the Germany button and then select Munich. You'll see that the map renders Munich.

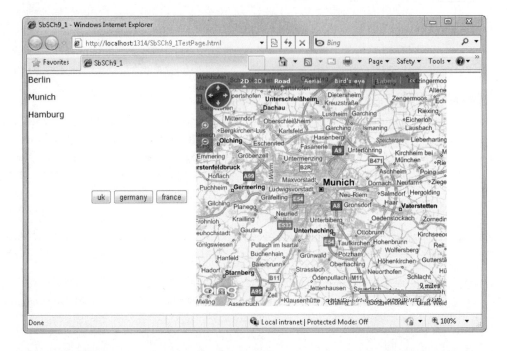

14. Now click the France button and select Toulouse. You'll see that the map jumps to Toulouse.

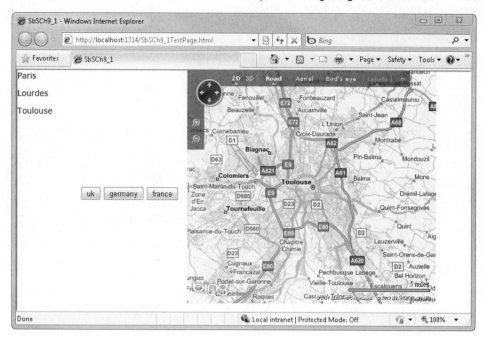

You're now able to call a JavaScript API and manipulate an object on the page through JavaScript and AJAX—all initiated by your Silverlight application. This barely scratches the surface of the many possibilities, but it should serve as a good primer for integrating Silverlight 4 as a first class browser citizen within your Web applications.

Understanding the Silverlight Object

You saw that you use the *<object>* tag to instantiate Silverlight within an HTML page. The *<object>* tag is a standard HTML tag and understanding it will help you build and support your applications more effectively.

Standard Object Tag Attributes

The full list of *<object>* attributes is beyond the scope of this book, but here's a list of the more common ones you'll use.

- The *Type* attribute specifies the MIME type of the object to load. For Silverlight applications, you use the *application/x-silverlight-2* MIME type. This instructs the browser to load the Silverlight plug-in to access the content. (You might wonder why the type specification ends with "-2" when this book covers Silverlight version 4. The reason is that the MIME type specification dates back to when Silverlight first became a .NET based application, which was in version 2.)

- The *Width* attribute specifies the control's width in either percent or pixels.

- The *Height* attribute specifies the control height in either percent or pixels.

- The *ID* attribute specifies the control name to be used in JavaScript programming.

Custom Silverlight Parameters

Because not every *<object>* supports the same set of configurable parameters, the HTML *<object>* tag allows you to specify non-standard parameters using a list of *<param>* elements. These *<param>* elements each specify a name/value pair. Table 9-1 shows the most common parameters used by the Silverlight object.

TABLE 9-1 Parameters Supported by the Silverlight Object

Parameter Name	Description
source	Specifies either the XAP file containing the application to load and run or a XAML document to render.
width	Sets the width of the control in pixels or by percent.
height	Sets the height of the control in pixels or by percent.
background	Determines the background color of the control. You can use an ARGB value, such as *#FFAA7700*, or a named color, such as *Black*.
framerate	Sets the maximum frame rate to allow for animation. It defaults to 24.
isWindowless	This is a Boolean value. When set to *true*, Silverlight content gets rendered behind the HTML content so that HTML content can be written on top of it.
enableHtmlAccess	Determines whether content hosted in the Silverlight control is accessible from the browser DOM. It defaults to true. If you set it to false none of the browser bridge functionality will work.
minRuntimeVersion	Determines the minimum version of Silverlight to support.
onLoad	Specifies a JavaScript function to run when the control is loaded.
onError	Specifies a JavaScript function to run when the control hits an error.
onFullScreenChange	This event fires when the *FullScreen* property of the Silverlight control changes.
onResize	This event fires when the *ActualWidth* or *ActualHeight* property of the Silverlight control changes.

Using HTML Fallback

One nice feature of the *<object>* tag is that it is stackable in the sense that if the initial *<object>* instantiation fails, the browser will render the fragment of HTML that is included within the *</object>* tag after all the *<param>* declarations. This makes it easy to create a simple banner that will appear on the screen if Silverlight is not installed.

The bold HTML code in the following example illustrates how to create a banner that appears only when a user doesn't have Silverlight installed.

```
<object data="data:application/x-silverlight-2," type="application/x-
silverlight-2" width="100%" height="100%" id="slControl">
  <param name="source" value="ClientBin/SbSCh9_1.xap"/>
  <param name="onError" value="onSilverlightError" />
  <param name="background" value= "white" />
  <param name="minRuntimeVersion" value="4.0.41108.0" />
  <param name="autoUpgrade" value="true" />
  <a href="http://go.microsoft.com/fwlink/?LinkID=149156&v=4.0.41108.0"
     style="text-decoration:none">
   <img src="http://go.microsoft.com/fwlink/?LinkId=161376"
        alt="Get Microsoft Silverlight" style="border-style:none"/>
  </a>
</object>
```

In this situation, if Silverlight is not present on the system, the browser renders the hyperlink (*<a>* tag) embedded within the object tag. This displays a link that users can click to install Silverlight.

Key Points

- You saw how to create a Silverlight application that's accessible from JavaScript hosted in your HTML.

- You learned how to call JavaScript in an HTML page from a Silverlight application.

- You learned about using JavaScript-based APIs from within your Silverlight applications.

- You explored the HTML *<object>* tag and how you can use it to render Silverlight on your page.

Chapter 10
Accessing Network Services

After completing this chapter, you will be able to:

- Build a financial data service that handles requests and returns data.

- Reformat a list of comma-separated values into XML.

- Use the *WebClient* class to connect to a Web site.

- Use LINQ to XML.

- Use the *WebRequest* and *WebResponse* classes to send and receive data.

- Use cross-domain policy files to control cross-domain access.

In this chapter, you'll look at how to build connected applications with Microsoft Silverlight. Silverlight offers a number of data connectivity APIs, and you'll get a good look at how to use them to connect to a hosted service and retrieve data from it.

You'll start with the simplest means of connection in Silverlight, the *WebClient* class, and then delve into more powerful functionality enabled by the *WebRequest* and *WebResponse* classes. You'll also explore how to support cross-domain access in your Silverlight applications using the cross-domain policy files.

It goes without saying that for connecting to a service, you'll need a service you can connect to. So the discussion will cover building a live service that will handle your requests and dispatch data back to your application.

Creating a Financial Data Service

In the next few sections, you'll look at building a data service from which Silverlight can consume data. You'll use Yahoo! Historical Quotes, which provides a list of comma-separated values (CSV) when called.

Its API is pretty simple—just call the URL *http://ichart.finance.yahoo.com/table.csv*. You specify the data that you want to get back by passing in the parameters shown in Table 10-1.

TABLE 10-1 Parameters and Values for the Yahoo! Historical Quotes.

Parameter	Value
s	Stock Ticker
a	Start Month (0=January through 11=December)
b	Start Day
c	Start Year
d	End Month (0=January through 11=December)
e	End Day
f	End Year
g	Always use the letter "d"
ignore	Always use the value ".csv"

For example, to get the time series data for Microsoft (MSFT) from January 1, 2009 to January 1, 2010, you would use the following URL: *http://ichart.finance.yahoo.com/table.csv?s =MSFT&a=0&b=1&c=2009&d=0&e=1&f=2010&g=d&ignore=.csv.*

Creating the Helper Class

To work through the examples in this chapter, the first step is to create a helper class that consumes the data from Yahoo!, taking in the CSV and converting it into an XML document that Silverlight can consume.

Create the helper class

1. Create a new Silverlight solution and name it **SbSCh10_1**. Specify that you want a Web project.

2. Right-click the Web project, SbSCh10_1.Web, and select Add New Class.

3. Give your new class the name **FinancialHelpers**.

4. Make sure you have the following code at the top of your class (in addition to the existing *using* statements):

```
using System.Text;
using System.Xml;
using System.Net;
using System.Data;
using System.IO;
```

5. Add a public string function called *BuildYahooURI* to this class. Let it take a ticker, a start date, and an end date as string parameters.

```
public string BuildYahooURI(string strTicker, string strStartDate, string
strEndDate)
{
}
```

6. Enter the following code into the *BuildYahooURI* function. Here is the complete code, which will build a URI to the service:

```
public string BuildYahooURI(string strTicker, string strStartDate, string
strEndDate)
{
  string strReturn = "";
  DateTime dStart = Convert.ToDateTime(strStartDate);
  DateTime dEnd = Convert.ToDateTime(strEndDate);
  string sStartDay = dStart.Day.ToString();
  string sStartMonth = (dStart.Month - 1).ToString();
  string sStartYear = dStart.Year.ToString();
  string sEndDay = dEnd.Day.ToString();
  string sEndMonth = (dEnd.Month - 1).ToString();
  string sEndYear = dEnd.Year.ToString();
  StringBuilder sYahooURI = new
      StringBuilder("http://ichart.finance.yahoo.com/table.csv?s=");
  sYahooURI.Append(strTicker);
  sYahooURI.Append("&a=");
  sYahooURI.Append(sStartMonth);
  sYahooURI.Append("&b=");
  sYahooURI.Append(sStartDay);
  sYahooURI.Append("&c=");
  sYahooURI.Append(sStartYear);
  sYahooURI.Append("&d=");
  sYahooURI.Append(sEndMonth);
  sYahooURI.Append("&e=");
  sYahooURI.Append(sEndDay);
  sYahooURI.Append("&f=");
  sYahooURI.Append(sEndYear);
  sYahooURI.Append("&g=d");
  sYahooURI.Append("&ignore=.csv");
  strReturn = sYahooURI.ToString();
  return strReturn;
}
```

This code is straightforward. It simply builds up a string for the URI based on the incoming parameters. You'll notice that the Yahoo! URI requires month, day, and year to be separate parameters, so this splits the incoming strings into separate strings. It then appends them as described.

Note that for a real service, you should validate and scrub the incoming parameters to make sure they really are dates, and not something that someone could use to inject malicious script.

7. Add a function called *getXML* that returns an *XmlDocument*. This function calls the Yahoo! service and receives the data back from it. The Yahoo! service returns the data in CSV format, but you'll convert it to XML, which is easier to handle. Here's the complete code for the *getXML* function:

```
public XmlDocument getXML(string strTicker, string strStartDate, string
strEndDate)      {
  XmlDocument xReturn = new XmlDocument();
  DataSet result = new DataSet();
  string sYahooURI = BuildYahooURI(strTicker, strStartDate, strEndDate);
  WebClient wc = new WebClient();
  Stream yData = wc.OpenRead(sYahooURI);
  result = GenerateDataSet(yData);
  StringWriter stringWriter = new StringWriter();
  XmlTextWriter xmlTextwriter = new XmlTextWriter(stringWriter);
  result.WriteXml(xmlTextwriter, XmlWriteMode.IgnoreSchema);
  XmlNode xRoot = xReturn.CreateElement("root");
  xReturn.AppendChild(xRoot);
  // This is a hack -- the process of writing out a timeseries from the dataset
  // puts this dummy record at the end...we want to remove it

  string strXML =
    stringWriter.ToString().Replace("<TimeSeries><Date /></TimeSeries>", "");

  // END OF HACK
  xReturn.LoadXml(strXML);
  return xReturn;
}
```

The *getXML* function calls the Yahoo! URI, and reads the returned values into a stream called *yData*. It then passes the stream to *GenerateDataSet*, getting a *DataSet* called *result* back. The *DataSet* provides a *WriteXml* method that makes it easy to write out the data as XML into an *XmlDocument*, which you return to the caller. Note the little hack. For some reason, when the XML is written out to a string, some dummy data is written at the end. This hack will strip out the dummy data.

8. The *getXML* function calls *GenerateDataSet*, which does the actual CSV parsing and conversion. Here's the code:

```
public DataSet GenerateDataSet(Stream yData)
{
  DataSet result = new DataSet();
  StreamReader sRead = new StreamReader(yData);
  string[] columns = sRead.ReadLine().Split(',');
  result.Tables.Add("TimeSeries");
  foreach (string col in columns)
  {
    // Remove Spaces from any names
    string thiscol = col.Replace(" ", "");
    // Add the column name
    result.Tables["TimeSeries"].Columns.Add(thiscol);
  }
  string sData = sRead.ReadToEnd();
  string[] rows = sData.Split('\n');
  foreach (string row in rows)
  {
    string[] items = row.Split(',');
    result.Tables["TimeSeries"].Rows.Add(items);
  }
  return result;
}
```

With that code in place, you've completed your helper class.

Creating the Data Service

Now you need to write a data service that uses the helper class. Here's how.

Write a data service

1. Open the SbSCh10_1 solution.

2. Right-click the Web Project and select Add New Item. This time specify a Generic Handler and call it **Financial.ashx**.

3. Open the code-behind for your new Generic Handler. It should be called Financial.ashx.cs. Add a *using* statement to the top of the code page below any existing *using* statements. The new *using* statement should look like this:

```
using System.XML;
```

4. Update the code, including the *ProcessRequest* handler, so it looks like this:

```
public class Financial : IHttpHandler
{
  FinancialHelpers fh = new FinancialHelpers();
  public void ProcessRequest(HttpContext context)
  {
    string strTicker, strStartDate, strEndDate;
    if (context.Request.Params["ticker"] != null)
      strTicker = context.Request.Params["ticker"].ToString();
    else
      strTicker = "MSFT";

    if (context.Request.Params["startdate"] != null)
      strStartDate = context.Request.Params["startdate"].ToString();
    else
      strStartDate = "1-1-2009";
```

```
      if (context.Request.Params["enddate"] != null)
        strEndDate = context.Request.Params["enddate"].ToString();
      else
        strEndDate = "1-1-2010";

      XmlDocument xReturn = fh.getXML(strTicker, strStartDate, strEndDate);
      context.Response.ContentType = "text/xml";
      context.Response.Write(xReturn.OuterXml);
    }

    public bool IsReusable
    {
      get
      {
        return false;
      }
    }
  }
```

5. Your basic financial service is now ready to go. Press F5 to run it. You can't set an ASHX file as a start page (because it isn't a page), so your browser will open to *http://localhost:XXXX/SbSCh10_1TestPage.aspx*, where *XXXX* is a random port number. In this address, replace SbSCh10_1TestPage.aspx with **Financial.ashx** and you'll see the results of the query.

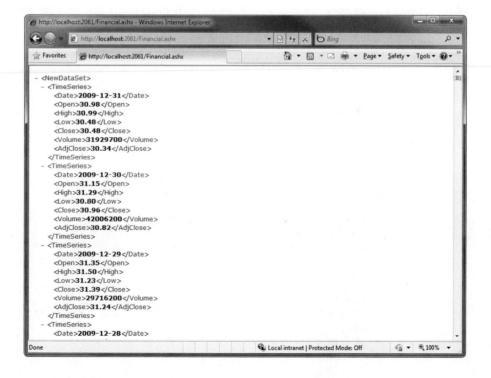

6. You can change the parameters of the query by changing the URI. In the preceding screenshot, the URI is *http://localhost:2061/Financial.ashx*. That URI returns the default data set—stock prices for Microsoft on days that the stock was traded between January 1, 2009 and January 1, 2010. You can change this by using the *ticker*, *startdate*, and *enddate* properties. Here's an example: *http://localhost:2061/Financial.ashx?ticker=VII&startdate=10-1-1996&enddate=12-12-2000*.

Using WebClient to Get Data

When you're using HTTP connectivity to get information across the Web, such as XML over HTTP, the *WebClient* class is a great solution for your needs. It's easy to use, simple to initialize, and performs well. It also supports basic header manipulation.

In the previous section, you built a service that can be called with the following URL: *http://servername:serverport/Financial.ashx?ticker=[ticker]&startdate=[startdate]&enddate=[enddate]*. Now you will take a look at how you can consume this service from a Silverlight client.

Consume your service

1. Open the SbSCh10_1 solution. Note that in the previous section, you edited the Web project. This time, you need to edit the Silverlight project.

2. In the Silverlight project, add a reference to *System.Xml.Linq*. You can find this in *Program Files\Microsoft SDKs\v 4.0\Libraries\Client*.

3. Edit the MainPage.xaml file so it contains an *ItemsControl*. As you may recall, you can use an *ItemsControl* for data binding. Remember that, in this case, its name is *_items*. You'll need that name a little later in this exercise.

```xml
<Grid x:Name="LayoutRoot" Background="White">
    <ItemsControl x:Name="_items">
        <ItemsControl.ItemTemplate>
            <DataTemplate>
                <StackPanel Orientation="Vertical">
                    <TextBlock FontWeight="Bold" Text="{Binding open}" />
                </StackPanel>
            </DataTemplate>
        </ItemsControl.ItemTemplate>
    </ItemsControl>
</Grid>
```

4. The preceding code data binds to a field named *open*. This will contain the opening value of the requested stock ticker. But remember that Silverlight will bind its data to local classes. So add a new class file to the Silverlight project and name it **TimeSeriesData**.

5. Your new *TimeSeriesData* class will store the data that comes back from the financial service. Its fields are *date, open, close, high, low, volume,* and *adjclose* (adjusted close). Here's the code for the class:

```
using System;
using System.Net;
using System.Windows;
using System.Windows.Controls;
using System.Windows.Documents;
using System.Windows.Ink;
using System.Windows.Input;
using System.Windows.Media;
using System.Windows.Media.Animation;
using System.Windows.Shapes;

namespace SbSCh10_1
{
    public class TimeSeriesData
    {
        public DateTime date { get; set; }
        public double open { get; set; }
        public double close { get; set; }
        public double high { get; set; }
        public double low { get; set; }
        public double volume { get; set; }
        public double adjclose { get; set; }

        public TimeSeriesData(DateTime dteIn, double openIn, double closeIn,
                double highIn, double lowIn, double volumeIn, double adjCloseIn)
        {
            date = dteIn;
            open = openIn;
            close = closeIn;
            high = highIn;
            low = lowIn;
            volume = volumeIn;
            adjclose = adjCloseIn;
        }
        public TimeSeriesData()
        { }
    }
}
```

6. Edit the *MainPage()* constructor so it uses the *WebClient* class to call the service you created earlier. So add the following line of code to *MainPage()*:

```
WebClient wc = new WebClient();
```

7. This creates a new *WebClient* class, which calls a URI asynchronously and raises an event when the result is returned. You create a URI using the *Uri* class. For example, here's how you create a URI to connect to the service you created a little earlier.

```
Uri uri = new Uri("http://localhost:2061/Financial.ashx?ticker=MSFT&startdate=
12-25-2009&enddate=12-31-2009", UriKind.RelativeOrAbsolute);
```

Remember that the 2061 shown in this book may change, based on the port that the development server assigns to you.

8. The *WebClient* class makes an asynchronous request, and then raises an *OpenReadCompleted* event when the data has been returned. You need to specify the name of the function to handle this event. You typically do this like so:

```
wc.OpenReadCompleted += new OpenReadCompletedEventHandler(wc_OpenReadCompleted);
```

9. Now all you have to do is call the *OpenReadAsync* method with the URI that you created earlier.

```
wc.OpenReadAsync(uri);
```

10. Here's the complete *MainPage()* constructor:

```
public MainPage()
{
  InitializeComponent();
  WebClient wc = new WebClient();
  Uri uri =
    new Uri("http://localhost:2061/Financial.ashx?ticker=MSFT&startdate=12-25-
            2009&enddate=12-31-2009", UriKind.RelativeOrAbsolute);
  wc.OpenReadCompleted += new
    OpenReadCompletedEventHandler(wc_OpenReadCompleted);

  wc.OpenReadAsync(uri);
}
```

11. You specified earlier that when the data read is complete, the event would be handled by the *wc_OpenReadCompleted* event handler. The data is returned as XML, so you'll need to read the XML into an *XDocument*. Before going any further, make sure you have the following *using* statements at the top of your document:

```
using System.IO;
using System.Xml;
using System.Xml.Linq;
```

12. To read the XML back from the service, you can use a *StreamReader* class, like this:

```
StreamReader read = new StreamReader(e.Result);
```

13. Read the XML into a string using the *ReadToEnd* method of the *StreamReader.*

```
string strXml = read.ReadToEnd();
```

14. Now that you have your XML in a string, you can load it into an *XDocument* class.

```
XDocument xmlDoc = XDocument.Parse(strXml);
```

15. Now you can start having some fun. Using LINQ, you can create an *IEnumerable* (which can be data-bound). Using generics, you can specify that your *IEnumerable* is of type *TimeSeriesData*. You're just binding to the *Open* value right now, so create an *IEnumerable* of *TimeSeriesData* and use LINQ to XML to extract the *Open* values. Here's the code:

```
IEnumerable<TimeSeriesData> myTimeSeries =
    from item in xmlDoc.Descendants("TimeSeries")
    select new TimeSeriesData()
    {
      open = Convert.ToDouble(item.Element("Open").Value)
    };
```

16. Now that you have an *IEnumerable*, you can set it to the *ItemsSource* property of the *ItemsControl* (remember that it was named _items).

```
_items.ItemsSource = myTimeSeries;
```

17. Press F5 to execute your application. It may not have the prettiest of UIs, but there is some good stuff happening here. Your Silverlight application calls the data service, which calls the Yahoo! service. In response to the request, Yahoo! provides data in CSV format and your data service converts it into XML. Your data service returns that XML,

which your Silverlight application loads into an *XDocument*. Then, through the magic of LINQ to XML, your application opens the stock prices and data binds that data to a *TextBlock* through an *ItemsControl*, rendering each of the opening prices. You've built the plumbing for a very complex and powerful application.

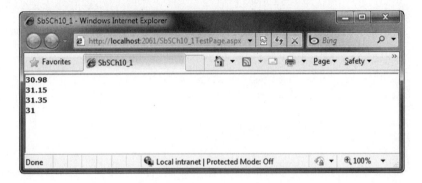

18. To see how easy it is to take this a little further, replace the *ItemsControl* with a *DataGrid*. To do so, remove the *<ItemsControl>* tag and all its children. Then place a *DataGrid* control onto the designer. Change its name to **TimeSeries** and your XAML should look like this:

```
<my:DataGrid x:Name="TimeSeries"></my:DataGrid>
```

19. Now go back to your *wc_OpenReadCompleted* event handler and fill out the LINQ to XML query so it extracts all the fields.

```
void wc_OpenReadCompleted(object sender, OpenReadCompletedEventArgs e)
{
    StreamReader read = new StreamReader(e.Result);
    string strXml = read.ReadToEnd();
    XDocument xmlDoc = XDocument.Parse(strXml);
    IEnumerable<TimeSeriesData> myTimeSeries =
        from item in xmlDoc.Descendants("TimeSeries")
        select new TimeSeriesData()
        {
            open = Convert.ToDouble(item.Element("Open").Value),
            close = Convert.ToDouble(item.Element("Close").Value),
            high = Convert.ToDouble(item.Element("High").Value),
            low = Convert.ToDouble(item.Element("Low").Value),
            adjclose = Convert.ToDouble(item.Element("AdjClose").Value),
            volume = Convert.ToDouble(item.Element("Volume").Value),
            date = Convert.ToDateTime(item.Element("Date").Value)
        };
    TimeSeries.ItemsSource = myTimeSeries;
}
```

20. Now press F5 to execute your application and you'll see that you have a data grid that renders all the values. And since you're using a data grid, the interface offers more advanced functionality, such as sorting.

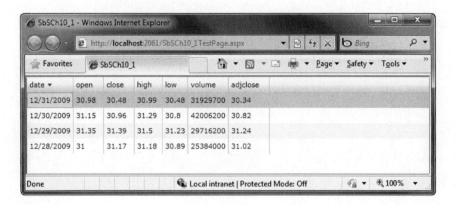

Using HTTP POST

The previous example uses an HTTP GET method that calls a URL and receives data back in response. This is the same mechanism used by a browser whenever you enter a URL into the address line and navigate to that URL.

Another common way to retrieve data from a service is to use an HTTP POST method, using an HTML *form*. With this approach, data isn't returned in a separate stream. Instead, the data is embedded within the HTTP headers themselves. It's important to understand how to read data from HTTP POST requests because you will likely encounter many Web APIs that share their data this way.

Building the HTTP POST Server

It's pretty easy to amend the ASHX file you created earlier to handle an HTTP POST method instead of the default HTTP GET method.

Prepare your code

1. Create a new Silverlight project and name it **SbSCh10_2**.

2. Right-click the Web project, select Add, and then select Existing Item. Find the FinancialHelpers.cs class file that you built for the SbSCh10_1 project and add it. Make sure you change its namespace from SbSCH10_1 to **SbSCH10_2**—you'll see the namespace near the top of the .cs file just after the *using* statements.

3. Add a new generic handler and name it **Financial.ashx**.

4. Edit the Financial.ashx.cs file so it contains the following code:

```
using System;
using System.Collections.Generic;
using System.Linq;
using System.Web;
using System.Xml;
namespace SbSCh10_2.Web
{
    public class Financial : IHttpHandler
    {
        FinancialHelpers fh = new FinancialHelpers();
        public void ProcessRequest(HttpContext context)
        {
            string strTicker, strStartDate, strEndDate;
            if (context.Request.HttpMethod == "POST")
            {
                if (context.Request.Form["ticker"] != null)
                    strTicker = context.Request.Form["ticker"].ToString();
                else
                    strTicker = "MSFT";
                if (context.Request.Form["startdate"] != null)
                    strStartDate = context.Request.Form["startdate"].ToString();
                else
                    strStartDate = "1-1-2009";
                if (context.Request.Form["enddate"] != null)
                    strEndDate = context.Request.Form["enddate"].ToString();
                else
                    strEndDate = "1-1-2010";
                XmlDocument xReturn = fh.getXML(
                                    strTicker, strStartDate, strEndDate);
                context.Response.ContentType = "text/xml";
                context.Response.Write(xReturn.OuterXml);
            }
        }
        public bool IsReusable
        {
            get
            {
                return false;
            }
        }
    }
}
```

This is very similar to what you used in the SbSCh10_1 project. The bold code highlights the difference between this and the earlier HTTP GET version.

This code simply checks to see if an HTTP POST has been performed and, if it has, the code will pull the values for the ticker, start date, and end date parameters from the HTTP POST form. It then passes these to the *getXML* function in the *FinancialHelpers* class, which handles the heavy lifting.

The data is then written back in the response stream. Note that if you call this ASHX without an HTTP POST form, an error message will be returned.

Press F5 to execute the application. You won't see anything because you don't have a client application to consume the service yet. But here you need to take note of the port that the Microsoft Visual Studio Development Server gives you. You'll see that the address is something like this: *http://localhost:XXXX/something*. You'll need the actual port—the numbers shown instead of the *XXXX*—in the next section.

Consuming the HTTP POST Server with Silverlight

The *HttpWebRequest* and *HttpWebResponse* classes give you some fine-grained control over HTTP communications. You can use these to perform an HTTP POST to the server and to process the data that comes back.

Using these classes may look a little convoluted at first, but you'll soon get the hang of it. The general approach is:

1. Create a new *HttpWebRequest* and initialize it.

2. Get the Request stream on an asynchronous callback when the request is ready to go.

3. When the request is ready to go, write the parameters to the request and set up the callback for the response.

4. When the response callback fires, pull the data you want.

Consume the HTTP POST server

1. Add a reference to *System.Xml.Linq* to your SbSCh10_2 project.

2. Use Add Existing Item to find the *TimeSeriesData* class you used in the SbSCH10_1 project. Edit the namespace within its class file to be **SbSCh10_2**.

3. Use the Toolbox to add a *DataGrid* to the XAML view for MainPage.xaml.

4. Change the name of the *DataGrid* to **TimeSeries**. Your XAML should look like this:

```
<UserControl
    xmlns:my="clr-namespace:System.Windows.Controls;
             assembly=System.Windows.Controls.Data"

    x:Class="SbSCh10_2.MainPage"
    xmlns=http://schemas.microsoft.com/winfx/2006/xaml/presentation
    xmlns:x=http://schemas.microsoft.com/winfx/2006/xaml
    xmlns:d=http://schemas.microsoft.com/expression/blend/2008
    xmlns:mc=http://schemas.openxmlformats.org/markup-compatibility/2006
    mc:Ignorable="d"
    d:DesignHeight="300" d:DesignWidth="400">
    <Grid x:Name="LayoutRoot" Background="White">
        <my:DataGrid x:Name="TimeSeries"></my:DataGrid>
    </Grid>

</UserControl>
```

5. Open the MainPage.xaml.cs file and add the following code to the top of it:

```
using System.IO;
using System.Xml;
using System.Xml.Linq;
```

6. To set up the *HttpWebRequest*, you need the URI of the service that you are calling. Replace the port number (the *XXXX)* in the following URI with the port number you noted in the previous section (the one you got from your development server):

```
Uri uri = new  Uri("http://localhost:XXXX/Financial.ashx");
HttpWebRequest request = (HttpWebRequest)HttpWebRequest.Create(uri);
```

7. Since this is a POST request, you need to specify that as the *Method* property for the request object. You also need to tell it to expect an HTTP form, which you can specify using the *ContentType* property.

```
request.Method = "POST";
request.ContentType = "application/x-www-form-urlencoded";
```

8. Now initialize the request stream. The request is performed asynchronously, so you need to specify a callback to handle the next step after the request stream is set up. In this case, the callback is called **RequestProceed**.

```
request.BeginGetRequestStream(new AsyncCallback(RequestProceed), request);
```

9. The *RequestProceed* callback should take a parameter of type *IASyncResult*. In this sample, that parameter is called *asyncResult*:

```
void RequestProceed(IAsyncResult asyncResult)
  {
  }
```

10. The *HttpRequest* variable isn't global, so there's no context to get it in this function. However, it is stored in the *asyncResult* variable's *AsyncState* property. Therefore, you can get a reference to it like this:

```
HttpWebRequest request = (HttpWebRequest)asyncResult.AsyncState;
```

11. With that reference in hand, the next step is to write the data with your parameters into the request so the data can then be passed to the service. You do this using a *StreamWriter*. The stream is available on the request object itself. Here's how to set it up:

```
StreamWriter postDataWriter = new
StreamWriter(request.EndGetRequestStream(asyncResult));
```

12. Writing the parameters is as easy as writing strings to this *StreamWriter*:

```
postDataWriter.Write("ticker=MSFT");
postDataWriter.Write("&startdate=1-1-2009");
postDataWriter.Write("&enddate=1-10-2009");
postDataWriter.Close();
```

13. At this point, you've written out everythinig to the request. The last thing to do is to start listening for the response. You use a callback here, so call the *BeginGetReponse* method of the request and tell it the callback function name (*ResponseProceed*, in this case).

```
request.BeginGetResponse(new AsyncCallback(ResponseProceed), request);
```

14. Now you need to catch the response and read the data from it. To do this, you need to use the *ResponseProceed* callback method, which takes an *IASyncResult* parameter.

```
void ResponseProceed(IAsyncResult asyncResult)
{}
```

15. Like before, you need to pull the reference to the request out of the *asyncResult*.
Additionally, you can get the response from the request object. Here's how:

```
HttpWebRequest request = (HttpWebRequest)asyncResult.AsyncState;
HttpWebResponse response = (HttpWebResponse)request.EndGetResponse(asyncResult);
```

16. Now that you have the response object, you can read the data from it using a
StreamReader, as follows:

```
StreamReader responseReader = new StreamReader(response.GetResponseStream());
string responseString = responseReader.ReadToEnd();
```

17. And now you're back in familiar territory. You have a string of XML data. You can
load this into an *XDocument*, use LINQ to get the data you want, put the data into an
IEnumerable, and then bind the data to the UI. Don't forget to add a *TimeSeriesData*
class to your project like you did in the *WebClient* project you did earlier.

```
XDocument xReturn = XDocument.Parse(responseString);
IEnumerable<TimeSeriesData> myTimeSeries =
  from item in xReturn.Descendants("TimeSeries")
  select new TimeSeriesData
  {
    open = Convert.ToDouble(item.Element("Open").Value),
    close = Convert.ToDouble(item.Element("Close").Value),
    high = Convert.ToDouble(item.Element("High").Value),
    low = Convert.ToDouble(item.Element("Low").Value),
    adjclose = Convert.ToDouble(item.Element("AdjClose").Value),
    volume = Convert.ToDouble(item.Element("Volume").Value),
    date = Convert.ToDateTime(item.Element("Date").Value)
  };
Dispatcher.BeginInvoke(() => TimeSeries.ItemsSource = myTimeSeries);
```

 Note You must make the binding on a *Dispatcher*. Because the call to this method was
not made on the UI thread, you can't bind to a UI control within it directly. However, by
using *Dispatcher.BeginInvoke()* as shown here, you'll be able to create the binding.

Here's the complete code for the code-behind Mainpage.xaml.cs:

```csharp
using System;
using System.Collections.Generic;
using System.Linq;
using System.Net;
using System.Windows;
using System.Windows.Controls;
using System.Windows.Documents;
using System.Windows.Input;
using System.Windows.Media;
using System.Windows.Media.Animation;
using System.Windows.Shapes;
using System.IO;
using System.Xml;
using System.Xml.Linq;
namespace SbSCh10_2
{
    public partial class MainPage : UserControl
    {
        public MainPage()
        {
            InitializeComponent();
            Uri uri = new Uri("http://localhost:10738/Financial.ashx");
            HttpWebRequest request = (HttpWebRequest)HttpWebRequest.Create(uri);
            request.Method = "POST";
            request.ContentType = "application/x-www-form-urlencoded";
            request.BeginGetRequestStream(
                    new AsyncCallback(RequestProceed), request);
        }
        void RequestProceed(IAsyncResult asyncResult)
        {
            HttpWebRequest request = (HttpWebRequest)asyncResult.AsyncState;
            StreamWriter postDataWriter = new

                StreamWriter(request.EndGetRequestStream(asyncResult));
            postDataWriter.Write("ticker=MSFT");
            postDataWriter.Write("&startdate=1-1-2009");
            postDataWriter.Write("&enddate=12-31-2009");
            postDataWriter.Close();
            request.BeginGetResponse(new AsyncCallback(ResponseProceed),
request);
        }
        void ResponseProceed(IAsyncResult asyncResult)
        {
            HttpWebRequest request = (HttpWebRequest)asyncResult.AsyncState;
            HttpWebResponse response =
                        (HttpWebResponse)request.EndGetResponse(asyncResult);
            StreamReader responseReader = new
                        StreamReader(response.GetResponseStream());
            string responseString = responseReader.ReadToEnd();
            XDocument xReturn = XDocument.Parse(responseString);
            IEnumerable<TimeSeriesData> myTimeSeries =
                from item in xReturn.Descendants("TimeSeries")
                select new TimeSeriesData
                {
```

```
            open = Convert.ToDouble(item.Element("Open").Value),
            close = Convert.ToDouble(item.Element("Close").Value),
            high = Convert.ToDouble(item.Element("High").Value),
            low = Convert.ToDouble(item.Element("Low").Value),
            adjclose = Convert.ToDouble(item.Element("AdjClose").Value),
            volume = Convert.ToDouble(item.Element("Volume").Value),
            date = Convert.ToDateTime(item.Element("Date").Value)
        };
        Dispatcher.BeginInvoke(() => TimeSeries.ItemsSource = myTimeSeries);
    }
  }
}
```

18. Press F5 to run the application. You'll see that it downloads the data and binds it to the grid.

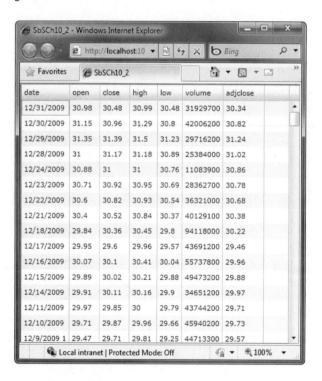

As you can see, using HTTP POST may be a bit more complicated than using an HTTP GET method that uses a *WebClient*. However, HTTP POST is still pretty straightforward, and you can use it to retrieve and bind to data in exactly the same way.

Making Cross-Domain Calls

So far, all the examples in this chapter have made calls within the same domain—likely *http://localhost*. In many instances, however, you'll need to call on data from services hosted on other machines. Silverlight uses a policy approach to cross-domain calls; the service being called must allow Silverlight to call it. Silverlight determines this by looking for a policy file in the root domain of the service it is calling. The policy file must be named clientaccesspolicy.xml.

When Silverlight sees a call to a service or other URL, it searches the root web at that URL for a clientaccesspolicy.xml file. If that file isn't present, Silverlight will not make the call, instead raising an error. If the policy file is present, Silverlight will parse the file. If the pending call is not allowed according to the policy, Silverlight will not make the call and instead will raise an error. Otherwise, Silverlight will attempt to make the call. Here's an example of a policy file:

```
<access-policy>
  <cross-domain-access>
    <policy>
      <allow-from http-request-headers="*">
        <domain uri="*" />
      </allow-from>
      <grant-to>
        <resource path="/" include-subpaths="true" />
      </grant-to>
    </policy>
  </cross-domain-access>
</access-policy>
```

Between the <allow-from> tags, the policy can define the domains from which calls are allowed. In this case, the URI is set to an asterisk (*), meaning anyone can call the service. Additionally, the grant-to section can specify which resources on the server a call may access, by defining the resource path and its sub-paths. This sample policy file specifies that anybody can access anything.

Key Points

In this chapter you explored some of the technologies available in Silverlight, including the following:

- You learned how to consume data from services located on your network and on the Internet.

- You reformatted CSV data as XML.

- You used the *WebClient* class to retrieve data from a data service and bind it to a Silverlight UI using LINQ to XML.

- You discovered how to enhance the data service to support HTTP POST.

- You used *HttpWebRequest* and *HttpWebResponse* to build an HTTP message, post the request to a service, and process the returned data.

Chapter 11
Windows Phone Development

After completing this chapter, you will be able to:

- Locate, download, and install development tools for building Windows Phone applications.

- Build a basic Windows Phone application.

- Build a real-world Windows Phone application that retrieves and displays nearly current stock quote data from a Web service.

Your Microsoft Silverlight skills aren't refined to the browser or the desktop. Starting with Windows Phone 7, you can use Silverlight to build rich mobile applications. In this chapter, you will see how to get and use the tools to build your first Windows Phone applications.

You can download the necessary tools from the Windows Phone for Developers site, which is located at *http://developer.windowsphone.com*. This chapter is based on the Community Technical Preview of the tools. If you have a later version of the tools, you may see some differences. If you get stuck, visit the homepage for this book at *http://www.microsoft.com/ press* where you'll find updates to breaking changes.

Getting Started

In this section, you will download and install the free tools that you need for Windows Phone development. The tools are:

- **Visual Studio 2010 Express for Windows Phone**   This is the main tool that you'll use for designing, coding, and debugging Windows Phone applications.

- **Windows Phone Emulator**   This is actually a virtual machine that runs the real Windows Phone operating system. Therefore, you can be sure your applications will run on the hardware—even if you don't have the hardware to test on yet.

- **Silverlight for Windows Phone**   This is a build of Silverlight that works on Windows Phone. It is the same Silverlight as used in the browser and on the desktop, so the skills you have acquired thus far will still apply to Windows Phone development.

- **XNA 4.0 Game Studio**   Games are a huge part of mobile development. This tool is a new version of the popular XNA Game Studio used for Xbox and Zune development. You can use it to build Silverlight-based games for the Windows Phone too! Building games is beyond the scope of this book, but the tools are available for you to explore on your own.

Get the tools

1. To get started, visit *http://developer.windowsphone.com* and click the Download The Tools Today link.

2. This will take you to the developer home page, where you can view a demo, read documentation, and download samples. For now, click the Download The Developer Tools link.

3. You'll see a download page where you can get an installer that will install Microsoft Visual Studio 2010 Express, Windows Phone Emulator, Silverlight, and XNA Game Studio 4.0.

4. Download and launch the installer using the link at the bottom of the download page and you should see the license agreement. If you agree, click the Accept button to continue.

5. Click the Install button. The installer will download and install each of the components. This may take a few minutes.

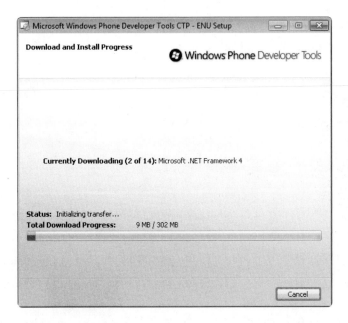

6. When the installation completes, you should see the following screen. You're now ready to begin building your first Windows Phone application.

Write Your First Windows Phone Application

Now that you have the tools, you're ready to build a Windows Phone application. Here's a step-by-step example that shows you what's involved.

Build a basic Windows Phone application

1. Launch Visual Studio 2010 Express for Windows Phone.

2. From the File menu, select New Project.

3. Name the new project **SbSCh11_1** and press OK.

4. Visual Studio will create the solution. The designer window provides a phone "skin" to help you design the look of your application. Note that this is not the emulator—you'll see the emulator shortly.

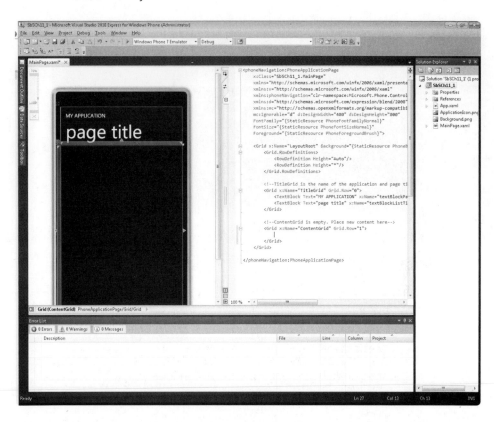

5. Open the Toolbox and add a *TextBlock*, a *TextBox*, a *Button*, and another *TextBlock*. When you're done, you should see something like this:

6. You can drag the controls around to tweak the layout. You can also use the Properties window to set such properties as *Font* and *FontSize,* as well as to change the contents of the controls. Try laying out the controls so the UI looks like this:

7. Notice that there's a separate *Grid* for the application and page title. Nonetheless, that's XAML and you can easily edit it. To do so, you can replace the two *TextBlocks* that Visual Studio generated or you can just edit the text in the existing *TextBlocks*. So, for example, you could change the top grid contents by using XAML like this:

```
<!--TitleGrid is the name of the application and page title-->
<Grid x:Name="TitleGrid" Grid.Row="0">
<TextBlock Text="My First Phone Application" x:Name="textBlockPageTitle"
Style="{StaticResource PhoneTextPageTitle1Style}"/>
<TextBlock Text="Hello, World!" x:Name="textBlockListTitle"
Style="{StaticResource PhoneTextPageTitle2Style}"/>
</Grid>
```

8. Double-click the *Button* to create an event handler, which will be called *button1_Click*. Next, edit this event handler so it contains the following code:

```
private void button1_Click(object sender, RoutedEventArgs e)
{
    textBlock2.Text = "Hello" + textBox1.Text;
}
```

9. Press F5 to run your application. It may be a little slow the first time you launch it, because the emulator needs to launch and it needs to load the virtual image of the operating system. Remember, this is a full version of the Windows Phone 7 operating system—so this is more than just a simple emulator!

10. When the application is running on the emulator, place your cursor in the text box. The virtual keyboard will appear, giving an exact representation of the behavior you would experience on a real phone.

11. Type your name into the text box and press Go. You'll see the second *TextBlock* update to say "Hello" followed by your name.

12. You can also debug your applications as they run on the phone or the emulator. To try this, switch back to Visual Studio while the application is still running in the emulator. Find the following line of code: *textBlock2.Text="Hello" + textBox1.Text* and press F9 to put a breakpoint on the line. You'll see a red dot in the margin and Visual Studio will highlight the code in red.

```
private void button1_Click(object sender, RoutedEventArgs e)
{
    textBlock2.Text = "Hello " + textBox1.Text;
}
```

13. Now switch back to the emulator and press the Go button again. This time, Visual Studio will stop on the line you highlighted in the previous step. As you can see, you have complete access to debugging your applications while they're running in the emulator.

14. Press F5 to get out of debug mode and continue running the application.

15. The emulator supports both portrait and landscape modes. You can test to see how your application looks in either mode by using the orientation buttons to the right of the emulator. Here you can see how your application looks in landscape mode.

Note You don't need to close down your emulator when changing between Visual Studio projects. In fact, if you leave it running in the background, the emulator will respond faster when you deploy new applications to it for testing.

Build a Service Client in Windows Phone

The simple "Hello, World" example is all very well, but it functions in isolation. Modern phones like the Windows Phone are usually connected to some form of data plan to give them Internet access. So here's a look at building an application that consumes a service—in this case, a stock quote service that provides basic stock quote data.

Create the Solution and Add the Service Proxy

In this section, you'll see how to build a Silverlight-based Windows Phone client that uses a stock quote Web service. For this task, you can use the Web service available at *http://www.webservicex.net/WCF/ServiceDetails.aspx?SID=19*. It provides that provides quotes that are delayed by 20 minutes.

Build a connected service

1. Create a new Windows Phone application and name it **SbSCh11_2**.

2. In Solution Explorer, add a reference to the *System.Xml.Linq* namespace.

3. You can automatically create a proxy class to the Web service by using Visual Studio if you know the location of the Web Services Definition Language (WSDL) file for the service that you want to consume. Fortunately, the stock quote service's WSDL is published at *http://www.webservicex.net/stockquote.asmx?WSDL*.

4. Right-click Service References in Solution Explorer and select Add Service Reference.

5. In the Add Service Reference dialog box, set the address to *http://www.webservicex.net/stockquote.asmx?WSDL* and click the Go button. Visual Studio will find the StockQuote service. In the Namespace field, give the service the name **StockService**.

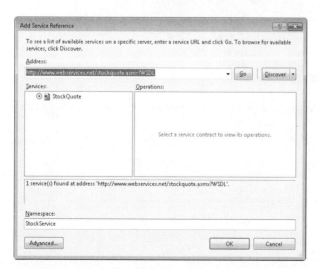

6. Click OK and Visual Studio will create a proxy class for communicating with this service. It will also add the new class to the Service References folder.

7. You now have all the pieces in place to consume the service. In the next section, you'll build a user interface to interact with the service.

Create the Stock Quote User Interface

In the previous section, you saw how to create a service proxy to consume data from the stock quote service. Now you need to create a user interface that will let you specify the stock ticker for which you want to retrieve data. Here you will learn that, as well as how to call the service proxy to get the data and display it in your user interface.

Here's the basic user interface that you'll build up. It's made up primarily of *TextBlock* controls along with a single *TextBox* and a *Button*.

Create the UI and call the service

1. Open the MainPage.xaml file in the SbSCh11_2 project.

2. Find the Grid named *TitleGrid*, and edit its contents to look like this:

```
<Grid x:Name="TitleGrid" Grid.Row="0">
  <TextBlock Text="Silverlight 4 Step By Step" x:Name="textBlockPageTitle"
            Style="{StaticResource PhoneTextPageTitle1Style}"/>
  <TextBlock Text="Stock Prices" x:Name="textBlockListTitle"
            Style="{StaticResource PhoneTextPageTitle2Style}"/>
</Grid>
```

3. Find the Grid control named *ContentGrid*. Add the *TextBlock*, *TextBox*, and *Button* controls to it. Lay them out as shown—or you can just use this code:

```
<Grid x:Name="ContentGrid" Grid.Row="1">
  <Button Content="Get Quote" Height="70" HorizontalAlignment="Left"
          Margin="282,10,0,0" Name="button1" VerticalAlignment="Top" Width="176"
          Click="button1_Click" />
  <TextBox Height="72" HorizontalAlignment="Left" Margin="91,10,0,0"
          Name="txtTicker" Text="" VerticalAlignment="Top" Width="209" />
  <TextBlock Height="36" HorizontalAlignment="Left" Margin="26,30,0,0"
          Name="textBlock1" Text="Ticker:" VerticalAlignment="Top" Width="124"
/>
  <TextBlock Height="36" HorizontalAlignment="Left" Margin="26,114,0,0"
          Name="textBlock2" Text="Last:" VerticalAlignment="Top" Width="81" />
  <TextBlock Height="36" HorizontalAlignment="Left" Margin="26,156,0,0"
          Name="textBlock3" Text="Change:" VerticalAlignment="Top" Width="81"
/>
  <TextBlock Height="36" HorizontalAlignment="Left" Margin="26,199,0,0"
          Name="textBlock4" Text="High:" VerticalAlignment="Top" Width="81" />
  <TextBlock Height="36" HorizontalAlignment="Left" Margin="26,244,0,0"
          Name="textBlock5" Text="Low:" VerticalAlignment="Top" Width="81" />
  <TextBlock Height="36" HorizontalAlignment="Left" Margin="26,287,0,0"
          Name="textBlock6" Text="Open:" VerticalAlignment="Top" Width="81" />
  <TextBlock Height="36" HorizontalAlignment="Left" Margin="123,114,0,0"
          Name="txtLast" Text="" VerticalAlignment="Top" Width="81" />
  <TextBlock Height="36" HorizontalAlignment="Left" Margin="123,156,0,0"
          Name="txtChange" Text="" VerticalAlignment="Top" Width="81" />
  <TextBlock Height="36" HorizontalAlignment="Left" Margin="123,199,0,0"
          Name="txtHigh" Text="" VerticalAlignment="Top" Width="81" />
  <TextBlock Height="36" HorizontalAlignment="Left" Margin="123,242,0,0"
          Name="txtLow" Text="" VerticalAlignment="Top" Width="81" />
  <TextBlock Height="36" HorizontalAlignment="Left" Margin="123,284,0,0"
          Name="txtOpen" Text="" VerticalAlignment="Top" Width="81" />
</Grid>
```

Warning The *TextBox* and several of the *TextBlock* controls (shown in bold text in the code above) are named as they will be referred to in code. Make sure you use the same names or else the following code will fail.

Note that might be able to make this XAML a lot neater by using layout controls. For example, if you used *StackPanel* controls as containers for all the *TextBlock* elements, you could eliminate the need for the *Margin* attributes.

4. Double-click the *Button* to create a *Click* event handler.

5. Create an instance of the service proxy in the *Click* event handler for the *Button*.

```
StockService.StockQuoteSoapClient myStock = new StockService.
StockQuoteSoapClient();
```

6. Calls to Web services are asynchronous in nature, so you need to specify a callback to catch the return values from the Web service.

```
myStock.GetQuoteCompleted += new
   EventHandler<StockService.GetQuoteCompletedEventArgs>(myStock_
GetQuoteCompleted);
```

7. Now all you need to do is call the Web service, passing it a string parameter that contains the ticker symbol of the stock for which you want to get a quote. You get this value as user input from the *TextBox* called *txtTicker*. If the *TextBox* has no content, just set a default ticker (in this case **MSFT**).

```
if (txtTicker.Text == "")
    txtTicker.Text = "MSFT";
    myStock.GetQuoteAsync(txtTicker.Text);
```

8. For reference, here's the complete event handler:

```
private void button1_Click(object sender, RoutedEventArgs e)
{

  StockService.StockQuoteSoapClient myStock =
      new StockService.StockQuoteSoapClient();

  myStock.GetQuoteCompleted += new
    EventHandler<StockService.GetQuoteCompletedEventArgs>(myStock_
GetQuoteCompleted);
  if (txtTicker.Text == "")
    txtTicker.Text = "MSFT";

  myStock.GetQuoteAsync(txtTicker.Text);

}
```

9. The Web service returns an XML document that contains the stock quote results. (You'll see that in a moment.) To use this, you will need a StockQuote class that you can load with the data. Here's the full listing for a simple class:

```
public class StockQuote
    {
        public double last { get; set;}
        public DateTime date { get; set; }
        public DateTime time { get; set; }
        public double change { get; set; }
        public double open { get; set; }
        public double high { get; set; }
        public double low { get; set; }
        public double volume { get; set; }
        public double prev { get; set; }


    }
```

10. You specified that the callback from the Web service should run a function called *myStock_GetQuoteCompleted*. Visual Studio should have automatically created the stub for you, but in case it hasn't, the code should look like this:

```
void myStock_GetQuoteCompleted(object sender,
  StockService.GetQuoteCompletedEventArgs e)
{}
```

11. To parse the XML returned from the Web service, the first thing you want to do is make sure you can use the LINQ to XML classes. If you haven't already added the *System.Xml. Linq* namespaces to the references, do so now and make sure your Mainpage.xaml.cs file includes the following line at the top:

```
using System.Xml.Linq;
```

12. The Web service returns the XML via the proxy as a string, which you can load into an XML document like this:

```
XDocument xReturn = XDocument.Parse(e.Result);
```

13. Now that you have the return values loaded into an *XDocument*, you can use LINQ to XML to generate an *IEnumerable* of the *StockQuote* by using the data in the *XDocument*.

```
IEnumerable<StockQuote> myQuote =
            from item in xReturn.Descendants("Stock")
            select new StockQuote
            {
                last = Convert.ToDouble(item.Element("Last").Value),
                date = Convert.ToDateTime(item.Element("Date").Value),
                time = Convert.ToDateTime(item.Element("Time").Value),
                change = Convert.ToDouble(item.Element("Change").Value),
                open = Convert.ToDouble(item.Element("Open").Value),
                high = Convert.ToDouble(item.Element("High").Value),
                low = Convert.ToDouble(item.Element("Low").Value),
                volume = Convert.ToDouble(item.Element("Volume").Value),
                prev = Convert.ToDouble(item.Element("PreviousClose").Value)
            };
```

14. For this exercise, you're interested only in the first *StockQuote* in the *IEnumerable*. (In fact, there is only one.) You can retrieve it like this:

```
StockQuote thisQuote = myQuote.ElementAt(0);
```

15. One way to make the UI a little nicer is to color some of the numbers based on the day's change in stock value. Red usually represents a down day and green usually represents an up day. Here's some code to add the colors:

```
if (thisQuote.change > 0)
{
    txtLast.Foreground = new SolidColorBrush(Colors.Green);
    txtChange.Foreground = new SolidColorBrush(Colors.Green);
}
else
{
    txtLast.Foreground = new SolidColorBrush(Colors.Red);
    txtChange.Foreground = new SolidColorBrush(Colors.Red);
}
```

16. The last thing you have to do is set the values of the *TextBlock* controls to the appropriate values from your StockQuote object.

```
txtChange.Text = thisQuote.change.ToString();
txtHigh.Text = thisQuote.high.ToString();
txtLow.Text = thisQuote.low.ToString();
txtLast.Text = thisQuote.last.ToString();
txtOpen.Text = thisQuote.open.ToString();
```

17. For reference, here's the complete callback function:

```
void myStock_GetQuoteCompleted(object sender,
  StockService.GetQuoteCompletedEventArgs e)
{
  XDocument xReturn = XDocument.Parse(e.Result);
  IEnumerable<StockQuote> myQuote =
              from item in xReturn.Descendants("Stock")
              select new StockQuote
              {
                  last = Convert.ToDouble(item.Element("Last").Value),
                  date = Convert.ToDateTime(item.Element("Date").Value),
                  time = Convert.ToDateTime(item.Element("Time").Value),
                  change = Convert.ToDouble(item.Element("Change").Value),
                  open = Convert.ToDouble(item.Element("Open").Value),
                  high = Convert.ToDouble(item.Element("High").Value),
                  low = Convert.ToDouble(item.Element("Low").Value),
                  volume = Convert.ToDouble(item.Element("Volume").Value),
                  prev = Convert.ToDouble(item.Element("PreviousClose").Value)
              };
          StockQuote thisQuote = myQuote.ElementAt(0);
          if (thisQuote.change > 0)
          {
              txtLast.Foreground = new SolidColorBrush(Colors.Green);
              txtChange.Foreground = new SolidColorBrush(Colors.Green);
          }
          else
          {
              txtLast.Foreground = new SolidColorBrush(Colors.Red);
              txtChange.Foreground = new SolidColorBrush(Colors.Red);
          }
          txtChange.Text = thisQuote.change.ToString();
          txtHigh.Text = thisQuote.high.ToString();
          txtLow.Text = thisQuote.low.ToString();
          txtLast.Text = thisQuote.last.ToString();
          txtOpen.Text = thisQuote.open.ToString();
  }
```

18. Press F5 to execute the application.

19. To test it, type a value into the Ticker *TextBox* and press the Get Quote button. The phone will call the Web service, get the stock quote data, and render the stock values on the screen. Here you can see a stock quote for IBM on an up day.

Key Points

- The tools necessary for building Windows Phone applications, including Visual Studio 2010 Express for Windows Phone and Windows Phone Emulator, are available as free downloads.

- The Windows Phone Emulator isn't so much an emulator as it is a virtual machine running the actual Windows Phone 7 OS and applications.

- You built your first Windows Phone application and tested it on a Windows Phone emulator.

- You created a more advanced application that consumed data from a Web service.

- The process and code involved in building Windows Phone applications is almost exactly the same as the process and code used to build Silverlight applications for the browser or the desktop. All the skills you've acquired thus far apply to the phone.

Chapter 12
Windows Phone Features

After completing this chapter, you will be able to:

- Recognize and adapt your applications to changes in phone orientation so they can run in both portrait and landscape modes.

- Write code that uses the hardware Back button on the Windows Phone, catching its events within your application.

- Add controls to and program the Application Bar.

- Use input scope to optimize the on-screen keyboard according to what a user is doing.

- Use typing intelligence and *Text* input scope to adapt the user interface to the user's typing.

- Use the Manipulation APIs to program the touch system, including multi-touch.

- Understand other available phone capabilities, including accelerometers and location features.

In Chapter 11, "Windows Phone Development," you took a look at developing for the Windows Phone 7 and built a simple stock quotes application. You saw how building applications for Windows Phone is similar to building applications for desktop Microsoft Silverlight applications and how you can re-use your skills for Windows Phone development.

This chapter introduces some Windows Phone–specific features. You'll see some areas where—even though you are still working with Silverlight—you will have to write your application differently to work on the new platform.

Be sure to work through the examples in Chapter 11 before reading this chapter. It will guide you through the process of downloading, installing, and configuring the development tools you'll need, as well as the Windows Phone emulator.

Using Orientation

One feature users expect from phone applications is for the applications to respond to the current orientation of the phone. Typically, people hold a phone in portrait mode when making a telephone call and in landscape mode when watching video or interacting with media. A good Windows Phone application should be able to react to the phone orientation, so you need to provide your user interface with the ability to redraw itself based on that orientation.

Redraw the UI based on orientation

1. Create a new Windows Phone application using Microsoft Visual Studio 2010 Express for Windows Phone. Name the new application **SbSCh12_1**.

2. Take a look at the *MainPage()* constructor in MainPage.xaml.cs. You'll see that Visual Studio has pre-populated it with this line of code:

```
SupportedOrientations = SupportedPageOrientation.Portrait |
SupportedPageOrientation.Landscape;
```

The pipe (|) character signifies a bitwise OR operation. In other words, this line of code says "Supported Orientations are either *Portrait* or *Landscape*." In other words, your application will support either portrait or landscape orientation.

3. If you want the application to support only portrait mode, you can alter the line to:

```
SupportedOrientations = SupportedPageOrientation.Portrait
```

4. To support both orientations, you can specify the *PortraitOrLandscape* value. Change the line of code to look like this:

```
SupportedOrientations = SupportedPageOrientation.PortraitOrLandscape;
```

5. Press F5 to execute your application.

6. The application will run in portrait mode, like this:

7. Now press the Change Orientation button:

The phone emulator will flip to landscape mode. You can see that both the title of the application and the page have been adjusted to the new orientation, making them more landscape-friendly.

8. Stop your application, but do not close the emulator. It can keep running and you can attach to it the next time you run your app.

Thus far you've set up code that allows the application to run in portrait or landscape mode, but while the user can see the orientation, the application doesn't. So, in the next few steps, you'll add a button that, when pressed, will check the current orientation.

Check the orientation

1. Open Mainpage.xaml in Visual Studio.

2. Add a *Button* control to the design surface for the phone interface. Adjust the width of the button so that it is a wide rectangle.

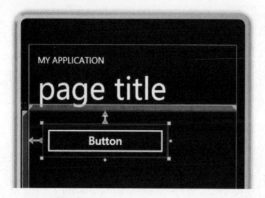

3. Double-click the *Button* in the designer to create an event handler and code.

4. Edit the code in the *button1_Click* event so it looks like this:

```
private void button1_Click(object sender, RoutedEventArgs e)
{
    textBlockListTitle.Text = this.Orientation.ToString();
}
```

5. Press F5 to run the application.

6. Press the button and the text in the label will change to match the orientation. In the screenshot, you can see the label specifies LandscapeLeft as the orientation.

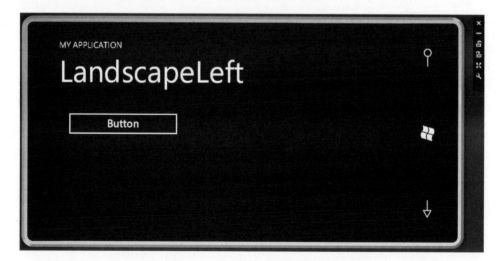

7. Press the Change Orientation button, to change the orientation by 180 degrees. Then press your new button again.

As you can see, there are two landscape modes—with left and right being based on the location of the screen, not the controls. Thus, Landscape Right displays when you hold the phone with the screen to the right of the controls.

> **Note** The emulator also supports a portrait mode, but only when the screen is facing upwards, as shown below. Portrait mode is not supported for when the screen is flipped 180 degrees to hold the hardware controls to the top.

In this case, the orientation was detected based on user input (pressing the Change Orientation button) rather than being detected automatically. Detecting the orientation is an event-driven task. So now you will add an event that automatically detects the orientation—the user will not need to press a button to trigger the change of the label.

 8. Stop the application from running.

 9. Go to the *MainPage* constructor and type **this.or**, and then wait for IntelliSense to fill in. You'll see that there are two events related to Orientation: *OrientationChanged* fires when the orientation change is complete, and *OrientationChanging* fires while the phone is being moved from one orientation state to another.

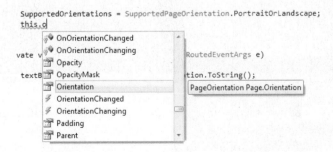

10. Add an event handler for each event. Remember that you can use *<Tab><Tab>* to create the code stubs automatically.

```
InitializeComponent();
SupportedOrientations = SupportedPageOrientation.PortraitOrLandscape;

this.OrientationChanging += new
    EventHandler<OrientationChangedEventArgs>(MainPage_OrientationChanging);

this.OrientationChanged += new
    EventHandler<OrientationChangedEventArgs>(MainPage_OrientationChanged);
```

11. Edit the event handlers to update the *TextBlocks* when the orientation changes.

```
void MainPage_OrientationChanged(object sender, OrientationChangedEventArgs e)
    {
        textBlockListTitle.Text = this.Orientation.ToString();
    }

void MainPage_OrientationChanging(object sender, OrientationChangedEventArgs e)
    {
        textBlockPageTitle.Text = "Changing Orientation!";
    }
```

12. Press F5 to execute the application. Now when you change orientation, the text will update automatically—you don't need to push the button.

 Note On a real phone, you see the transition as the application changes from one orientation to another. But in the emulator, an application simply jumps from one orientation state to another. As a result, you don't really see the *OrientationChanging* event occur in the emulator.

Using the Back Button

You may have noticed that Windows Phone provides a Back button. It's on the control pad to the left of the Start button. With a little code, you can support this button in your applications.

Add support for the Back button

1. Create a new Windows Phone application and name it **SbSCh12_2**.

2. Using the designer, add a new *TextBlock* to the design surface. Make sure it's wide enough to hold some text.

3. Open the MainPage.xaml.cs code file and find the *MainPage()* constructor.

4. Add an event handler for *this.BackKeyPress*.

```
this.BackKeyPress += new
    EventHandler<System.ComponentModel.CancelEventArgs>(MainPage_BackKeyPress);
```

5. Edit the code for the *Mainpage_BackKeyPress* event handler so it changes the value of the *TextBlock* whenever a user presses the Back key.

```
void MainPage_BackKeyPress(object sender, System.ComponentModel.CancelEventArgs e)
    {
        textBlock1.Text = "Back Key Pressed!";
    }
```

6. Press F5 to run the application.

7. Press the Back button. The label will change to Back Key Pressed, but then the application will close and you will go back to the phone's application list screen.

   The application closed because the Back button is a system button, not an application button. In this case, the most recent action taken by the phone was to load your application. Thus, pressing the Back button reverses that action and closes your application. But you can override this default behavior.

8. Take another look at the *MainPage_BackKeyPress* event handler. You'll see that the second argument is of the type *System.ComponentModel.CancelEventArgs*, which lets you cancel the system event. Using this feature, your application can respond to the button press event and then cancel the system event after you've handled it. Thus your application can use the button directly, without system events overriding your application.

9. Change the event handler to look like this:

```
void MainPage_BackKeyPress(object sender, System.ComponentModel.CancelEventArgs e)
    {
        textBlock1.Text = "Back Key Pressed!";
        e.Cancel = true;
    }
```

10. Press F5 to run your application.

11. When you press the Back button this time, you'll see the *TextBlock* change, but the phone will no longer close the application.

Using the Application Bar

Windows Phone applications can use an application bar. Think of this as a software-based extension to the hardware system buttons (Back, Start, and Search).

For a good example of an application bar, check out the built-in version of Windows Internet Explorer on the Windows Phone. Just below the colored portion of the screen, you can see three buttons (Add To Favorites, View Favorites, and View Open Pages) and an ellipsis button that opens a menu that provides additional options.

In this section, you will learn to add both buttons and menus to your own applications.

Create an application bar

1. Create a new Windows Phone application and name it **SbSCh12_3**.

2. In Solution Explorer, find the References folder, right-click, and choose Add Reference.

3. Find the Microsoft.Phone.Shell component, select it, and click OK.

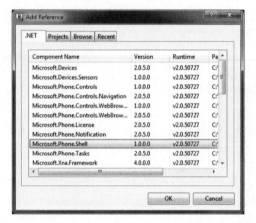

4. Your buttons will need to be 48 x 48 pixel transparent .png files. You can create these buttons yourself or you can use the ones that are provided with the code download for this book.

5. Create a new folder within your solution by rightclicking the project, and selecting Folder from the Add New menu. Name the folder **images**.

6. Copy your .png files to this new folder. This example uses three files: 1.png, 2.png, and 3.png. (Make sure you add them to the images folder in Solution Explorer in Visual Studio.)

▲ 📁 images
    🖼 1.png
    🖼 2.png
    🖼 3.png

7. Select one of the images. In the Properties window, set the build action for the image to **Content**. Do this for each of the images. If you don't see the Properties window, press F4.

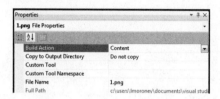

8. The application bar functionality is not available from the Toolbox. You have to add the XAML to define it manually. Don't worry, that's pretty easy to do. Open the Mainpage.xaml file. Within the opening *<phoneNavigation:PhoneApplicationPage>* tag at the top of the page, type **xmlns:shell=**. IntelliSense will give you a list of options for the shell namespace. Select *Microsoft.Phone.Shell*.

9. You want to place the application bar definition beneath this tag, and above the *Grid* named *LayoutRoot*.

10. Start defining your application bar with the *<phoneNavigation.PhoneApplicationPage. ApplicationBar>* tag.

```
<phoneNavigation:PhoneApplicationPage.ApplicationBar>
</phoneNavigation:PhoneApplicationPage.ApplicationBar>
```

11. Between these tags, you can define your application bar using the *ApplicationBar* control. This control exists in the *Microsoft.Phone.Shell* namespace, which you added in step 8, so you can define it using *shell:ApplicationBar*. If you set the *IsMenuEnabled* attribute to *True*, you'll get the ellipsis button at the right side of the application bar. When a user presses the ellipsis, the menu will open. When a user selects a menu item, the menu will close.

```xml
<shell:ApplicationBar IsVisible="True" IsMenuEnabled="True">
</shell:ApplicationBar>
```

12. Now you can define the buttons using *<shell:ApplicationBar.Buttons>* tags. You define the event handlers for these buttons in the XAML. (For a refresher on defining handlers, look back to Chapter 1, "Introducing Silverlight," and Chapter 2, "Silverlight Controls.")

```xml
<shell:ApplicationBar.Buttons>
    <shell:ApplicationBarIconButton IconUri="/images/1.png"
            Click="ApplicationBarIconButton_Click"/>
    <shell:ApplicationBarIconButton IconUri="/images/2.png"
            Click="ApplicationBarIconButton_Click_1"/>
    <shell:ApplicationBarIconButton IconUri="/images/3.png"
            Click="ApplicationBarIconButton_Click_2"/>
</shell:ApplicationBar.Buttons>
```

This code defines three buttons. Their visual presentations, respectively, are the three .png files you added to the images folder.

13. You define the menu using a collection of *<shell:ApplicationBar.MenuItems>* tags. As with the buttons, you can use XAML to define the event handlers for these items. Be sure to use IntelliSense to ensure that Visual Studio Express will add the event handler stubs for you automatically.

```xml
<shell:ApplicationBar.MenuItems>
    <shell:ApplicationBarMenuItem Text="Menu Item 1"
            Click="ApplicationBarMenuItem_Click" />
    <shell:ApplicationBarMenuItem Text="Menu Item 2"
            Click="ApplicationBarMenuItem_Click_1" />
</shell:ApplicationBar.MenuItems>
```

14. Look at the bottom of the page and you'll see a *Grid* control named *ContentGrid*. Use the following XAML to define a *TextBlock* within it:

```
<Grid x:Name="ContentGrid" Grid.Row="1">
    <TextBlock Height="44" HorizontalAlignment="Left" Margin="34,40,0,0"
        Name="textBlock1" Text="TextBlock" VerticalAlignment="Top" Width="379" />
</Grid>
```

15. Here's the full XAML. It defines the namespace for the *Microsoft.Phone.Shell*
namespace, your application bar, and the *TextBlock*.

```
<phoneNavigation:PhoneApplicationPage
    x:Class="SbSCh12_3.MainPage"
    xmlns="http://schemas.microsoft.com/winfx/2006/xaml/presentation"
    xmlns:x="http://schemas.microsoft.com/winfx/2006/xaml"
    xmlns:phoneNavigation=
    "clr-namespace:Microsoft.Phone.Controls;assembly=Microsoft.Phone.Controls.
Navigation"
    xmlns:d="http://schemas.microsoft.com/expression/blend/2008"
    xmlns:mc="http://schemas.openxmlformats.org/markup-compatibility/2006"
    xmlns:shell="clr-namespace:Microsoft.Phone.Shell;assembly=Microsoft.Phone.
Shell"
    mc:Ignorable="d" d:DesignWidth="480" d:DesignHeight="800"
    FontFamily="{StaticResource PhoneFontFamilyNormal}"
    FontSize="{StaticResource PhoneFontSizeNormal}"
    Foreground="{StaticResource PhoneForegroundBrush}">
    <phoneNavigation:PhoneApplicationPage.ApplicationBar>
        <shell:ApplicationBar Visible="True" IsMenuEnabled="True">
            <shell:ApplicationBar.Buttons>
                <shell:ApplicationBarIconButton IconUri="/images/1.png"
                    Click="ApplicationBarIconButton_Click"/>
                <shell:ApplicationBarIconButton IconUri="/images/2.png"
                    Click="ApplicationBarIconButton_Click_1"/>
                <shell:ApplicationBarIconButton IconUri="/images/3.png"
                    Click="ApplicationBarIconButton_Click_2"/>
            </shell:ApplicationBar.Buttons>
            <shell:ApplicationBar.MenuItems>
                <shell:ApplicationBarMenuItem Text="Menu Item 1"
                    Click="ApplicationBarMenuItem_Click" />
                <shell:ApplicationBarMenuItem Text="Menu Item 2"
                    Click="ApplicationBarMenuItem_Click_1" />
            </shell:ApplicationBar.MenuItems>
        </shell:ApplicationBar>
    </phoneNavigation:PhoneApplicationPage.ApplicationBar>
    <Grid x:Name="LayoutRoot" Background="{StaticResource PhoneBackgroundBrush}">
        <Grid.RowDefinitions>
            <RowDefinition Height="Auto"/>
            <RowDefinition Height="*"/>
        </Grid.RowDefinitions>
        <!--TitleGrid is the name of the application and page title-->
        <Grid x:Name="TitleGrid" Grid.Row="0">
            <TextBlock Text="MY APPLICATION" x:Name="textBlockPageTitle"
                    Style="{StaticResource PhoneTextPageTitle1Style}"/>
            <TextBlock Text="page title" x:Name="textBlockListTitle"
```

```
                                    Style="{StaticResource PhoneTextPageTitle2Style}"/>
        </Grid>

        <!--ContentGrid is empty. Place new content here-->
        <Grid x:Name="ContentGrid" Grid.Row="1">
            <TextBlock Height="44" HorizontalAlignment="Left" Margin="34,40,0,0"
                       Name="textBlock1" Text="TextBlock"
                       VerticalAlignment="Top" Width="379" />
        </Grid>
    </Grid>
</phoneNavigation:PhoneApplicationPage>
```

16. You're almost ready to try it out. This application defined three buttons and two menu items, complete with event handlers named *ApplicationBarIconButton_Click*, *ApplicationBarIconButton_Click_1*, and so on. Switch to your MainPage.xaml.cs code file and add code for these events. Here's some simple code for demonstration purposes:

```csharp
private void ApplicationBarIconButton_Click(object sender, EventArgs e)
{
    textBlock1.Text = "You Pressed Button 1";
}
private void ApplicationBarIconButton_Click_1(object sender, EventArgs e)
{
    textBlock1.Text = "You Pressed Button 2";
}
private void ApplicationBarIconButton_Click_2(object sender, EventArgs e)
{
    textBlock1.Text = "You Pressed Button 3";
}
private void ApplicationBarMenuItem_Click(object sender, EventArgs e)
{
    textBlock1.Text = "You Pressed Menu Item 1";
}
private void ApplicationBarMenuItem_Click_1(object sender, EventArgs e)
{
    textBlock1.Text = "You Pressed Menu Item 2";
}
```

17. Press F5 to run the application. You'll see your application bar at the bottom of the screen when you're in portrait mode.

18. Selecting the ellipsis on the right side opens the menu. The menu closes when you select an item. Alternatively, you can click the ellipsis again to close the menu.

19. Notice that when you select a button or a menu item, the *TextBlock* updates with the name of the item you pressed.

Keep in mind that when you add an application bar to an application, you should limit the number of buttons and menu items you provide. Otherwise, you could end up with very little screen space left for your application. And it's worth noting that Microsoft offers a number of icons that are ready to use in your own application bars. You can download them for free at *http://go.microsoft.com/fwlink/?LinkId=187311.*

Using Input Scope

When using Silverlight on a computer, users are accustomed to typing on the keyboard whenever they see a text entry field. The experience on a phone, however, can be a bit different. The on-screen keyboard appears only when you need it. And due to the limited screen space, the keyboard doesn't provide all the same keys as a physical keyboard.

With this in mind, it's important to make it a little easier for the user to use different input types according to the expected input scenario. For example, a text entry field intended for a phone number should provide the numeric keypad by default. A text field intended for a URL or e-mail address, on the other hand, should display the alphanumeric keyboard. This concept is referred to as input scope. The following example will demonstrate how to apply input scope for a number of different input types.

Define input scope

1. Create a new Windows Phone application and name it **SbSCh12_4**.

2. Add four *TextBlock* controls and four *TextBox* controls, laid out like this:

 Important   You don't need to name the *TextBlock* controls, but be sure to name the *TextBox* controls using the following names: *txtEmail*, *txtURL*, *txt-Phone*, and *txtSMSP*.

3. You will define their input scope using code in the code-behind. Open the MainPage.xaml.cs file and find the *MainPage()* constructor.

4. To set the input scope, you assign the *InputScope* property of the control to a new instance of the *InputScope* class. Because there is no constructor that accepts the scope name as a parameter, you must set its *Names* property to a new instance of an *InputScopeName* class with a specified *NameValue*. You'll find *NameValue* in the *InputScopeNameValue* enumeration. Fortunately, doing all this is a lot less complex than it sounds! Here's the code for the e-mail *TextBox*, named *txtEmail*.

```
txtEmail.InputScope = new InputScope()
{
    Names = { new InputScopeName()
            { NameValue = InputScopeNameValue.EmailSmtpAddress }
        }
};
```

5. Using the enumeration values in the *InputScopeNameValue* object, you can define the desired behavior. For a full list of these enumerations, take a look at the documentation for *InputScopeNameValue* available at *http://msdn.microsoft.com/library/system.windows.input.inputscopenamevalue(v=VS.96).aspx*.

6. Here's the code for the other three *TextBox* controls. The code specifies the name scope for each as *TelephoneNumber*, *Chat*, and *Url*, respectively.

```
txtPhone.InputScope = new InputScope()
{
  Names = { new InputScopeName()
            { NameValue = InputScopeNameValue.TelephoneNumber } }
};

txtSMSP.InputScope = new InputScope()
{
  Names = { new InputScopeName()
            { NameValue = InputScopeNameValue.Chat } }
};

txtURL.InputScope = new InputScope()
{
  Names = { new InputScopeName() { NameValue = InputScopeNameValue.Url } }
};
```

7. Press F5 to run your application.

8. Place your cursor in the Email Address text field. A keyboard appropriate for e-mail entry will appear. This keyboard even includes an extremely convenient ampersand (@) key in the bottom row!

9. Now place your cursor in the URL field. The keyboard changes to one that's more appropriate for entering Web addresses—the @ is removed and the carriage return icon changes to a "Go" icon (an arrow pointing to the right).

10. Place your cursor in the Phone # field and you'll see a more drastic change. The phone has detected that the input scope is a phone number and changes the input keyboard to a number pad.

11. Finally, place the cursor in the Text Message field. If the input space is covering the Text Message field, just click anywhere in the main UI (other than in one of the text input boxes) to make the keyboard disappear. When you put the cursor in the Text Message field, the keyboard changes to yet another keyboard layout. It has no @ key or .com key, but does provide a smiley face emoticon key.

 Note Windows Phone supports several emoticons, which you can access by pressing the smiley face key. The emulator, however, doesn't support all of the emoticons at the moment. (It appears the developers weren't very happy when they built this screen!)

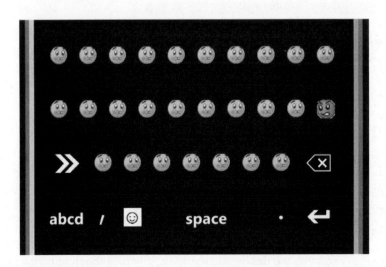

12. Although this example offers a good start to using *InputScope*, the code is a little complex. Fortunately, there's a shortcut. If you know the names of the different available scopes, you can set the *InputScope* attribute on the *TextBox* controls within your XAML rather than writing all the C# code shown above. Here's an example of what this looks like:

```xml
<Grid x:Name="ContentGrid" Grid.Row="1">
  <TextBox Height="31" InputScope="EmailSmtpAddress"
          HorizontalAlignment="Left" Margin="6,23,0,0"
          Name="txtEmail" Text="" VerticalAlignment="Top" Width="468" />
  <TextBox Height="31" InputScope="Url"
          HorizontalAlignment="Left" Margin="6,119,0,0"
          Name="txtURL" Text="" VerticalAlignment="Top" Width="468" />
  <TextBox Height="31" InputScope="TelephoneNumber"
          HorizontalAlignment="Left" Margin="6,214,0,0"
          Name="txtPhone" Text="" VerticalAlignment="Top" Width="468" />
  <TextBox Height="31" InputScope="Chat"
          HorizontalAlignment="Left" Margin="6,309,0,0"
          Name="txtSMSP" Text="" VerticalAlignment="Top" Width="468" />
</Grid>
```

Using Typing Intelligence

One special *InputScope* to consider when building your applications is the *Text* input scope. This provides users with the full range of typing intelligence features that are built into Windows Phones. These features include:

- Text suggestions while the user types or when the user taps on a word.

- Auto-correction.

- Automatic addition of an apostrophe when using English.

- Automatically placing an accent in a word that requires an accented letter.

- Automatic capitalization of the first letter of a sentence.

You don't need to do anything special to take advantage of these features when using the *Text* input scope, but it is worth exploring them a little.

Work with the *Text* input scope

1. Create a new Windows Phone application and name it **SbSCh12_5**.

2. Add a new *TextBox* to the design surface. Make it large enough to contain multiple lines of text. Here's an example:

```
<TextBox Height="367" HorizontalAlignment="Left" Margin="9,63,0,0"
        Name="textBox1" Text="TextBox" VerticalAlignment="Top" Width="464" />
```

3. Add an *InputScope* attribute to the XAML and set its value to *Text*. Be sure to clear the *Text* property.

```
<TextBox Height="367" HorizontalAlignment="Left" Margin="9,63,0,0"
        Name="textBox1" Text="" VerticalAlignment="Top" Width="464"
        InputScope="Text" />
```

4. Press F5 to run the application. You'll see the phone screen with the text input box open. Because it is empty, the keyboard will default to capital letters. This is so the first word you type will be capitalized.

5. Type the letter **H**. The first letter appears as a capital and then the keys change to lower case letters.

6. Type the letters **e**, **l**, and **l**. You can do this on your computer's keyboard or you can press the appropriate keys on the emulator.

7. In the space above the keys but below the text box, you'll see some suggested words. Possibilities include words that require an apostrophe, so the letters you typed (**H**, **e**, **l**, and **l**) could mean you are typing the contraction "he'll" (meaning "he will"). You could also be typing a word that begins with "h-e-l-l," such as "hello," or you could have mistyped a common word, such as "bell."

Using the Multi-Touch Interface

Windows Phone allows the user to manipulate the UI with multiple touch points. For instance, you can scroll across a wide image by dragging it with one finger or you can zoom out of an image by "pinching" the image with two fingers. And you can use Silverlight to build interfaces that use multi-touch on the phone. The emulator supports the same interface as your computer, so if you have a single or multi-touch screen, you'll be able to test the application as a single or multi-touch application. If you do not have a touch screen, you can use the mouse to emulate a single touch screen.

Build a touch-enabled interface

1. Create a new Windows Phone project and name it **SbSCh12_6**

2. Add a new *Image* control to the design surface and use its *Source* property to add an image to the project.

3. Name the *Image* control **img**. Your XAML will look something like this:

```xml
<!--ContentGrid is empty. Place new content here-->
<Grid x:Name="ContentGrid" Grid.Row="1">
  <Image x:Name="img" Height="150" HorizontalAlignment="Left"
      Margin="133,133,0,0" Stretch="Fill"
      VerticalAlignment="Top" Width="200"
      Source="/SbSCh12_6;component/Images/bucky.jpg" />
</Grid>
```

4. Go to the MainPage.xaml.cs code-behind file.

5. Above the *MainPage()* constructor, add the following three lines of code:

```csharp
private TransformGroup transformGroup;
private TranslateTransform translateTransform;
private ScaleTransform scaleTransform;
```

TranslateTransform is used to determine the movement of the picture. As you slide your finger around the phone, you determine the parameters of the translation and, in turn, that determines the location of the picture. Similarrly, *ScaleTransform* manages the *size* of the image. If you have a multi-touch device, pinching two fingers inward or spreading them outward on the screen will provide scaling information which—when applied to the transform for the image—will resize the image.

Note that you can stack these into a single transform within a *TransformGroup* object.

6. Within the *MainPage()* constructor, set up a *ManipulationDelta* event for the application:

```
this.ManipulationDelta +=
    new EventHandler<ManipulationDeltaEventArgs>(MainPage_ManipulationDelta);
```

7. Set up the *transformGroup*, the *translationTransform* and the *scaleTransform* for the application.

```
this.transformGroup = new TransformGroup();
this.translateTransform = new TranslateTransform();
this.scaleTransform = new ScaleTransform();
```

8. Add the private *translateTransform* and *scaleTransform* objects to the *transformGroup*.

```
this.transformGroup.Children.Add(this.scaleTransform);
this.transformGroup.Children.Add(this.translateTransform);
```

9. Finally, specify that you are going to use the *transformGroup* on the *Image* control. Remember that you used the name *img* for the *Image*.

```
this.img.RenderTransform = this.transformGroup;
```

10. Here's the complete *MainPage()* constructor:

```
private TransformGroup transformGroup;
private TranslateTransform translateTransform;
private ScaleTransform scaleTransform;
public MainPage()
{
    InitializeComponent();
    SupportedOrientations =
        SupportedPageOrientation.Portrait | SupportedPageOrientation.Landscape;
```

```
    this.ManipulationDelta +=
      new EventHandler<ManipulationDeltaEventArgs>(MainPage_ManipulationDelta);

    this.transformGroup = new TransformGroup();
    this.translateTransform = new TranslateTransform();
    this.scaleTransform = new ScaleTransform();
    this.transformGroup.Children.Add(this.scaleTransform);
    this.transformGroup.Children.Add(this.translateTransform);
    this.img.RenderTransform = this.transformGroup;
}
```

11. You set up the *ManipulationDelta* event earlier. It detects actions on the
touch system and turns them into manipulations. It takes a parameter of type
ManipulationDeltaEventArgs, where the manipulation conversion has taken place. So,
for example, if you spread your fingers outwards (the gesture for making something
larger), then the *Scale.X* and *Scale.Y* sub-properties of this object will be greater than
one. You can then simply multiply the current scale by those values to get the new desired size.

 Note When you're running the emulator for the phone, the *Scale* events will return zero
on a non-touch screen. Check that they are greater than zero before you apply them to
the scale or the image will be scaled to zero and effectively vanish!

12. Here's the complete code for the *ManipulationDelta* event handler:

```
void MainPage_ManipulationDelta(object sender, ManipulationDeltaEventArgs e)
{
  if ((e.DeltaManipulation.Scale.X > 0) && (e.DeltaManipulation.Scale.Y > 0))
  {
    this.scaleTransform.ScaleX *= e.DeltaManipulation.Scale.X;
    this.scaleTransform.ScaleY *= e.DeltaManipulation.Scale.Y;
  }
  this.translateTransform.X += e.DeltaManipulation.Translation.X;
  this.translateTransform.Y += e.DeltaManipulation.Translation.Y;
}
```

13. Press F5 to run your application. You'll see the image on your page. You can use the
mouse to emulate a single-finger touchpoint to slide the image around the screen. If
you have a multi-touch screen, you should be able to use it to resize the image.

Other Services

Windows Phone supports many other services that have not been covered in this book because they're not supported on the emulator. These include:

- **Location Awareness**   The phone can detect your location based on its built-in GPS using the *GeoCoordinateWatcher* class.

- **Accelerometer**   When a user tilts or moves the phone, the built-in accelerometers raise events that your application can capture. You can use the current tilt of the phone to drive your user interface. To do this, you use the *AccelerometerSensor* classes in the *Microsoft.Devices.Sensors* namespace.

- **Trial Applications**   The Windows Phone market is designed to allow users to easily find and purchase applications. As a developer, you may want to provide a trial version that either provides limited functionality or expires after a defined time. The Silverlight APIs allow you to do this using the License APIs, which include an *IsTrial* method. Silverlight also provides a *MarketPlaceLauncher* API that you can use to provide Buy It Now functionality.

- **Push Notifications**   These allow phone applications to subscribe to services in such a way that, when information from the service changes, the application will receive a notification, allowing the application to update itself. This is commonly used, for example, to retrieve updates to sports scores or social networks.

Key Points

- Silverlight for Windows Phone 7 is the same Silverlight as what you get on the desktop and in a browser. But it supports many additional services designed for today's mobile devices.

- You learned how to use the orientation service to build applications that adapt to how a user is holding the phone—in either portrait or landscape mode.

- You saw how to use the hardware Back button on the Windows Phone, catching its events within your application and overriding its default system functionality.

- You built a functioning application bar, complete with buttons and menu items.

- You explored input scope and how it can create a better experience for users who need to input text into your application by automatically providing a context-appropriate keyboard.

- You explored the typing intelligence features that are built into Windows Phone to streamline text input.

- You implemented multi-touch support, which allows users to interact with your application with touch and gestures. These capabilities rely on the Manipulation APIs.

Chapter 13
Expression Blend for Windows Phone

After completing this chapter, you will be able to:

- Find, download, and install the tools you need to develop Windows Phone applications with Silverlight.

- Use Expression Blend to build Silverlight user interface elements.

- Build a Silverlight application that runs on Windows Phone.

This chapter provides an introductory look at the Microsoft Expression Blend interactive designer tool. Note that support for Windows Phone will be part of Expression Blend 4. This book uses the first Beta release of Expression Blend 4 and the details in this chapter may differ slightly from the final release, but the principles should remain the same. The links that are shown in this chapter are for the Beta release of Expression Blend 4 and for the preview versions of the add-in and the SDK.

Before you being working through this chapter, you should visit *http://www.microsoft.com/expression/try-it/Default.aspx* and download the 60-day trial of Expression Studio Ultimate, which includes Expression Blend 4 and all the tools and SDKs for Windows Phone development."

Create Your First Windows Phone Application with Expression Blend

After installing all the tools, you're ready to use Expression Blend to create Windows Phone applications. Microsoft Expression Blend was designed to increase the speed and efficiency in which you can take your project from concept to completion. It was built with designers in mind, providing tools for designers to create engaging user experiences while implementing UI elements with the same code base developers work with. Therefore, when you're using Expression Blend, you'll notice that it is built on a visual paradigm—what you see is what you get.

Now it's time for you to use Expression Blend to build a simple application, end-to-end. And you'll do this without writing any code.

Build a Windows Phone application

1. Launch Expression Blend 4 Beta from your Start menu. If you see the Startup Wizard, close it to go directly to Expression Blend.

2. Select the New Project option on the File menu and the New Project dialog box will open.

3. If you've installed everything correctly, the New Project dialog box will include templates for a Windows Phone Application and a Windows Phone Data-Driven Application. Select the Windows Phone Application option.

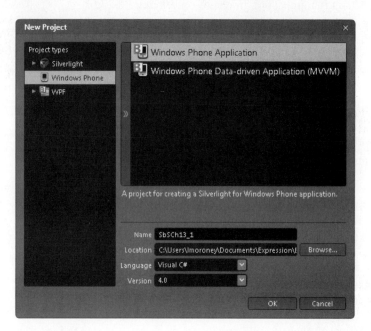

4. Enter **SbSCh13_1** in the Name field for your new project and click OK to continue.

Expression Blend will create your application solution and you'll see the phone design surface on the art board, just like in Microsoft Visual Studio.

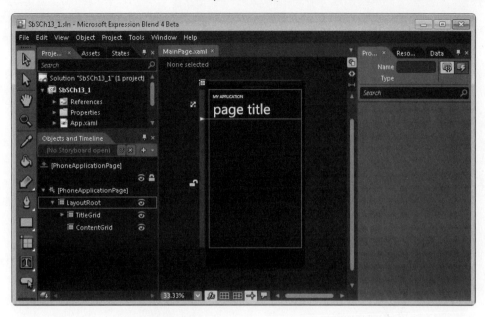

At the top-left corner of the screen, you'll see the Projects window. This should look familiar if you've used Visual Studio (and you should have if you have been working through this book). The Projects window includes the project file and the source XAML and CS files. Along the left side of the screen you'll see the Toolbox.

5. To save space, Expression Blend groups tools together. So if you look at the Rectangle tool, for example, you'll see there's a small arrow in the lower-right corner. When you click the Rectangle tool, you get the shape shown on the toolbox (a rectangle). But if you hold the mouse down, you'll see all the controls available in that family—in this case, the Rectangle, the Ellipse, and the Line.

6. Select the Ellipse tool and draw an *Ellipse* on the design surface. Note that the Toolbox image changes to an ellipse now instead of the rectangle.

7. Select the *Ellipse* on the design surface by clicking on it. In the Properties window on the right of the screen, select the *Fill* setting and make sure the Solid Color tab is selected. Then, on the color board, drag the indicator to a solid color—for example, a shade of light blue.

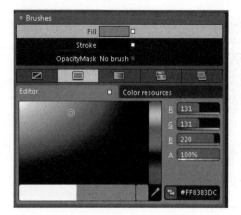

You should now have a colored ellipse on the design surface.

8. Expression Blend supports two different styles of workspace: the one you're currently using is the Design workspace and it is used to—as its name suggests—design assets. The other workspace is the Animation workspace, which you use to set up timeline-based animations. You can switch between the workspaces either by choosing the appropriate workspace item from the Window menu at the top of the screen or by pressing F6. So press F6 and the screen will change to the animation workspace.

9. Near the bottom of the screen you'll see the Objects And Timeline panel. You can use this to define your animations visually and control how they run on a timeline. To get

started, press the plus sign (+) button at the upper right of the Objects And Timeline window to add a new Storyboard. (Note that a storyboard provides the description for how an animation will work—it defines the time that the animation takes to complete, the objects that will be changed, and what the changes will be.)

10. The Create Storyboard Resource dialog box will appear. Name your new animation **Bounce** and then OK.

The Objects And Timeline window will change to show the timeline. The yellow vertical bar shows the current position on the timeline. By default, it's at 0 because you haven't started running the timeline yet. You can drag the bar to a particular point to test the animation at that point.

1. Drag the yellow vertical bar to the two-second point on the timeline.

2. Select the Ellipse control and press the Record Keyframe button near the top of the timeline beside the time readout—it looks a little like an egg with a + beside it. After you click the Record Keyframe button, there will be a keyframe indicator on the timeline beside the ellipse.

3. On the design surface, drag the ellipse until it is at the bottom of the screen. By doing this, you are telling Expression Blend where you want the ellipse to be at two seconds into the animation.

4. Press the Play button and you'll see the animation play. The ellipse will drop from the top of the screen to the bottom, taking two seconds to do so.

5. Click the arrow beside the ellipse in the Objects And Timeline window to see *RenderTransform* and select it. Note that the animation works by manipulating the *RenderTransform*. For more details on how this works, see Chapter 7, "Transformation and Animation."

6. In the Properties section, find the Easing window and select the *EasingFunction* option.

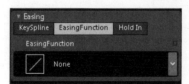

7. From the *EasingFunction* drop down, find the Bounce functions and select the middle one. This is the Bounce Out *EasingFunction*, where Out refers to the end of the animation. In refers to the beginning of the animation, and InOut means both.

8. You can select both the number of bounces and the bounciness. You'll also find more details on these in Chapter 7 (which you should have read already). For now, keep the default values: **3** bounces and a bounciness value of **2**.

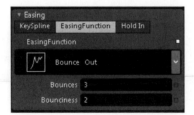

9. In the Objects And Timeline Window, press the Play button again. Now the ball falls to the bottom of the screen and bounces three times before coming to a rest.

10. Press F5 to deploy and test this application.

11. You'll see a Change Device Selection screen. This gives you a choice between using the Windows Phone 7 Emulator or a physical Windows Phone 7 Device. Select your desired target (in this case, I'm using the emulator) and press OK.

After a few moments, your application will run within the emulator. But wait. You won't see the animation. That's because you haven't yet defined when the animation should play—you were able to test it in Expression Blend, but you didn't specify that it should happen in response to any event.

12. Here's how you can fix this issue. You'll configure it so the animation will start (meaning the ellipse will bounce) when you click the ellipse. Go back to the design surface and change to the XAML view. To do that, click the button at the top-right corner of the designer that looks like two angle brackets (<>).

13. In the XAML, find the declaration for the Ellipse, click somewhere inside the closing angle bracket and add a *MouseLeftButtonDown="StartMe"* event definition.

```
<Ellipse x:Name="ellipse" Fill="#FF8383DC" HorizontalAlignment="Left"
    Margin="29,34,0,0" Stroke="Black" Width="135" Height="114"
    VerticalAlignment="Top" RenderTransformOrigin="0.5,0.5"
    MouseLeftButtonDown="StartMe" >
```

14. This code specifies that when the user clicks the ellipse, the code in the function called "StartMe" should execute. So you'll need to create the *StartMe* function. Using the Projects window, find MainPage.xaml.cs, open it, and add this code:

```
private void StartMe(object sender, MouseEventArgs e)
{
        Bounce.Begin();
}
```

15. Press F5 to execute the application again within the emulator. This time, click on the ellipse using the mouse (or touch it with your finger if you have a touch screen). Now the ellipse bounces!

Key Points

- Expression Blend is a tool created with designers in mind. It lets you create visual effects and UIs without writing any code.

- You installed the necessary tools and built a simple Windows Phone application using Expression Blend.

Chapter 14
Getting Started with XNA Game Development for Windows Phone

Microsoft XNA is a set of software, services, resources, and communities that are focused on enabling game developers to develop for various gaming platforms. Traditionally, XNA has focused on the Xbox and Windows platforms, but with Microsoft Silverlight and the new tools for Windows Phone, you can now use XNA to build games for Windows Phone 7.

XNA Game Studio is an integrated development environment, based on Microsoft Visual Studio, that lets you build games on the XNA framework for a variety of devices. If you followed the procedures in Chapter 11, "Windows Phone Development" to install the developer tools for Windows Phone, XNA 4.0 Game Studio will already be installed on your system. If not, go back to that chapter and follow the installation process and then you'll be ready to go.

XNA is worthy of several books in its own right, so in this chapter you're just going to skim the surface of what is possible. You'll build a simple game-like experience that shows how you can manage sprites, user input, collisions, sound, and a game loop.

Creating an XNA Application and Adding Content

To get started, launch Visual Studio 2010 Express for Windows Phone. This is the same tool you've been using to build Silverlight projects in the previous chapters. Visual Studio 2010 Express for Windows Phone has XNA built in.

Prepare your game content

1. From the File menu in Visual Studio, select New Project and you'll see the New Project dialog box. From the Installed Templates list on the left, select XNA Game Studio 4.0 to create a new XNA game project.

2. Enter **SbSCh14_1** as the project name and press OK to create the application.

   In Solution Explorer, you'll see that your new application has two projects. The SbSCh14_1 project contains all your code and resources. The project named SbSCh14_1Content should contain all the content that your application will use, including any graphics and sound files.

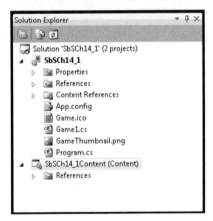

3. Next, you need to add some graphics to your application. The first graphic will be your main character and for this you'll use what is called a sprite sheet. A sprite sheet contains all the pieces of animation for your character in a single image. With XNA, you take the appropriate slice off the sprite sheet to make it look like your character is animated.

Here's the sprite sheet for a girl character in your new game, courtesy of the nice folks at *gamepoetry.com*. This sheet is tweaked a little from the original—the girls are always at the same spot in a 32 x 64 rectangle.

Later on, depending on which direction the girl is walking, and depending on which frame of the animation you want to show, you'll cut one of the images out using a rectangle and draw it inside the sprite on the screen. This will have the effect of animating the girl walking. The sprite sheet is a .png file (called NPCFemale1.png) with a transparent background, so you don't need to worry about the girl's rectangle blanking out the surrounding area. For a real game, you might want to do this a little differently—using masking—but this chapter uses the transparent .png file to keep things simple.

 Note You can get this graphic and the rest of the assets from this chapter in the downloadable code for this book.

4. Add the NPCFemale1.png file to your project and to the Content project. You can simply drag it from your file system onto the project and then drag it from your project into your Content project. Solution Explorer should look like this now:

5. Select the graphic in the Content project, as shown in the previous screenshot. Then, in the Properties window, note the Asset Name. You'll need the Asset Name later when you refer to the graphic in code. The property defaults to the name of the file without the extension—in this case, it's NPCFemale1.

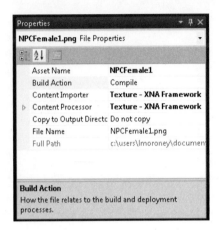

 Note In game development, NPC typically stands for Non-Player Character. This graphic was originally created to be an NPC, hence its name. However, in this example, the graphic is the player's character.

The NPC in this game will be a barrel that moves around the screen automatically. You'll need to move the player to avoid hitting the barrel. As before, the graphic is a .png file with a transparent background. Because the barrel doesn't animate (it only moves), it isn't a sprite sheet—it's just a single small image.

6. In the same way as before, add the barrel picture to both your project and the Content project in Solution Explorer. When you're done, Solution Explorer should look like this:

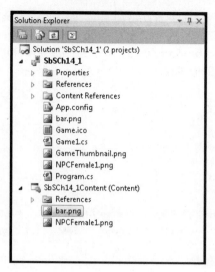

The Asset Name for the barrel will be bar, following the convention that the Asset Name is the file name without the extension.

7. Finally, add a sound file. You can record one yourself if you like. Just make sure you use a .wav file and not a .wma file. As before, add it to both the project and the Content project.

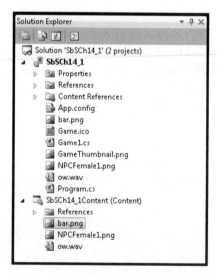

You now have everything you need to create the game. In the next section, you'll add the code.

Writing the Code for Your Game in XNA

When you create your game using Visual Studio, the IDE creates a lot of stub code in the *Game1* class. First, you'll explore the generated code and then you'll see what you need to do to edit it.

Visual Studio creates two class level variables:

```
GraphicsDeviceManager graphics;
SpriteBatch spriteBatch;
```

GraphicsDeviceManager handles the configuration and management of the graphics device by your game. You can use it to, for example, find out the dimensions of the phone's screen.

You use the *SpriteBatch* to draw sets of sprites in a batch, at the same time, using the same settings.

Both of these classes are best understood through demonstration. As you work through the code for your game, you'll see them in action.

Next you'll see the class constructor for *Game1*, which initializes the *GraphicsDeviceManager*, sets the directory from which content will be loaded, and sets the frame rate at which your game will run. It defaults to 30 frames per second (fps).

```
public Game1()
{
    graphics = new GraphicsDeviceManager(this);
    Content.RootDirectory = "Content";
    // Frame rate is 30 fps by default for Windows Phone.
    TargetElapsedTime = TimeSpan.FromSeconds(1 / 30.0);
}
```

The *Initialize()* function gets called just before your game starts to run. If you are using any external services—or anything else that may need initialization (other than loading content)—you should do it here.

```
protected override void Initialize()
{
    // TODO: Add your initialization logic here
    base.Initialize();
}
```

You should load your content in the *LoadContent()* function. Later, you'll use this function to load your graphics and sound files. The basic version provided by the template initializes the *spriteBatch* you created earlier.

```
protected override void LoadContent()
{
    // Create a new SpriteBatch, which can be used to draw textures.
    spriteBatch = new SpriteBatch(GraphicsDevice);

    // TODO: use this.Content to load your game content here
}
```

The *Update()* function is the workhorse of your game. It is called repeatedly, so this is the function you use to update your game world. In the *update* function, you'll check user input, set up how your sprites move around, and check for collisions.

```
protected override void Update(GameTime gameTime)
{
    // Allows the game to exit
    if (GamePad.GetState(PlayerIndex.One).Buttons.Back == ButtonState.Pressed)
        this.Exit();
    // TODO: Add your update logic here
    base.Update(gameTime);
}
```

Finally, you use the *Draw()* function to draw and update your screen during game time. You'll use this to batch-draw the sprites later.

```
protected override void Draw(GameTime gameTime)
{
    GraphicsDevice.Clear(Color.CornflowerBlue);
    // TODO: Add your drawing code here
    base.Draw(gameTime);
}
```

Those are the primary functions that XNA provides in the *Game* class to support writing games. In the rest of this section, you'll add code to these functions to implement your game. When the game is running on your Windows Phone, it will look something like this:

Now you can take a look at how to write the code to implement the game.

Creating the Class Variables

In this section, you'll create and initialize the class-level variables that the application will use across functions. In your *Game1* class file, add this code before the *Game1()* constructor.

Write the class variables

1. First, create three variables to hold the top, left, and direction values for the girl sprite. This game uses the conventions of 0 when the sprite's direction is downward, 1 when she's moving left, 2 for right, and 3 for upward. These values correspond to the rows of sprites in the sprite sheet.

```
int nDirection;
int xPos = 200;
int yPos = 200;
```

2. To hold the sprite for the girl, you use a *Texture2D* instance. You'll load the image that represents the current animation frame into *Texture2D*. You'll also need a rectangle that holds the area of the screen that she occupies. You'll use this rectangle for collision detection.

```
Texture2D theGirl;
Rectangle theGirlBounds;
```

3. The barrel will move automatically, but you'll need a *Texture2D* to render it and a vector to indicate its current direction. Another vector will indicate its speed in that direction. And you'll need another rectangle to hold the bounds of the barrel.

```
Texture2D barrel;
Vector2 barrelDirection;
Vector2 barrelSpeed = new Vector2(50.0f, 50.0f);
Rectangle theBarrelBounds;
```

4. To animate the girl, you need a timer and an interval, so you'll need to initialize a couple of variables to hold those, starting at time 0 and defining a 500 ms interval.

```
float timer = 0f;
float interval = 500f;
```

5. Each animation state for the girl has four frames. Study the sprite sheet and you'll see what this means—there are four states for moving up, four for moving down, and so on. You need to keep track of the current animation frame, so add an integer variable for that.

```
int currentFrame = 1;
```

6. Each animation frame for the girl sprite is 32 pixels wide and 64 pixels high. Create two variables to hold these values.

```
int spriteWidth = 32;
int spriteHeight = 64;
```

7. You need a rectangle to define which of the images on the sprite sheet you slice and draw on the screen to represent the girl walking.

```
Rectangle sourceRect;
```

8. And you need to know the center of the current animation frame when drawing the girl on the screen. You'll see more about this when you get to the *Draw()* function.

```
Vector2 origin;
```

9. Finally, when the barrel and the girl collide, she screams, so you need to have a *SoundEffect* object to access the .wav file so you can play back the scream.

```
SoundEffect ow;
```

Loading the Content

In XNA, you use the *LoadContent()* function to load all the content that your application is going to use. In this case, you need to load the graphics for the girl and the barrel and the sound effect so the girl can scream when the barrel hits her. You'll also use the *LoadContent()* function to set up the collision rectangles.

Load the game content

1. Find the *LoadContent()* function in the *Game1* class and add the following code to load the sprites. Keep any existing code in this function. Earlier you assigned Asset Names for the images and sound file. You'll use those Asset Names here.

```
// Load the sprites for the girl and the barrel
theGirl = Content.Load<Texture2D>("NPCFemale1");
barrel = Content.Load<Texture2D>("bar");
```

2. Next, set up the bounding rectangles for the bar and the girl. These will be used to track the position of the graphics, but won't be drawn themselves. When they overlap, a collision will occur.

```
// Set up the collision rectangles
theBarrelBounds.Height = barrel.Height;
theBarrelBounds.Width = barrel.Width;
theGirlBounds.Height = 64;
theGirlBounds.Width = 32;
```

3. Now you'll load the sound effect. This follows the same principle as the graphics, except you are loading it into a SoundEffect object instance named "ow".

```
ow = Content.Load<SoundEffect>("ow");
```

4. Here's the completed *LoadContent()* function:

```
protected override void LoadContent()
{
    // Create a new SpriteBatch, which can be used to draw textures.
    spriteBatch = new SpriteBatch(GraphicsDevice);

    // TODO: use this.Content to load your game content here
    // Load the sprites for the girl and the barrel
    theGirl = Content.Load<Texture2D>("NPCFemale1");
    barrel = Content.Load<Texture2D>("bar");

    // Set up the collision rectangles
    theBarrelBounds.Height = barrel.Height;
    theBarrelBounds.Width = barrel.Width;
    theGirlBounds.Height = 64;
    theGirlBounds.Width = 32;

    // Load the sound effect
    ow = Content.Load<SoundEffect>("ow");
}
```

With the content in place, you can fill in the *Update()* function, which manages the user input and updates the status of the game world accordingly.

Updating the Game World

The *Update()* function is where the logic for updating the game world should reside. In the *Update()* function, you check for collisions, gather input, and do other game-processing tasks. By default, Visual Studio inserts basic code that checks for a game exit when a user clicks the Back button.

You're going to add support for the directional arrows so users can move the character. You'll also check to see if she has gone off screen and update her animation frames. Note that on a real phone, you'd probably use the accelerometer, but because that feature isn't currently supported in the emulator, this example uses the arrow keys.

You'll also process the automatic movement of the barrel that the girl has to avoid, and check to see if the two collide.

Code the game world functionality

1. To start, add the Keyboard handlers, using the *Keyboard.GetState().IsKeyDown()* function and checking for a particular key. For example, to check for the keyboard arrow down, you'd write code like this:

```
if (Keyboard.GetState().IsKeyDown(Keys.Down)){}
```

2. Add the code to check for all the arrow keys, set the girl's direction based on the key pressed, and then change either the *X* position or *Y* position of the sprite.

```
if (Keyboard.GetState().IsKeyDown(Keys.Down))
{
  nDirection = 0;
  yPos += 2;
}
if (Keyboard.GetState().IsKeyDown(Keys.Left))
{
  nDirection = 1;
  xPos -= 2;
}
if (Keyboard.GetState().IsKeyDown(Keys.Right))
{
  nDirection = 2;
  xPos += 2;
}
if (Keyboard.GetState().IsKeyDown(Keys.Up))
{
  nDirection = 3;
  yPos -= 2;
}
```

Note that the user can hold down multiple keys simultaneously and this method will capture them. This allows users to move the sprite diagonally by pressing two arrow keys.

3. Now that you've updated the *xPos* and *yPos* of the sprite based on the user's key input, you should check the bounds. For this example, the *Y* position must be more than 120 pixels from the top and more than 120 pixels from the bottom. Similarly, it must be at least 20 pixels from the left and 20 pixels from the right.

Note that the early preview of the emulator doesn't seem to be very accurate when it comes to pixel measurements of the bounds. Just adjust the values as necessary to keep the sprite working within the screen area.

```
// Check Screen Bounds
if (yPos < 120)
      yPos = 120;
if (yPos > GraphicsDevice.Viewport.Height - 120)
      yPos = GraphicsDevice.Viewport.Height - 120;
if (xPos < 20)
      xPos = 20;
if (xPos > GraphicsDevice.Viewport.Width - 20)
      xPos = GraphicsDevice.Viewport.Width - 20;
```

4. Remember that the girl sprite had an associated collision rectangle. You'll need to update this rectangle with the new position, like so:

```
theGirlBounds.X = xPos;
theGirlBounds.Y = yPos;
```

5. To animate the girl sprite, update her position every 500 ms. The *gameTime.ElapsedGameTime.TotalMilliseconds* property will return the elapsed time because *Update* was last called. If that time is greater than 500 ms, you need to display the next frame in her animation. Because there are only four frames, make sure you use a frame number from 0 to 3.

```
//Increase the timer by the number of milliseconds since update was last called
timer += (float)gameTime.ElapsedGameTime.TotalMilliseconds;

if (timer > interval)
{
  currentFrame++;
  timer = 0f;
}

if (currentFrame == 4)
{
  currentFrame = 0;
}
```

6. Now that you know the right frame, you need to find the rectangle in the sprite sheet that corresponds to the current animation frame and load that into the origin. You do this by creating a rectangle. As parameters to the rectangle's constructor, pass the *X* and *Y* coordinates of the top-left corner and the *width* and *height*.

To find the correct animation frame on the sheet, pass the *X* coordinate, which is the current frame times the width. In other words, to display frame 0, *X* will be 0; to display frame 1, *X* will be 32 (32 × 1); to display frame 2, *X* will be 64 (32 × 2), and so on. Similarly, you find the *Y* coordinate by multiplying the direction value by the frame height. So the *Y* coordinate of the down frames is 0, the Y coordinate of the left frames is 64, and so on.

To get the second frame for the girl walking left, as shown in the following image, the current frame is 1 and the image width is 32, so the *X* coordinate will be 32. The current direction is 1 and the image height is 64, so the *Y* coordinate is 64. That gives you the upper-left corner of the image. Because the image rectangle is always 32 × 64, you can cut out that frame and load it into the origin.

You'll use the origin when drawing the sprite later. Here's the code:

```
sourceRect = new Rectangle(currentFrame * spriteWidth,
                           nDirection * spriteHeight,
                           spriteWidth,
                           spriteHeight);
origin = new Vector2(sourceRect.Width, sourceRect.Height);
```

7. Update the barrel's position and check for collisions. (You'll write the necessary functions in the next steps.)

```
// Then we update the position of the barrel.
UpdateSprite(gameTime, ref barrelPosition, ref barrelSpeed);

// And check if they collide!
CheckForCollision();
```

8. Finally, continue the game loop by calling *Update* again—the stub code generated by Visual Studio already does this.

```
base.Update(gameTime);
```

That's it for the *Update* function. Next, you'll write the *UpdateSprite* function that moves the NPC (the barrel).

Moving the Non-Player Character

In the previous section, you saw the *Update* function and how it's used to move the player character and update the animation frames. In this section, you'll create the *UpdateSprite* function used to move the barrel (the NPC). Remember, *UpdateSprite* gets called from the *Update* function. Visual Studio Express doesn't provide any stub code for this, so you'll have to write it all yourself.

Write the code for the NPC

1. The *UpdateSprite* function takes the current *gameTime* (so it can be synchronized with the player character movement), position, and speed of the NPC as parameters. (The previous section covered how the function is called from the Update section.)

```
void UpdateSprite(GameTime gameTime,
                  ref Vector2 spritePosition,
                  ref Vector2 spriteSpeed)
{ ... }
```

2. Moving the sprite is pretty simple. You have a vector for its position and a vector for its speed. The speed vector is specified in pixels in the *X* and *Y* direction. To calculate the new position, you simply add the result of multiplying the speed by the time that has elapsed. In the "Creating the Class Variables" section, you defined a *barrelSpeed* vector, specifying that the speed is 50 pixels on *X* and 50 pixels on *Y* per second. Therefore, If 100 ms (.1 of a second) has passed, you add 5 to the *X* value of the current position and 5 to the *Y* of the current position.

```
spritePosition += spriteSpeed * (float)gameTime.ElapsedGameTime.TotalSeconds;
```

3. When the barrel hits any screen edge, you should change its direction. You can do this by changing the sign of the corresponding portion of the speed vector. For example, when moving left on the screen, set the *X* part of the speed vector to be negative. Here's the code:

```
if (spritePosition.X > graphics.GraphicsDevice.Viewport.Width)
{
    spriteSpeed.X *= -1;
    spritePosition.X = graphics.GraphicsDevice.Viewport.Width;
}
else if (spritePosition.X < 0)
{
    spriteSpeed.X *= -1;
    spritePosition.X = 0;
}
if (spritePosition.Y > graphics.GraphicsDevice.Viewport.Height)
{
    spriteSpeed.Y *= -1;
    spritePosition.Y = graphics.GraphicsDevice.Viewport.Height;
}
else if (spritePosition.Y < 0)
{
    spriteSpeed.Y *= -1;
    spritePosition.Y = 0;
}
```

Now you have the code that will update the position of the NPC. Here's the full function:

```
void UpdateSprite(GameTime gameTime, ref Vector2 spritePosition,
                  ref Vector2 spriteSpeed)
{
  spritePosition += spriteSpeed * (float)gameTime.ElapsedGameTime.TotalSeconds;
  if (spritePosition.X > graphics.GraphicsDevice.Viewport.Width)
  {
    spriteSpeed.X *= -1;
    spritePosition.X = graphics.GraphicsDevice.Viewport.Width;
  }
  else if (spritePosition.X < 0)
  {
    spriteSpeed.X *= -1;
    spritePosition.X = 0;
  }
  if (spritePosition.Y > graphics.GraphicsDevice.Viewport.Height)
  {
```

```
        spriteSpeed.Y *= -1;
        spritePosition.Y = graphics.GraphicsDevice.Viewport.Height;
    }
    else if (spritePosition.Y < 0)
    {
        spriteSpeed.Y *= -1;
        spritePosition.Y = 0;
    }
}
```

Checking for Collision

Earlier, in the *Update* function, you called a *CheckForCollision()* function. This simply checks for a collision between the bounding rectangles for the Player character and the NPC. For this example, when there is a collision, you will play the sound and move the character back to the upper-left position.

Write the collision code

1. Add a new void function called *CheckForCollision*.

    ```
    void CheckForCollision()
    { ... }
    ```

2. Update the bounding rectangle of the girl sprite to *xPos* and *yPos* as its upper left corner.

    ```
    theGirlBounds.X = xPos;
    theGirlBounds.Y = yPos;
    ```

3. Update the bounding rectangle for the NPC based on its current coordinates.

    ```
    theBarrelBounds.X = (int)barrelDirection.X;
    theBarrelBounds.Y = (int)barrelDirection.Y;
    ```

4. If the two rectangles intersect, you have a collision, at which point you can play the screaming sound and reset the position of the player sprite. Note that the *play* function lets you change the pitch of the sound for a little variety.

```
if (theGirlBounds.Intersects(theBarrelBounds))
{
  xPos = 0;
  yPos = 0;
  ow.Play(1.0f, 1.0f, 0.0f);
}
```

And that's it for the game logic. For your convenience, here's the full *CheckForCollision* function:

```
void CheckForCollision()
{
  theGirlBounds.X = xPos;
  theGirlBounds.Y = yPos;
  theBarrelBounds.X = (int)barrelDirection.X;
  theBarrelBounds.Y = (int)barrelDirection.Y;
  if (theGirlBounds.Intersects(theBarrelBounds))
  {
    xPos = 0;
    yPos = 0;
    ow.Play(1.0f, 1.0f, 0.0f);
  }
}
```

Drawing the Sprites to the Screen

All that you need to do now is draw out the sprites on the screen in the draw loop, which XNA calls automatically. Visual Studio provides a stub function as part of the generated template.

Draw the sprites

1. First, you need to clear the screen to erase the current positions of the sprites.

```
graphics.GraphicsDevice.Clear(Color.CornflowerBlue);
```

2. XNA can draw sprites in batches, which is a feature worth taking advantage of. Back at the beginning of this chapter, you set up an object called *spriteBatch*. To start the batch processing, you simply use its *Begin()* method.

```
spriteBatch.Begin();
```

3. Now draw the girl and the barrel. The *Draw* function has many different overloads—to draw the girl, you want to use the clipping rectangle of the sprite sheet to draw her using the origin rectangle. The barrel is a little easier—just draw the texture at the position indicated by the *barrelDirection* vector.

```
spriteBatch.Draw(theGirl,
                new Vector2(xPos, yPos),
                sourceRect, Color.White,
                0f,
                origin,
                2.0f,
                SpriteEffects.None,
                0);

spriteBatch.Draw(barrel, barrelDirection, Color.White);
```

4. End the batch and call the *Draw* function on the base to go back into the game loop.

```
spriteBatch.End();
base.Draw(gameTime);
```

That's it. You've created your first Windows Phone game using XNA! Press F5 to deploy the application to your emulator and execute it. Congratulations and welcome to the world of game development for the Windows Phone.

Key Points

- All the necessary tools to get started developing games for Windows Phone 7 are available to download for free.

- You added images and sounds to your project, and learned how to use sprite sheets to animate your characters.

- You discovered how to use the keyboard to capture user input and update the game world.

- You created a non-player character (NPC) that moves automatically and checked for collisions between the player character and the NPC.

- You used batch drawing to redraw your screen.

Index

Symbols

3-D model, 84
3-D simulation of scene, 99
3-D space, 136
* (asterisk), for flexible grid column size, 56
| (pipe) character, 242

A

"About" menu, 38
Accelerometer, in Windows Phone, 266
AcceptsReturn property, of TextBox control, 44
Add Internal Link (Deep Zoom Composer), 91
Add New Domain Service Class dialog, 78
Add New Item dialog box, 70, 184
Add Reference dialog box, 160–161
Add Service Reference dialog box, 233
administrator account for SQL, password, 5
ADO.NET Entity Data Model, 74–77
Advanced Stream Redirector (ASX) playlists, 112
affine matrix, 134
allow-from tag, 224
Angle property, of RotateTransform, 128
AngleX property, 133
AngleY property, 133
animation, 140–147
 creating, 140–142
 defining parameters, 141
 easing, 145–147
 Expression Blend for defining, 148–152
 key frames, 142–144
Animation workspace in Expression Blend, 148, 277
ApplicationBar control, 252
application bar, in Windows Phone, 249–255
Application.Current.Install() function, 159
applications. See also out-of-browser applications
 accessing webcam from, 123–125

browser bridge for controlling, 184–188, 190–193
 creating, 22
 with MediaElement control, 112–113
 with MouseMove event, 35–37
Application Storage, 172. See also isolated storage
Area tool, 91
ASHX file, 209
ASP.NET, 3
Asset Names in XNA game, 286, 287, 293
asterisk (*), for flexible grid column size, 56
asynchronous request, from WebClient class, 212
asyncResult variable, AsyncState property of, 219
attached Properties, 54
attributes, 26
audio formats, MediaElement control support, 111
AutoGenerateColumns property of DataGrid control, 79
automatic updates to out-of-browser applications, 159–163
AutomationFactory object, 179
AutoReverse property, of animation, 142

B

Back button, in Windows Phone, 247–249
BackEase class, 147
background parameter, of Silverlight object, 200
BackKeyPress event handler, 247
backside, viewing image from, 139
banner, when Silverlight not installed, 201
BeginGetReponse method of request, 220
BeginStoryBoard tag, 141
binding
 DataGrid to collection, 80
 on Dispatcher, 221
binding data
 ItemsControl for, 188, 210
Bing Maps API, 194–195
bodyLoaded function, 106, 107, 108

BounceEase class, 147
bounce easing function, 145
bounciness, 280
bounds for game, checking, 295–296
breakpoint, 178, 232
browser bridge, 183
 application control with, 184–188
 opening, 189–190
 for Silverlight application control, 190–193
browser functions, calling from Silverlight, 194–199
brush, video as, 122–123
btnIn_Click function, 98
BuildYahooURI function, 205
Button.Content tags, 63
 XAML in, 32
Button controls, 27–34
 adding, 17, 23, 62
 adding functionality, 17–18
 code for action, 24
 Properties window for, 25
 Style property, 65
 for video playback, 114
buttons in HTML, input tag for, 191

C

callback, for Web services, 236–237
callback function, 239
calling browser functions, from Silverlight, 194–199
Canvas control, 53–55, 66
Canvas.Left property, of control, 54
Canvas.Top property, of control, 54
CaptureDeviceConfiguration. RequestDeviceAccess() function, 123–124
CaptureSource object, 124
caret button, 29
center of transformation, 128
 for skew, 133
CenterX property
 of RotateTransform, 128, 129
 of SkewTransform, 133
CenterY property
 of RotateTransform, 128, 129
 of SkewTransform, 133
Change Device Selection screen, 281

X

Y

Z

What do you think of this book?

We want to hear from you!

To participate in a brief online survey, please visit:

microsoft.com/learning/booksurvey

Tell us how well this book meets your needs—what works effectively, and what we can do better. Your feedback will help us continually improve our books and learning resources for you.

Thank you in advance for your input!

Stay in touch!

To subscribe to the *Microsoft Press® Book Connection Newsletter*—for news on upcoming books, events, and special offers—please visit:

microsoft.com/learning/books/newsletter